ATTACK PROOF

THE ULTIMATE GUIDE TO PERSONAL PROTECTION

Master John Perkins

Founder, Perkins Self-Defense Systems

8th degree black belt

Major Al Ridenhour, USMC

4th degree black belt

Matt Kovsky

3rd degree black belt

Human Kinetics

Library of Congress Cataloging-in-Publication Data

Perkins, John, 1951 Mar. 31-
    Attack proof: the ultimate guide to personal protection / John Perkins, Al Ridenhour,
Matt Kovsky.
    p.   cm.
    Includes bibliographical references and index.
    ISBN: 0-7360-0351-7
    1. Crime prevention. 2. Violent crimes--Prevention. 3. Self-defense. I. Ridenhour, Al, 1964-
II. Kovsky, Matt, 1957- III. Title.

HV7431 .P453 2000
362.88--dc21   99-059762
                                                                                                          CIP

ISBN-10: 0-7360-0351-7
ISBN-13: 978-0-7360-0351-3

Acquisitions Editor: Jeff Riley; **Developmental Editor:** Julie Rhoda; **Assistant Editor:** Carla
Zych; **Copyeditor:** Bonnie Pettifor; **Proofreader:** Jim Burns; **Indexer:** Nan N. Badgett; **Graphic
Designer:** Robert Reuther; **Graphic Artist:** Kimberly Maxey; **Cover Designer:** Keith Blomberg;
Photographer (cover): Tom Roberts; **Photographer (interior):** Timothy J. Carron, TLC Photo,
Inc., 1587 Central Park Ave., Yonkers, NY 10710 (914-395-1300); **Printer:** United Graphics

Human Kinetics books are available at special discounts for bulk purchase. Special editions or
book excerpts can also be created to specification. For details, contact the Special Sales Manager
at Human Kinetics.

Printed in the United States of America   10   9

Human Kinetics
Web site: www.HumanKinetics.com

United States: Human Kinetics
P.O. Box 5076, Champaign, IL 61825-5076
800-747-4457
e-mail: humank@hkusa.com

Canada: Human Kinetics
475 Devonshire Road Unit 100, Windsor, ON N8Y 2L5
800-465-7301 (in Canada only)
e-mail: orders@hkcanada.com

Europe: Human Kinetics
107 Bradford Road, Stanningley, Leeds LS28 6AT, United Kingdom
+44 (0) 113 255 5665
e-mail: hk@hkeurope.com

Australia: Human Kinetics
57A Price Avenue, Lower Mitcham, South Australia 5062
08 8277 1555
e-mail: liaw@hkaustralia.com

New Zealand: Human Kinetics
Division of Sports Distributors NZ Ltd., P.O. Box 300 226 Albany, North Shore City, Auckland
0064 9 448 1207
e-mail: info@humankinetics.co.nz

Dedicated to Coy Perkins, Sr., who started it all.

—John Perkins

CONTENTS

Part III   Guided Chaos for Superior Self-Defense   125

ACKNOWLEDGMENTS

Sincere thanks and appreciation to the following individuals who made this book possible:

- Human Kinetics acquisitions editor Jeff Riley for recognizing the difference
- HK developmental editor Julie Rhoda for her patience, charm, and insight
- Bryan Hopkins, A.K.A. Dr. Macintosh, for his computer expertise
- Tim Carron of TLC Photo, Inc. of Yonkers, NY, for his flawless photography
- David Randel, Killeen Good, and Samantha Fox for modeling their technique and expertise for the photographs
- David Pirell for his peerless artistry
- Mary Ann Celente for her organizational precision
- Phyllis O. Burnett (you know why)

Master John Perkins would like to thank Professor Bradley J. Steiner for his inspiration, Grandmaster Ik Jo Kang for his patient teaching, Master Waysun Liao for his philosophy, and Dr. Drew Miller for his insights. Special thanks to Dr. Peter Pizzola and Dr. Peter DeForrest for their guidance in the world of forensic science. Most of all, he would like to thank his sweetheart Cheryl Adler for her wisdom and support.

Major Al Ridenhour would like to acknowledge his wife, Lani, and his son, Spencer, for all their love and support over the years and without whom none of this would be possible.

Matt Kovsky would like to thank his wife, Kerri, for her love and endurance through the lengthy birth of this book.

INTRODUCTION

LIFE ON THE STREETS

There are hundreds of martial arts styles out there and many times that number of books about them. Nevertheless, most are pretty much the same, both in content and approach. What you are about to read, however, is unlike any other self-defense book you've ever come across.

We're not going to sugar-coat it for you; self-defense is warfare. In war, there is a distinct difference between what works and what doesn't, between what is real and what we would like to be real. War is a filter for figments of the imagination. Through a deadly process of attrition, whether you like it or not, useless knowledge is disposed of. What you're left with are survival skills.

In the modern era, the focus of hand-to-hand combat training has become lost, especially for civilians. The reasons for this are varied but include economic, cultural, and egotistical influences; political and personal rivalries overseas between individuals and governments have spawned secretiveness, repression, and financial hardship among many old-world masters, and financial greed in many new-world disciples. In fact, an entire volume could be written on just this subject, but that is beyond the scope of this work. What we need to recognize is, whether by plan or accident, self-defense training on almost all levels has become inadequate, overstylized, and unnatural. To teach large numbers of people in a short time, defensive moves are often boiled down into simple, regimented, robot-like techniques that bear no resemblance to actual fighting. Similarly, some originally authentic systems of fighting have developed into highly artistic and dance-like art forms that are appropriate for demonstration purposes only. Marketed as self-defense, they are now too elaborate and cumbersome for the violent mayhem of real-life situations.

The methodologies in this book are the result of extensive real-world testing and have nothing necessarily to do with belts, tournaments, rankings, egos, or preserving traditions that no longer reflect the effectiveness of their original forms. Their creator, John Perkins, is a retired New York police detective and an expert on the dynamics of violence at homicide scenes. His research experiments for Dr. Peter Deforrest (head of Forensic Science at John Jay College of Criminal Justice) and Dr. Peter Pizzola (of the Yonkers, New York crime lab), involving thousands of experiments in blood spatter pattern interpretation, were crucial to Perkins's understanding of various aspects of very violent events. These experiments revealed to Perkins that fights to the death don't "go down" the way most people think.

John Perkins has applied the reality principles that arose from his work, life-long martial arts training, and personal involvement in more than 100 armed and unarmed confrontations as a police officer to the development of a unique and dynamic fighting system. This system is currently used by some highly trained Marines, SWAT teams, and FBI hostage rescue personnel, as well as state and local law enforcement officers. As stated earlier, this self-defense methodology is probably different from anything else you've ever come across. It has to be, to address the paradox that has plagued the field of self-defense for some time: If all life-and-death struggles are hell-storms of unchoreographed chaos and confusion, then why do other systems train you with repetitive, patterned techniques? In everything from formalized katas to standardized punching, the nervous systems and reflexes of students and professionals are being trained from the beginning for a reality that doesn't exist—preplanned fighting.

This book prepares the highly skilled martial artist and the nonmartial artist to face their two most dangerous adversaries: the psychopathic violent criminal and ignorance. Self-defense, although it may be raised to the level of an art form, is neither a game nor sport. The psychopathic violent criminal is not a movie character but a living beast who enjoys senseless acts of brutality—the maiming or killing of innocent people—to release his seething rage. She may be lucid or acting under the influence of mind-altering substances. He may be a prison-trained monster or he may have learned as he went. He or she may be anyone from a next door neighbor or an ex-husband to a rogue police officer or seemingly innocent mother. He attacks instantly and decisively, relying on surprise or subterfuge, either armed or bare-handed. He gives no quarter and cares little about being killed himself. This is what you may come up against.

The bottom line for you is to prepare for potential confrontations, both physically and mentally. As such, you're going to have to learn to do things a little differently. To deal with real-life mayhem, learning some special technique is not going to help you. Neither is retreating into Eastern or New Age mysticism. You need to take a swan dive into reality with both eyes and all your senses wide open. With the help of this book, you're going to become a master of **guided chaos**. You're going to learn how to deal with violence the way it really happens.

This book provides martial artists with unique principles to learn that enhance what they already know, and novices with the bare bones of survival as well as a methodology of training that will enhance their overall coordination, timing, balance, and inner and outer harmony. But, as is not the case with purely meditative training, that inner peace will become more profound with training because it will be based on physical and mental abilities and a true representation of fighting dynamics.

This fighting methodology is different from other organized "styles" of martial arts in many ways, yet it can complement most of them. How different is it? Foremost, the methods presented here have no forms. That is, there are no set and sanctified techniques, no prearranged responses to specific types of attacks, and no learn-by-the-numbers choreography to clog the mind and reflexes with unnecessary strategic calculations. How is this possible? We invert the entire learning process. With guided chaos, we start your training where most systems end—with grace—and work backward from there. We do this because during a real fight for your life, it is virtually impossible to deliver a stylized technique effectively; the speed, chaos, viciousness, confusion, and utter terror associated with a real fight preclude this. Your nervous system simply becomes overloaded with the flood of sensory stimuli. You can't treat your brain like an electronic dictionary of self-defense responses and expect it to select the right "technique" to counter a "matching" attack under extreme duress. It simply doesn't work that way. If you've been programmed by practicing a specific response to a specific attack, your defense will fail if the attack changes by even one inch from the way you've trained.

This is true whether you know one technique or one thousand. How will your body know when to deliver the strike if the sensory data it is being bombarded with has no correlation to your practice? Remember, all serious (nonsparring) fights are literally hell-storms of chaos; therefore, you cannot rely confidently on choreographed training. This is not conjecture. It has been proven through exhaustive experience, countless police and morgue reports, and testimonials of police officers with high-ranking belts from various martial arts styles whose classical training failed them when the spit hit the fan.

This book contains documented examples of real people under horrific circumstances. It helps to be reminded that violence rarely unfolds the way it does in the martial arts school, or the way it's depicted on TV or in the movies.

 # YONKERS BLOODBATH

John Perkins

In one documented example, a police officer responded to a radio call for help from an injured colleague at an infamous Yonkers, New York lounge. The responding officer was highly trained in various styles of karate and kung fu and plunged through the open door of the bar, ready for action.

As he ran across the threshold, his first step into the dimly lit room was straight into a pool of blood. As if on ice, he slipped and slammed down hard on his back. Immediately, a huge brute dove on him and began whaling at his face while trying to strangle him. In a frenzy, the officer grabbed his nightstick and swung it wildly at the attacking man. The heavy nightstick crashed against a bar stool and blew apart before it made contact with the thug's head. As a traditional weapon, it was now useless.

What saved the officer was that as a child, he had been trained by his father in Native American fighting principles that embodied looseness, spontaneity, and unbridled viciousness. These now emerged. He began to use the broken nightstick as a stabbing and bludgeoning weapon, pounding it against the thug's temple. This, working in concert with his raging adrenaline, enabled him to evade strikes, adapt to the broken nightstick, and avoid serious injury to himself.

PSYCHOTIC REACTION

John Perkins

A fact of life is that no matter how strong, large, or fast you are, there's always someone stronger, larger, or faster. Typically, these are the people who attack you. Also, no matter what the attacker looks like, you never know who you're dealing with. An otherwise diminutive individual can become so enraged by drugs, psychosis, or sheer terror, that he or she literally has the strength of a lion.

For example, police officers found a small homeless woman lying motionless in the street, muttering to herself. When they asked her to move, all hell broke loose. To make a long story short, between the street where she was discovered and the mental hospital where she was finally locked down, one cop had his uniform torn to shreds, another had flesh ripped from his body, and two large hospital orderlies who tried to contain her were seriously injured while begging for assistance. Caught unaware, a 220-pound cop with a black belt hit her with a reverse punch square in the solar plexus that sent her crashing against a wall. This only enraged her. She let out a deep, guttural growl that would have made an exorcist cower in fear and then exploded into violence. The first thing available with which to subdue her without serious injury was a 200-pound iron hospital bed. Needless to say, despite her size, the woman was a human tornado.

This book offers a proven alternative form of thinking, training, and fighting that takes the following issues head-on:

- Training in a "hard" style of martial arts that emphasizes brute strength may not adequately prepare you for real life-and-death confrontations.
- Training in a "soft" style with technically complex forms can clog the mind when every millisecond of a real fight is totally unpredictable.

Now don't get us wrong. With time, dedication, talent, and first-class teaching, classical training has turned out (and continues to turn out) superb fighters. Nevertheless, we submit a different approach to learning realistic self-defense, one that's more focused on the end result. Weigh the arguments carefully and draw your own conclusions. Our methodology focuses on training in a noncooperative manner from the start, stressing the unexpected.

In contrast, in one popular soft style martial art's training routine, when a person attacks, it's in a preset manner, with both parties knowing the precise technique that will be used. An example of this is where one person faces another, pretending to attack with a knife. He slowly moves forward, holding the knife about waist-high. The defender steps confidently to one side while brushing the knife away. Next, grabbing the offender's arm, he twists his wrist. The attacker then jumps into the air, flips over, and lands on his side, whereupon the defender puts the knife hand into a wrist lock, supposedly vanquishing him. This is as close to pure choreography as you can get, yet it's a scene duplicated in many martial arts schools. Often, students are told that these techniques will work in the real world. This is a dangerous fallacy. Police reports show that an enraged, untrained 100-pound woman with a large knife can slice a trained martial artist to ribbons in seconds.

Train unrealistically and unnaturally, and you cannot fight for real. As obvious as this concept seems, more often than not it is one of the most overlooked

THE BEFUDDLED MASTER

John Perkins

A great master of the soft style mentioned on page x (who was second only to the style's creator), "lost" in a mock fight with an untrained cameraman who was filming him. On a whim, the master had decided to use this cameraman in an impromptu demonstration. Unfortunately, this cameraman, as you can actually see in the film, did not know how to "cooperate" with the master, who had a difficult time trying to put him on the ground. In fact, it took quite a long time and much effort to win. The fight was a clumsy mess and probably very embarrassing for the master. Surprisingly, this did not serve as a lesson—the art is still taught today as if cooperation is always going to be present.

aspects of martial arts training. This is because many people who say they want to learn self-defense really want a sport—or a religion. This is why so many martial arts schools concentrate on the superfluous instead of the essential.

Don't misunderstand—it is always helpful to be fit to have the best chance in an attack. That is, achieving and maintaining cardiovascular fitness and muscular strength and endurance means that you will be better able to move quickly and protect yourself. However, since the reality is that most real fights last less than four seconds, adrenaline and trained reflexes are the true keys to survival. Even if you win the fight, however, you could still lose: if you're not in shape, your body can suffer cardiovascular and structural trauma simply recovering from the stresses your adrenaline-fired responses placed on it. We will help you develop only those physical attributes necessary for self-defense at the expense of those that would help you win a body-building contest, an arm wrestling match, or a triathlon.

OVERQUALIFIED?

John Perkins

In one of our seminars, an arrogant teacher of a particular style that emphasizes knife work (who also happened to be a police trainer) thought he was overqualified for a particular drill using rubber knives. He was matched with an untrained, five-foot-two-inch woman. Before the exercise began, she was pulled to the side and told to imagine that she was a Native American warrior and that settlers had come and captured her family. The only thing standing between her and her children was the self-assured man standing in front of her. She was given permission to do whatever she wanted. She proceeded to annihilate him. With a yell, she ran straight at him. At the last second, she slid on her knees and stabbed him five times in the groin with the rubber knife. Stunned, her opponent managed one feeble swipe at her head (which she blocked), before falling backward on the ground. The woman jumped on top of him and finished him with a "stab" to the throat.

Not surprisingly, the police instructor was crestfallen. He was obviously highly skilled, but he suffered from a reactive handicap—pattern recognition. Because what the woman had done resembled no pattern he had ever practiced, he could not respond to her movement effectively.

Classical training is very often beautiful, cooperative, and predictable while combat is ugly, nasty, and chaotic. Board-breaking, high flashy kicks, and Russian splits are all great and praiseworthy athletic accomplishments. But they all have one thing in common: they have absolutely nothing to do with self-defense. It's very simple—the way you practice is the way you fight. So if you can't depend on fixed techniques, and you can't rely on muscling your assailant, what are you left with?

To free the mind and allow it to function at the gross "animalistic" level best suited for survival, you need to train in what amounts to a paradox: principles of movement that are simultaneously random, spontaneous, and free, yet singularly effective. What we mean by principles of movement are the laws of inertia, momentum, speed, ballistics, weight, balance, looseness, sensitivity, coordination, and body unity that characterize and are best suited for the human (and animal) body in mortal combat.

This is what we call an education in guided chaos. During a fight, the only constant is change—change in direction, attack angles, weapons, balance, environment, lighting, number of assailants, friction, speed, force, tactics, footing, emotions, pain, and any number of other variables. Therefore, in this methodology, what you will be learning and practicing are principles and exercises to help you to become a master of motion, randomness, and change rather than a master of techniques.

> *In the real world, attacks are not choreographed. They happen when least expected, and under the worst circumstances. They are anarchic and spontaneous by nature and require a different mind-set and method of training.*

Now an army may be likened to water, for just as flowing water avoids the heights and hastens to the lowlands, so an army avoids strength and strikes weakness. And as water shapes its flow in accordance with the ground, so an army manages its victory in accordance with the situation of the enemy. And as water has no constant form, there are in war no constant conditions. Thus, one able to gain the victory by modifying his tactics in accordance with the enemy situation may be said to be divine.

Sun Tzu, *The Art of War*, 1963

This is as true today as it was over 2,000 years ago.

Because our approach to self-defense is unusual, the material in *Attack Proof* is laid out differently from what you might expect. There are virtually no conditioning exercises nor repetitive drills. Although we detail many physical exercises that may double as effective low-impact aerobics, the mission of *Attack Proof* is to teach you principles of motion that can help you save your life.

In part I we detail and dispose of certain faulty preconceptions about handling violence. Chapter 1 prepares you mentally for what is to follow. If this sounds frightening, don't worry; once you begin to understand what you are dealing with and how you are going to deal with it, you will build a new perspective on self-defense—and perhaps life—that is both calming and fortifying. You will also learn the single most important tool of self-defense, which, ironically, has nothing to do with fighting. Chapter 2 briefly describes basic strikes, some obvious and some unusual, that make up the elementary tools you'll defend yourself with. We have culled these from a system used to train United States soldiers during WWII to deal with the prospect of going hand to hand with Japanese troops allegedly proficient in judo and karate. A simplified system called **close combat** has been devised from these methods that alone is lethal and, with little training, provides effective self-defense for the average person. We round out chapter 2 with some very unusual drills to unify the mental principles described in chapter 1 with the physical principles explained in chapter 2. It is important, however, that you do not attempt to perfect the strikes in chapter 2 or you will fall into the most common trap in martial arts: fixating your mind and body on a technique. What you'll learn is that the strike itself is not as important as how you get the opportunity to deliver it.

Learning this close combat material first will ensure that you develop the right attitude for self-preservation before launching into the heart of this book—the study and training of guided chaos and its related principles in parts II and III.

What, then, is the relationship between the close combat described in part I and the guided chaos described in parts II and III? We believe that learning to punch and kick is the easy part. All you need is the knowledge to discriminate between useless and effective striking; that's what close combat is. Then, once you understand what basic strikes are and what they're supposed to do, you can focus your attention on the real business of learning self-defense: how to make them work. That's where guided chaos comes in. Guided chaos is the language of fighting. We cannot emphasize enough that great physical strength, hand-toughening routines, and extraordinary balletic splits aren't required. All you need are gravity, perseverance, and an open mind.

Part II explains in detail the four primary principles of guided chaos. Their chief purpose is to make your movements free and creative. Each chapter has its own unique exercises for integrating the principles into unified mind-body responses. We say "unified" because as you'll see, your own mind can be your biggest enemy.

Part III shows you how to apply the principles of part II while fighting. By explaining additional modifying principles and exercises in chapter 7 ("Applying the Principles to Motion") and chapter 8 ("Economy of Movement"), you begin to apply the "guided" in guided chaos. Chapter 9 ("Grabs and Locks") uses the preceding principles to protect you from one of the most dangerous traps in fighting: falling in love with controlling tactics. Finally in chapter 10, we explain the guided chaos approach to ground fighting, as well as defending yourself against kicks, sticks, knives, guns, and multiple attackers. (Guided chaos as applied to gun fighting is a unique and complete art in itself and beyond the scope of this book; please refer to the references and resources section for specific resources on this topic.) In addition, throughout *Attack Proof* we present various self-defense awareness tips that make up a body of street smarts, covering everything from hotel safety to safe jogging to thwarting carjackings.

One last comment about the methods in this book: Are you an advanced black belt? Do you want to put teeth into your tai chi? You needn't dispose of whatever hard-won competence you already have. It's all valuable. Rather, as one student who has been through the training outlined in this book has observed, "It's the grease that makes all my other skills work better."

DRILL FINDER

DRILL NAME	CLOSE COMBAT	LOOSENESS	BALANCE	BODY UNITY	SENSITIVITY	GRIP	TENDON STRENGTHENERS	GUN AND KNIFE DEFENSES	PARTNER	PAGE NUMBER	PART NUMBER
Anywhere Strikes I	•									34	I
Anywhere Strikes II	•									35	I
Anywhere Strikes III	•									35	I
Back Walk					•				•	107	II
Ball Compression					•					110	II
Basic Knife Fighting Drill								•	•	193	III
Battle-Ax Box Step			•							83	II
Beanbag					•					109	II
Body Writing				•						69	II
Box Step			•							81	II
Circle Clap		•								63	II
Coin Chase					•				•	107	II
Coin Dance					•				•	107	II
Contact Flow					•				•	118	II
Dead-Fish Arms		•								55	II
Finger Creep						•				169	III
Fold Like a Napkin		•							•	54	II
Free-Striking Box Step			•						•	82	II
Fright Reaction I	•								•	28	I
Fright Reaction II	•								•	29	I
Fright Reaction III	•								•	29	I
Gang Attack I	•								•	33	I
Gang Attack II	•								•	37	I
Gang Attack III								•	•	183	III
Gun Defense I								•	•	198	III
Gun Defense II								•	•	199	III
Hula		•								56	II
Interview	•								•	30	I
Iso-Strike							•			170	III
Knife Skip Drill								•	•	192	III
Leg Mania								•		182	III

DRILL NAME	CLOSE COMBAT	LOOSENESS	BALANCE	BODY UNITY	SENSITIVITY	GRIP	TENDON STRENGTHENERS	GUN AND KNIFE DEFENSES	PARTNER	PAGE NUMBER	PART NUMBER
Meet Jason	•								•	31	I
Mexican Hat Dance	•									36	I
Modified Anywhere Stikes	•									159	III
Moving Behind a Guard	•									128	III
Ninja Walk			•							77	II
Opening the Door				•						70	II
Polishing the Sphere I					•					111	II
Polishing the Sphere II					•					112	II
Polishing the Sphere III					•					112	II
Psycho-Chimp		•								62	II
Relaxed Breathing		•								54	II
RHEM					•					116	II
Rolling the Energy Ball					•					113	II
Row the Boat	•									159	III
Run and Scream	•									27	I
Sand Bucket						•				169	III
Small Circle Dance		•								61	II
Solo Contact Flow		•								60	II
Speed Flow							•			170	III
Split-Brain Air-Writing		•								64	II
Stair Steps					•					109	II
Starting the Mower				•						70	II
Sticks of Death		•							•	61	II
Sticky Fingers		•							•	61	II
Stumble Steps					•				•	108	II
Swimming		•								57	II
Swimming Sidestroke		•								59	II
Turning		•								56	II
TV-Cut Drill					•					109	II
Two-Minute Push-Up							•			170	III
Vacuum Walk			•							79	II
Washing the Body					•					114	II
Weaving Python		•							•	55	II
Whirling Dervish Box Step			•							84	II
Wood-Surfing			•							85	II

PART ONE

CLOSE COMBAT BODY AND MIND PRINCIPLES

Before we launch into the methodology that makes our approach so different from other martial arts, part I provides you with some close combat fighting basics that should be part of every serious self-defense student's knowledge. These consist of fighting mind-sets and body positions (chapter 1) and basic close combat strikes (chapter 2). As noted in the introduction these close combat methods alone are lethal and, with little training, provide effective self-defense for the average person. They also provide the necessary foundation on which you can build your knowledge and practice of guided chaos, which is presented more fully in parts II and III.

CHAPTER ONE

AWARENESS

The concept of awareness is so simple you may be tempted to ignore it. Ironically, though, it's one of the most effective forms of self-defense available. There are also many misconceptions about it. Consider this scenario: You're walking to some destination on a city street. You need to turn left and walk down Main Street. As you do so, you notice two men loitering against a car. They don't necessarily look dangerous, but there's just something, a feeling, that disturbs you slightly about them. Do you

a. walk down the opposite side of the street and avoid eye contact so you won't seem confrontational;

b. walk straight toward them, confident, head held high, as you may have learned in your assertiveness training class; or

c. reach into your pocket (handbag, holster) and rest your fingers lightly on your knife (mace, pistol) and get ready to use it?

The correct answer? None of the above. Rather, you use your awareness and walk down another street. It's logical: if you're not there, they can't attack you. No one is going to pin a medal on you for bravery if you're already dead. Let the next person be the hero.

Learn to respect your intuition and to use your awareness in any situation. Everyone has it, yet many people ignore their better judgment. A gross example of this is people who walk around with their heads down, contemplating some inner scenario, completely oblivious to their surroundings. This behavior is an accident waiting to happen. Granted, most of us look where we're going, yet we don't really see anything.

Even if you are licensed to carry a handgun and have sought the necessary professional training to be able to use your gun safely and effectively, it's important that you still are extremely aware so that you can reach for it in time. Without adequate hand-to-hand fighting knowledge, you won't be able to get your gun out before you're overpowered. And your assailant may get to it first, which could really escalate the seriousness of the situation. We've done workshops in which gun owners had their worlds rocked by a simple test. They found that if they were charged at by a knife-wielding attacker from all the way across a large room, they were cut down long before they could pull their weapons. Even so, we remind you that if you do own a gun, seek out the proper professional training to ensure you know how to use it effectively.

By being aware of your surroundings, we are not talking about descending into some gobbledygook, New Age, Zen-like state of mind, but about the importance of training yourself to casually notice your surroundings all the time. This is vital because in nearly 100 percent of assaults, the victim had a feeling that something was wrong before anything happened. It's not about having 20/20 hindsight, either. Our primitive instincts are still fully functional, screaming at us; we're just not listening to them.

Try this simple exercise every time you're on the street: Decide to look for something during the course of your walk. For example, look for people with red shirts or men with mustaches. This gets you to open your awareness to your surroundings on a regular basis.

You don't have to go around in a continuously paranoid state, however. Simply keep your attention outward, and if something looks amiss, you'll notice it. Best of all, if you are aware, any predator out there will notice that you're aware of your surroundings and therefore that you aren't an easy target.

Learn to trust your feelings. For example, if a complete stranger insists on helping you fix a flat, carry packages, or any other unsolicited favor, you may feel a tightness in your stomach and ignore it, because you want to be polite. Predators count on this. They approach you this way to earn your trust and get you to a private location. Don't back down. Seek out a third person, like a store employee or a neighbor, if they're insistent. Or start screaming; there are more dead polite people than you'd like to know about. The best self-defense is never having to use it in the first place.

Learn Awareness Strategies

The following tips provide some specific ways to be aware and prevent robbery, assault, and murder (some ways to combat rape are discussed in chapter 2). Whether you're at home, at the office, in a parking lot, at an ATM, in a car, or on a train, the best self-defense is awareness. Keep in mind that fear can actually stifle your sensitivity. Simply take notice of your environment and responsibility for your safety—daydream only when you know you're safe.

Being Aware at Automated Teller Machines (ATMs)

ATMs are potentially dangerous anytime but especially at night and when you're alone. Avoid using the ATM at night or in an isolated area. Robberies are bad enough, but assault, rape, and murder are sometimes part of the equation. There's some safety in numbers, however. Carefully stick to these guidelines to help protect yourself:

- Scan the area before leaving your car to approach an ATM.
- At drive-up ATMs, keep the car in drive or in gear with the clutch depressed. Keep your foot securely on the brake. If something goes wrong hit the gas.
- If a vehicle pulls out ahead of you and suddenly stops, the driver may be counting his money—and maybe not. Don't enter any area where your car can be immobilized. Wait until there's no potential for blockage.

It's important to train yourself to casually take notice of your surroundings all the time.

- Only use ATMs in the public eye. Naturally, criminals prefer darkness and isolation.
- Some criminals study the habits of regular ATM users. Don't visit ATMs on a schedule. Vary the days, times, and ATMs you visit.
- If your ATM card is lost or stolen, you may be contacted by telephone. The caller may sound official and ask for your PIN number. Don't give it to him or her. Instead, offer a reward if he or she turns your lost property over to the police. Or meet him or her in a public place and bring a friend.

Staying Safe When Traveling

Be especially vigilant when traveling. Hotels and motels are prime crime areas. Follow these tips to help you stay safe when traveling:

- Call the front desk if someone suspicious is lurking about or tries to gain entry to your room, using some excuse such as that he or she "must check your TV."
- Watch out for ruses. Many travelers fall victim to criminals posing as employees. Always verify by calling the front desk. Some criminals manipulate legitimate employees to gain access to your room.
- If you're going on a trip or are a constant traveler, purchase one or two portable door alarms that attach to the doorknob. You can find these alarms in electronics supply stores. If someone tries to enter your front door or the door between your room and an adjacent one, he or she will activate a high-pitched siren. You can also purchase portable alarms with a built-in delay to place on the inside of the door while you're out. Be aware, however, that the delay feature is not good for direct personal protection when you're in.
- If you have valuables, put them in the hotel safe.
- If you suspect that something is wrong before entering your room, have a staff member check it first.
- You can always have your room cleaned while you're present.
- Keep a "Do not disturb" sign on your door and a radio or TV playing while you're out.
- Always find out who's calling you in your room. Don't give your name until you're satisfied you've got a legitimate caller. If the caller says they're from room service, ask their name and verify by calling room service. If they say they're calling from the front desk, call the front desk back and verify.
- If you're out partying, whether away from home or not, be aware that there are many kinds of drugs that can be slipped into your drink by a person who has gained your confidence. Do not leave your drink unattended. Get to know who you're dealing with. Allowing them to return to your room with you is dangerous.
- Keep conversations with cab drivers or hotel personnel courteous, but don't give out personal information. It may be used for criminal purposes.
- Remain sober while traveling. The need may arise for you to take physical steps to survive.

Distinguishing Phony Police

A person posing as a police officer is a disturbingly popular scam used by the most heinous predators. Here are some tips to help you distinguish phony from real police:

- If you're going about your business and are accosted by a person or persons flashing badges and IDs in plain clothes, be extremely wary, especially if you know you've done nothing wrong. If they ask you for nonpersonal information and their IDs look legitimate, you could answer their questions.
- If they want to place you in a vehicle or move you to another location or if you have doubts, be courteous and ask them to communicate with headquarters and call for a uniform patrol car to respond. Don't jump into an unmarked car with potential masqueraders.
- If you're in an unmarked car and something they say or do clearly tells you they're not real police, then crash the car (see page 11).
- If you receive a phone call from someone claiming to be a police officer, find out which precinct he or she is calling from and call back to verify.
- If you're approached on foot by someone flashing a badge, don't just follow blindly if asked—demand a uniform patrol car.
- If you're driving lawfully and carefully in an isolated area and a suspicious unmarked car pulls up with a plain clothes driver asking you to pull over, take no chances. Even if you see a flashing dashboard and single roof light, be careful. Anyone can buy a badge or light for his car. Authentic-looking uniforms can be purchased by anybody. Signal to the suspect officer to follow you to a safer, crowded area. If you're stopped, request that a uniform patrol car be sent. Keep your car locked, windows up, and engine running. Ask for the phone number of his precinct. Call 911 if you feel you're in danger, and let them see you doing it. This all points to the importance of always carrying a cellular phone; it's no longer a luxury—it's an absolute necessity.

Avoiding Purse Snatchers, Pickpockets, and Muggers

Carry your valuables such as license, keys, and credit cards separate from your wallet or purse, especially when traveling. Purchase a money belt or pouch that can be easily concealed. Follow these tips as well:

- If a purse snatcher grabs your bag, don't fight him. Let it go. Many have been injured or killed because they valued their possessions more than their personal safety.
- Most street robberies are perpetrated by one or more criminals who use a diversion. It could be as simple as asking the time or some other question. You're being assessed as a potential target.
- Don't stop on the street. Keep walking and politely decline requests for information, directions, the time, or money. Say you're in a hurry, you have no money, whatever. If the person attempts to physically stop you, be ready to escape. If you can't, be ready to fight.
- Keep in mind that you don't know if the person accosting you is working with an accomplice and setting you up for rape, robbery, assault, or mur-

der. In the case of panhandlers in public places, you could have some loose change to drop, but don't ever go into your purse or wallet to get change. If you're actually being robbed, and they ask for your money, don't fish around for bills. Give them the whole purse or wallet.

- If you're walking and somehow become cornered by one or more people and your inner alarm goes off, attack immediately and ruthlessly (study the section on multiple attackers, page 186). As soon as you can, escape. Hit hard and fast, disable the one closest to you, push him aside, and run through the gap. If escape is impossible, you'll need everything you will learn in this book. You can survive.

Defending Yourself at Home

More than half of all rapes and a great percentage of robberies, assaults, and murders happen in the home. Defend your home or apartment like a castle:

- Most criminals avoid homes with dogs. Some breeds work better than others, so do some research.
- Keep your windows clear of shrubbery, which can hide a burglar or rapist while they're jimmying your window.
- Get outdoor motion sensor lights.
- Consider installing an alarm system from a reputable security company.
- Join your Neighborhood Watch program, or form one if it doesn't already exist.
- Keep your valuables out of easy sight and away from ground floor windows.
- Make sure that your garage door is secure. Many thieves or more violent criminals gain access this way.
- Have a peep sight and/or an intercom system installed in your front and rear door. Don't open your door for anyone. If they're in an emergency, call 911 for them. Rapists, robbers, and murderers often use this ruse. They may pose as plumbers, letter carriers, or telephone or power company employees. They may be women or children with adult male backup. Fake injuries are also used to get past your front door.
- If you reach the door to your house or apartment and the key won't go into the lock or your entry is damaged, get away immediately and call the police. Don't enter your home without the police checking it out first.
- If you're on your way home and suspect you're being followed, you can verify this by making four left or right turns around a block. If the vehicle is still behind you, don't go home. Criminals simply follow and jump you in your own driveway. Drive to the local police or fire department or some other highly public area. Use your cell phone and call 911.
- Reinforce your bedroom door with a secure lock to slow down an intruder. Keep a cell phone and gun (that you've been trained to use) by the bed. This may seem extreme, but think of the simple logic behind this plan: If the intruder is not discouraged by motion lights, alarm, and dog and is still determined to get in, you've got a serious problem. All the previously listed obstacles and the reinforced door are meant to slow him down, while the cell phone gets around a cut phone line. You know what the gun's for. If it's come to this, don't hesitate to empty it into him.

- This is all well and good if you've got no children or there's no other exit. Remember: the first line of defense is awareness and the second is escape. Create and practice an evacuation plan for your entire family. Everybody tries to get out through the nearest window or door and get a neighbor's attention.

Safe Jogging

Pepper spray has limited effectiveness against an enraged and determined attacker. In John Perkins's personal experience it has only worked about half the time, even when it's shot straight in the eyes at close range. Use it in conjunction with a defensive strategy: spray and run, or spray, hit, and run. Here are more commonsense tips for jogging safely:

- Never jog with headphones on; you jeopardize your awareness, making yourself a sitting duck.
- Stay away from unlit, thick shrubbery adjacent to trails and paths. Remain at least 10 feet away from the sides of buildings and parked cars as you round blind corners. This can provide the critical space you need to defend yourself against an ambush.
- Do not jog alone.
- Vary your jogging times and routes. Predictability aids a predator's planning.
- Wear a personal alarm that you can set off with one hand.
- If you believe at any time you're being followed by a vehicle as you're out jogging, turn around immediately and run in the opposite direction—preferably toward home or another secure area. Don't be assertive. Don't be coy. Just get out of there!

Awareness can prevent you from getting into other potentially hazardous situations, from entering a strange bar at 4 A.M. on New Year's Eve to leaving your drink unattended (and susceptible to a "date rape drug" cocktail). In addition to the awareness guidelines provided throughout this chapter, two excellent books that promote self-defense awareness are *Strong on Defense* by Sanford Strong and *The Gift of Fear* by Gavin de Becker.

Establish Your Personal Comfort Zone

It's an unfortunate fact of life, but there are people in this world who simply can't live in peace with their fellow human beings. You try to cultivate a "love your neighbor" philosophy, and then some mutant wrecks it by jumping you. Regrettably, it's that one violent encounter that can cut short a lifetime of good deeds. So you must make a personal decision either to be wholly trusting (and vulnerable) or ever-vigilant. Vigilance doesn't mean you have to walk around angry. Indeed, if you take the emotion out of it, vigilance merely becomes a relaxed practical exercise for fully participating in life.

For example, establish a personal comfort zone that no stranger is allowed to enter. At a minimum, the zone is about as far as you can extend your arm. Maintaining this zone may require that you walk around people so they don't get too close. Refusing to give space needlessly is a senseless provocation and another liability of so-called assertiveness training. Don't create or let yourself be pulled into senseless confrontations. You never know who you are dealing with. Maintaining your personal comfort zone is difficult in a crowded subway or elevator, but in these situations your awareness is already heightened. Also, potential attackers are discouraged from attacking in such crowded conditions: there are witnesses, and the attacker's escape route is usually obstructed.

Practice Hostile Awareness

What you think and do before a fight is often more important than the fight itself. We'll call this next section your "prefight orientation" because you have to make some decisions about your attitude as a victim. But first, try this: from time to time, strictly as an exercise, when you walk down a busy sidewalk with people going by at different angles, directions, and speeds, visualize how you would respond to a random attack from a stranger. Calmly imagine counterattacks that are appropriate to their position in space in relation to yours. How would you strike? When could you run? Do you have sturdy shoes with which to kick? If you're really aware, you may need to make a practical decision about your footwear. Shoes can be stylish and still pack a punch. Are there natural weapons (bricks, sticks, bottles, and the like) nearby? Perhaps you have a ballpoint pen handy to use as a stabbing weapon to the head or soft body parts. Don't get nervous, this is your life we're talking about protecting. This is only a drill, but drills are best practiced while you are calm; it will become easier as you learn and practice the methodologies in this book. After a while, it will become second nature, and your subconscious won't be so startled if the real thing should happen. The point is, practicing hostile awareness isn't an exercise in creating social or emotional dysfunction. Instead, you're looking for potential hostility in your environment, not building your own. This prepares your nervous system to respond in an attack.

Remember, anger can be detrimental to your self-defense, because it robs you of your ability to stay loose and be physically sensitive. You're merely engaging in neural programming, what's called visualization in advanced sports training.

The Decision-Making Process

Does this attitude of passive vigilance seem extreme? Remember we're giving you your prefight orientation here so you can make some important philosophical decisions. Perhaps some sobering statistics are in order. If you're involved in a mugging or some other form of assault in which the assailant attempts to take you to another place (in other words, a kidnapping, carjacking, or a robbery moved to a remote location), do you

a. try to reason with your captors,

b. go along quietly so you can escape or be rescued later, or

c. tell him that you're expected someplace and that people will come looking for you?

Once again, the correct answer is none of the above. Police statistics show that if you go along with the attacker to a second crime scene, the odds of being killed or being so severely injured that you might wish you had been killed are extremely high. By the same token, if you make your stand right there and either run (if you can) or fight for your life, the odds are reversed. So, you see, your decision-making process is greatly simplified. But let's be absolutely clear about what we mean by this:

- If you're asked for money by a mugger, be very polite and respectful, and give it to him. Give him whatever he wants, quickly. In some situations where you have a little distance, you can throw your wallet and run the other way.

- However, if the mugger wants you to come with him, it's because he has a lot more in mind.

This is the moment of truth. We detail what you actually should do in your counterattack in chapter 2, but it's important to know the reality of the situation. Despite what you may have been told or seen in movies, there's no magic solution that will get you out of this situation completely unscathed. You'll probably sustain some sort of injury even if you get away successfully. The key thing, however, is that you survive. If you don't run or fight back, you probably won't.

Now, for example, with a knife right against your throat or a gun in your face, this changes, but only to the extent that your attacker needs to be taken slightly off guard. We detail specific maneuvers to increase your chances in these situations in chapter 10, but the point we are trying to make now is you still shouldn't wait until the attacker has taken you to a secure location. By the way, keep in mind that most assaults take place without a weapon being introduced, at least initially.

Using Hostile Awareness During a Carjacking

Hostile awareness can be extended to other dangerous circumstances that demand immediate action to prevent later tragedy. What if you're in your car, boxed in by traffic, and one or more carjackers come in suddenly through carelessly unlocked doors and windows and demand to take you someplace? Prevent the assault from moving to a second crime scene by doing whatever it takes to crash the car quickly. Bite, scratch, and rip his eyes out; then grab the wheel and smash into something big. Carjackers lose interest in you fast when this happens, and the injuries you might sustain will probably be less than any the attacker might give you. A crash also attracts a lot of attention. In short, don't go with them if you want to live.

Here are some other tips to help you survive a carjacking:

- Scan the parking area before you approach your car. Have your keys ready. Once inside, lock the windows and doors.

- Avoid driving through bad areas of town. If you must and you get a flat tire, drive on the rim as far as you need to in order to leave the area. The cost of a new wheel is a small price to pay for your life. If while you're driving, someone points to your wheel and says you've got a flat, say "thank you" and keep driving to the nearest safe area. They may even have put a slow leak in your tire and followed you. This phony good Samaritan scenario is the oldest trick in the book.

- Always carry a cell phone with an extra battery.

- When in traffic, always maintain some space in front and behind your car so you can escape or at least ram another car and then escape.

- Beware of fender-bender scams. If you're hit, never pull over in a deserted area. Signal to the other driver that you want to drive to a populated area or some business establishment where you can trade insurance information. If he doesn't like it, too bad. You can tell the judge you were afraid for your safety. Better to be judged by 12 than carried by 6.

- If you're stopped on the highway with severe car trouble, your cell phone won't connect, and someone stops to "help" you, tell them you just called the highway police for assistance, but you'd also like to call AAA and your battery died. Ask if they could go to a phone and call for you. If they insist on helping you and then get out of their car, leave the ignition key and get out immediately, putting distance between you and the good Samaritan. Don't get trapped in your car. Remember, a law-abiding person would never put you through this.

- Prepare your family for carjacking incidents. Practice escaping through the nearest window or door and scattering in different directions at the first indication of danger or at a prearranged signal from you (e.g., "Run!").

- If you're alone and a predator suddenly enters through a window or door before you can hit the gas, leave the keys and run out the other door. Give him the car.

- Don't go with your abductor. Crash the car. Hard. If the abductor is driving, wait until you're doing at least 25 mph and then scratch his eyes out, bite his ear off, go berserk, and make him lose control. That's what you want. Grab the wheel. Don't reach for the keys; it's a dangerous waste.

- If you're placed in the car's trunk, rip out as many wires as you can once the car starts moving. Inoperative tail lights may attract a cop's attention. In many cars you can punch out the tail lights from inside the trunk and actually stick your hand out and wave to attract attention.

- Always scan the area before parking your car. Always park in well-lit areas. Scan again before leaving your car. When returning to your car, scan the area before approaching. This applies especially to parking lots in malls. If something looks suspicious, go back to the mall, tell a security guard or use your cell phone to call the police—don't second guess yourself. Many recent horrific tragedies in the news could have been prevented by following this ridiculously easy and simple advice.

- Fill your tank in the daytime. Scan the gas station and the store before pulling up.

The three linchpins of self-defense awareness are

- scan,
- avoid, and
- carry a cell phone.

Understand Your Perspective as a Victim

Law enforcement personnel are in an unenviable position. With their lives on the line, they must subdue and arrest extremely dangerous individuals who are often quite willing to take their heads off. The question each cop in such a situation asks is, "Does this suspect actually harbor this intent or is he just bluffing? Can I take the risk?" Then, once a fight begins, only "reasonable force" may be used. In the heat of battle, every cop is expected to have a legal computer implanted in his skull to weigh the results of his actions and to avoid "excessive" tactics that may save his life and those of innocent victims, yet provoke a lawsuit by the perpetrator.

The impending legal implications of every action have created a market for tactics that don't use lethal force (locks and holds rather than strikes and chokes), which protect the criminal more than the cop or other victim. Even so, the effectiveness of these nonlethal tactics is also controversial. This book is not the place to discuss this issue in depth without getting into an argument over department policy, local politics, and civil rights; however, we will say that geared-down "lethal" force training often winds up being safer for both perpetrator and policeman than locks and holds: a cop who can't fight will more likely use his gun. The point is that as a civilian you are under no such constraints.

For example, a melee took place one Thanksgiving Day at a football game in Yonkers, New York. Knives were involved and many people were hurt. A police officer, who also happened to be an instructor of control tactics, applied a wrist lock to one extremely large and belligerent individual and was actually raised off the ground by his lock and tossed like a toy against a four-inch iron pipe protruding from a fence. This teaches us the following:

- Training for life-and-death situations by practicing controlling tactics is like taking major league batting practice with a flyswatter. In both cases, you'll strike out big time.

- As a private citizen, you're under no obligation to respect the rights of someone who is trying to maim or kill you. You have the right to fight back and be left alone.

- By training to use deadly force instead of training to contain the attacker, you have the ability to decide the level of punishment. You can always back off from maximum force.

Challenge No One

We are teaching the pacifism of a warrior. Unless you or a loved one are in imminent physical danger, no fight is worth it, because you never know who you are dealing with. Even when you win, you can be seriously injured. Remember that self-defense isn't about honor, it's about survival, and macho posturing is a form of insecurity. What are we talking about? Suppose you are in a bar and someone bumps you, then makes some remark intended to insult your sexual orientation or claims to have intimate knowledge of your sister. You say "Excuse me," admit you're a eunuch, and wish him well with your sister. If necessary, claim you're a coward and leave. Walking away from confrontation has three advantages:

1. You avoid petty squabbles and later entanglement with the legal system.
2. It restricts fights to those you absolutely must undertake to physically save your hide.
3. It relieves you of moral indecision and guilt when you have no other choice but to do what you have to do.

The principle of challenging no one, although philosophical, will also prepare you for its vital physical counterpart when we launch into the guided chaos principles in part II.

THE BATTERED KICKBOXER

John Perkins

Mercy can be a liability, even for the well-trained. Mary (not her real name), a competitive kickboxer, was assaulted out of nowhere by a man who spat Fritos in her face and then lunged at her. To her credit, she reacted instantly, punching and kicking him with full force. The man fell to the ground, apparently hurt badly.

Unfortunately, what she did next almost got her killed. Mary leaned over him to make sure he wasn't seriously injured. Suddenly, he leapt up, struck her face, and started pummeling her. She recovered and again fought back, only to be suddenly pulled off him by the authorities. At first, they thought he was the victim because he was covered with blood. In actuality, his first strike at her face had been with a concealed punch knife, and it had pierced her nasal cavity between the eye and the nose. The blood had poured out of her onto him. Mary was lucky to survive. After much reconstructive surgery, she eventually healed.

The moral of the story? Do what's necessary, and then run. Often, weapons aren't pulled until later in the fight. If you can't get away, then finish the job. After all, he attacked you, and your family or loved ones won't be consoled if an act of pity deprives them of you forever.

Respond According to Your Environment

Your environment can play a part in your response. If you're in an area with other people, such as a crowded train, it's effective to be loud, assertive, and vocal to attract attention to your position, especially if it's a stealthy harassment situation with a pickpocket or a groper. Simply screaming at the offender will turn heads and discourage him. However, if the person is not discouraged, or if you're in an area where no one is likely to help you (or care), the material in chapter 2 comes into play.

Preventing Common Mistakes

- Trying to be polite with a stranger who gives you a "bad feeling" is potential suicide. Run.
- Self-defense skills are useless if you can't release and channel your fear.
- Memorized self-defense techniques are too slow for the nervous system to process in a rapidly changing crisis.
- Being inappropriately or unnecessarily assertive with a criminal is an invitation for disaster.
- Standing up to verbal bullying in a bar is not self-defense. Don't be manipulated.
- Don't resist a simple robbery. Do resist an abduction with everything you've got.
- Don't look on a conflict as a personal challenge. Avoid confrontations at all costs. Run away first. Fight only when you have no choice.
- Be a pacifist warrior. Obscurity is the best security.

CHAPTER TWO

BASIC STRIKES AND STRATEGIES

You've developed your awareness, you avoid dangerous situations, and you claim cowardice and walk away from confrontations. Nevertheless, some mutant has picked you as his target du jour. If you're jumped without notice or your attacker wants to move you to another location, you now know, at least mentally, that it is time to take your stand. But what do you actually do and how do you train for it?

The Interview and Preemptive Strike

Unless you're the victim of an assassination-style attack in which you're simply ambushed and executed, most confrontations begin with an "interview." The interview situation refers to an impending mugging or attack that be-

gins with a verbal distraction, such as "You got the time?" or "You got some change?" or the ever-popular "Do you know how to get to . . . ?" It also can refer to that all-important point in the beginning stages of a confrontation in which one person attempts to provoke you with "what-you-gonna-do-about-it" talk. If the person gives you the slightest bad feeling (a feeling based on your awareness, which you need to trust), your verbal response is to say "Nothing," "No," or "I don't know" and back away, keeping your eyes on him. In short, since you challenge no one (see chapter 1, page 12), you give him every opportunity to disprove your suspicions and reveal himself as relatively benevolent—while you retreat. A law-abiding person will accept your reluctance. You react to the interview in this way so you can take full responsibility for what might happen next.

Despite your withdrawal, if a stranger (or a

hostile acquaintance) physically enters your personal comfort zone (see page 8) with a gesture, strike, or attempt to touch you for the purpose of causing you harm, and you can't escape, you need to resort to a preemptive strike—an action that Bradley Steiner, President of the International Combat Martial Arts Federation, has coined as "attacking the attacker"—quickly and decisively.

You don't want to spar with the enemy. You want to disable him or her as quickly as possible and run. This may involve using deadly strikes to the eyes and throat immediately. Indeed, if a fight lasts longer than four seconds, you're in trouble.

In close combat there are some basic defensive postures that enable you to effectively use the preemptive strike.

The Jack Benny Stance

If you're old enough to know who the great comedian Jack Benny was, you'll picture this immediately (but it's no joke!). Jack used to stroke his chin while he pondered his next punch line. This is the same stance you want to take during the interview at the first inkling of danger (which you tend to feel almost immediately—even with scam artists).

To assume the Jack Benny stance, stand sideways to your aggressor (far enough away so that he must step forward to reach you) and bring your lead hand near your face with the elbow down in a seemingly nonaggressive position (figure 2.1a). Or this could be a nervous gesture of indecision such as scratching your head, rubbing your mouth, or, if cornered in an elevator, raising both hands up in a kind of meek "why me?" posture (figure 2.1b).

FIGURE 2.1

Don't attempt to look threatening with an "en guarde" attitude as if you know how to fight. The last thing you need is to get his adrenaline flowing faster than it already is. Instead, like Jack Benny, look small, confused, and harmless. Better yet, with your hands near your face, look relaxed, or, depending on the situation, terrified (and this may be closer to how you feel than you'd like), in other words, nonthreatening. This immediately lets the other guy think he won't have to break a sweat to get what he wants. If it's money, give it to him promptly. If he wants more than you can give and attempts to harm you, or especially if he wants you to go somewhere with him, you must act. In either case, he'll relax a little, because up to now, you've looked like "easy pickin's." This is good, because you'll be attacking him preemptively, by striking in the middle of a sentence, while you're cowering (attacking the attacker). If you're getting the idea that playing possum has its advantages, you're on the right track. In a nutshell, you're assuming a physical posture that does three things:

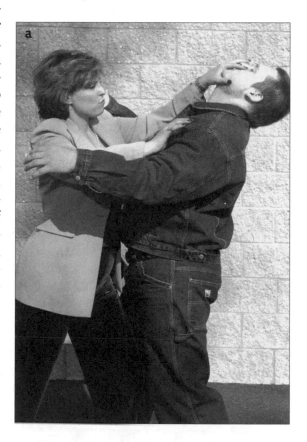

1. It makes you less threatening to the attacker and relaxes him slightly.
2. It automatically provides cover for your head and throat.
3. It aligns your arm for a straight shot to the thug's chin, eyes, or throat while deflecting a strike from him.

With your arms in the Jack Benny stance position, in the midst of acting meek, shoot your lead (upraised) hand straight out as you step forward onto your lead leg with all your weight moving in a falling motion. Simultaneously jab your attacker under the chin with your palm while you drive the fingers of your lead hand as deep into his eye sockets as you can (figure 2.2a). (This type of combination strike is called a chin jab.) Or chop to the front or side of the throat with the pinkie edge of your hand (figure 2.2b.) Follow instantaneously with the other arm by blasting your palm up under his chin again as you continue to step forward, as if launching a shot put. A relatively weak person, under adrenaline, can wrench a larger person's neck with this strike because the vertebral support is weak.

This is only the first in a series of rapid, straight, and screaming blows you should unleash like a wild, enraged cat. (You'll learn others, starting on page 19.) The key is to hunch your shoulders up and drop your head down so that you protect your face and neck. By doing this, your arms occupy the line your attacker might take to attack you. This accomplishes your deflection automatically.

FIGURE 2.2

No strike occurs in isolation.

When you're standing sideways in the Jack Benny stance, because both hands shoot out (one behind the other), you'll deflect a strike from either of his hands automatically if he should move first. This forms a kind of instantaneous defensive arc around your head. To understand how it works, imagine the hull of a boat, or better yet, an icebreaker. The V-shape of the hull cracks the ice at the prow or point. This is the area of maximum force combined with the narrowest surface area. The ice then slides around the sides. Similarly, without blocking, your hands go straight for the chin, eyes, and throat while your arms (the prow) shield against his attack.

If your energy is directed at blocking his hand, you'll be committed to this direction and will waste perhaps your only opportunity to strike unimpeded. Also, he'll probably overpower your block anyway. Since what you really want to do is disable the attacker, focus on driving his head back, spearing his eyes, or chopping the side of his neck. Because of the shape of your response (the position of your arms in the Jack Benny), you will block his attack incidentally anyway. If he reaches for or strikes at you from the outside left (figure 2.3a) he'll be deflected and struck at the same time. If he reaches or strikes from the outside right, the outcome is the same. If he reaches straight forward (figure 2.3b), he'll either be deflected or both your first strike and his will neutralize each other, except that your other hand, which has been simultaneously traveling to the same target, will hit its mark.

If he reaches for you with both hands (typically attackers don't hit with both hands simultaneously), the shape of your attack will split his two hands like a wedge. Remember, your chin jab, eye gouge, or chop is not happening in isolation. You are not posing to strike like Jean-Claude Van Damme. It's merely the first in a continuous barrage of screaming, ripping, wildcat-like, buzz-saw strikes. In short, forget about looking good or pausing to admire your handiwork. Just

FIGURE 2.3

go absolutely wild. Again, attacking the attacker is simply efficient, because you are only incidentally blocking. We detail these strikes as well as drills to help you practice using them later in this chapter.

Blind Attacks and the Fright Reaction

More dangerous than the interview is the blind attack. In the blind attack, you're ambushed with no prior warning (as described in "The Williams Brothers Attack," chapter 5, page 86). Provided you aren't killed instantly—with a knife or gun—your defense depends on your body's natural fright reaction, and not on a rigid, stylized technique. There's virtually no defense against a planned assassination, even if you're Mike Tyson armed with an AK-47. However, since most assaults have a different objective in mind (such as robbery, rape, or intimidation), you have some options.

It is a waste of time to block, since this may be the only opening you ever get. If the attacker reaches for you first, resist the temptation to stop his hand. Go straight for the eyes and throat. Done correctly, your strike will deflect his strikes.

The fright reaction uses your body's natural adrenaline-fired response to sudden shock or fear. Have you ever been attacked by a swarm of angry bees? What did you do the last time you heard a loud, unexpected noise in an isolated, dark place? Ever had a firecracker thrown at you? Or worse, ever heard unexpected gunfire near you? What did you do? Your whole body instinctively dropped its center of gravity, your back curved out protectively, your head sank low between your upraised shoulders, and your arms came up around your face and neck. Dropping your center of gravity in this way strengthens your stability and adds to your power and balance. This fundamental and instinctive reaction involves a motion principle we describe later in this chapter and enhance and capitalize on in the guided chaos principles in part II. For now, though, understand that simply lowering your head, hunching your shoulders, and raising your arms protects vital areas (especially your throat) from strikes and rear-approach strangling attacks. And you do this all without any training. This is an ideal defensive position and should not be discouraged by instead assuming a rigid, classically trained stance. What would classically trained martial arts skills such as an X-block, wheel kick, or reverse punch do against a swarm of bees anyway? It's the same with fighting people you may confront outside of a martial arts school. So why train this way?

What you do immediately after this split-second fright reaction is critical, and must be simple and focused. Turn toward the attacker and chin jab, strike his neck, or simply spear your fingers straight into his eye sockets. If you've ever been accidentally poked in the eye, such as in a basketball game, imagine how devastating a purposeful strike could be. We describe these and other follow-up strikes in the next sections.

Basic Close Combat Strikes

Many of the strikes detailed in this section can be lethal if practiced properly. They do not involve complicated movements. Most of them are culled from methods taught to United States soldiers during WWII to defeat the Japanese, who were all presumed to be skilled in judo, jujitsu, and karate. These strikes are also the elementary weaponry that we use in showing you how to apply guided chaos principles, beginning in chapter 3.

Speaking of guided chaos, there is one principle we briefly illustrate here because it is something that, although not originally part of close combat, can nevertheless augment all its strikes. Simply put, we want you to deliver every strike as if you were sneezing through the strike. Not straining, not winding up, but convulsing spasmodically, as if your strike had been shot out of your body like your breath during a sneeze. We call this principle dropping, and it involves an instantaneous and complete relaxation of the whole body. This principle will make more sense when we discuss it in relation to the energy principles in chapter 6, but for now, apply this sensation to every strike you practice.

Chin Jab

You direct this strike at the face while moving forward. The idea is to cause massive trauma to the head and spine by striking with the heel of the palm, especially underneath the chin. You actually walk through the strike, driving your attacker back. By striking under the chin, the head snaps back, creating pressure on the spinal cord and either knocking the assailant unconscious or breaking his neck.

Deliver these palm strikes exactly as if you were throwing a shot put or pushing half a grapefruit under someone's chin. A common mistake beginners make when delivering palm strikes is to get too close and overbend the elbows so that they wind up pitty-patting the target. Rather, drive through his head, not with muscular strength, but with your root—your connection with the ground. This is something you should do on all strikes. Your root is an esoteric principle from martial arts, but what it basically means here is your ability to drive all your strikes with your legs. You will train yourself to root automatically when you learn more about the principles in part II, but for now for the gross application of power, recognize that your legs are far stronger than your upper body. Therefore, drive from the ground through your legs at high speed, extending the energy through your hand to your fingertips, as if you were pushing a stalled car. When you come right down to it, it's your legs that'll get the car moving—not your upper body strength. Using your arm muscles exclusively will make you tight and slow. You only need enough muscle to keep the elbow joint from overbending (this is actually an example of tendon strength). Then use your fingers to gouge out the eyes or to drive through the eyes with power, pushing them back into their sockets. Yes, it's gory, but your goal is to survive.

You may wonder "Why not use a fist?" There are many disadvantages to using a closed fist (see page 24). One advantage of the chin jab over a closed fist strike is that it usually slips under an opponent's block because the hand is shaped more like a spear when it comes out, offering less surface area for the attacker to block.

Chops, Spears, Ridgehands, and Claws

You direct these strikes at the side of the neck, Adam's apple, eyes, or back of the neck at the base of the skull. A relatively unfamiliar but extremely effective target for the spear is the center of the armpit. Executed correctly, these blows are deadly.

When employing a chop, hold your hand flat with your wrist straight and your fingers together but relaxed. This is different than many styles where you are told to tighten your hand strongly; we have found this tightness slows the speed, power, and reaction time of your strikes significantly (see chapter 3). Aim for the soft tissue of the neck and strike with the pinkie side of your hand, using either the bony prominence of the wrist or the fleshy area one inch above it. Create a loose, dropping motion when striking to the side or back of the neck, using the weight of your body and not the tightening of your muscles. Drop your entire body weight like a sack of potatoes. When striking, you want to almost fall into the chop, so that the power is not a by-product of muscular exertion but of body mass in motion. You do this by lunging forward and relaxing the front leg so that for a split second your knee collapses about two inches. This dropping action adds power to the strike, because you're turning and dropping your body weight down onto the opponent's neck like an ax. If you look at old films of world champion boxer Jack Dempsey, you'll see that he would often step and suddenly drop his weight onto his lead leg as he jabbed. This augmented his punching power.

When hitting the throat, blast through it, using the same dropping motion. Again, this adds power to your attack, even if the chop is upward. The body propels the chop outward. The chopping shoulder moves to the inside, while the other shoulder moves away; this is because the whole body is turning like a windmill, as you can see in figure 2.4. You can deliver chops at an almost infinite number of angles. When you become familiar with the principles of guided chaos in parts II and III, you'll see how they're used in the context of a real fight. Ridgehands are similar to chops, except that you deliver them with the thumb side of the flat hand.

When using a spear hand strike, keep your fingers together and almost straight, aiming for the eyes and throat. These are your primary targets. No matter how big or strong a person is, no matter how much he lifts weights, there is nothing he can do to make his eyelids or throat stronger. Your eyelids will not stop a person's fingers from going through them. If your hand is in a clawing position, like a bear or a cat, you do not need to press your fingers together. At least one of your fingers will find an eye socket without precise aiming. Also, as a bonus, the momentum of a clawing strike sends your palm into the nose or chin. If you imagine you're throwing a shot put or a banana pie into someone's face, your hand will be in the right position.

A yoking, or V-shaped, spear hand strike to the Adam's apple is also potentially lethal. With your hand in a chopping position, move your thumb out about three inches to create a V, which you thrust out and drive into the throat. This is useful at close range, where you don't have to reach.

Rips and Tears

Contrary to what you may have been taught in classical methods of self-defense, rips and tears can comprise some of your most effective weaponry. Rips and tears have the effect of opening the attacker to other strikes. Rip using your hands to squeeze and tear at any soft tissue areas of the body. Any time someone pulls away from you, it presents an opportunity to rip and tear.

FIGURE 2.4

Pull at the eyes, neck, throat, ears, groin, lips, hair, fingers, or any lose fold of skin, like around the underarms, waist, corners of the mouth, or the like. This and pinching (discussed shortly) are the only tactics for which we recommend a regimen of pure strength training for the hands, because the stronger your grip, the more it will hurt your attacker.

Pinches

If, despite everything you've done, you wind up with your arms pinned to your opponent's body, dig your fingers in or grab some flesh between the bent second joints of your index and middle finger and pinch and twist with every ounce of strength in one, fast, convulsive movement. If your attacker is experiencing an adrenaline rush, a pinch may not cause him to collapse in pain (unless you pinch him in vital areas such as the throat, face, or groin). Pinches are dramatically more effective on some body types than others, but this is not a calculation you need to make. Nevertheless, pinches often provide an opening for you to hit through when he reacts. If it allows you to follow with a stab in the eye, perfect. One other particularly effective target for a pinch is the edge of the pectoral muscle where it overhangs the armpit. This can be very nasty—which leads us to the subject of biting.

Bites

You're being held tightly by his arms; you can't move. Chances are, however, that your mouth is free. If so you can use it to rip and tear into his flesh like a wild dog. Don't be shy: this is your life we're talking about, and you could die if you don't act. Worry about diseases later. The second he flinches, start gouging with your fingers, hitting with your elbows, and doing the following.

Head Butts

You've probably seen this in movies, but it's important to know what part of the head to hit with or you'll suffer more damage than you'll dish out. Use the thickest part, which is the front of the forehead, right at the hairline. The straight butt is particularly effective in an upward strike against tall opponents (figure 2.5). Your target can be any part of the face, temple, or jaw. Just don't hit your attacker's forehead. You can also slash with this part of the head sideways, not just straight on. Be sure to practice head butts at all possible angles, but remember to warm up and stretch your neck muscles first and start slowly.

Elbow Strikes

You can use elbow strikes anywhere: to the head, neck, throat, base of the skull, chin, upper and lower arm, hand, shoulder, chest, rib cage, and so on. When done correctly, an elbow strike is equivalent to hitting someone with a baseball bat, because the

FIGURE 2.5

elbow's striking power penetrates deep into the body with the devastation of a bludgeon. Moreover, you can use the elbow strike in a spearing motion. This tool is virtually limitless in its applications and the variety of angles at which you can deliver it. It is vastly underused in most martial arts. Practice elbow strikes using a variety of angles. (Part II teaches other uses for the elbow beyond striking.) The only limitation of this weapon is that you can only use it at short range.

Some of the less familiar angles that we recommend you practice include the up elbow (figure 2.6a) and the downward spearing elbow (figure 2.6b), delivered as a thrust with the upper body, rather than as a swing. The downward

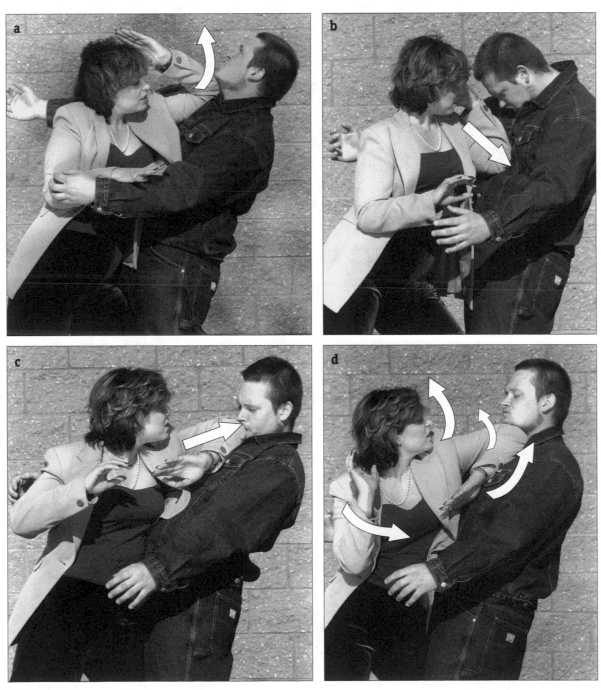

FIGURE 2.6

spearing elbow is similar to the horizontal spearing elbow (figure 2.6c). You deliver the inverted up elbow (figure 2.6d) like a shoulder shrug, and you can use it as part of an upward-turning body rotation that ends in a chop to the throat.

Closed-Fist Strikes

You may be wondering why we placed these strikes at the end of the list of offensive hand weapons: because, although these strikes are the most popular, they're the least effective for self-defense, especially when striking to the head. Ironically, using the fist is practically a conditioned response in most people.

Believe it or not, a fist has too much "give" in it to be an effective weapon unless it is highly trained; the wrist is likely to bend on impact. The hand itself is constructed of many small bones and tendons, each with the cushioning potential of a small shock absorber. When making contact, the hand must first compress until there is no more flex remaining before it can deliver any power. Along the way there is great potential for injury to the puncher. This is why boxers tape their wrists before a fight.

When you use an open-handed strike like the palm heel, it's already in the position it needs to be when it makes contact. There's little skeletal movement, because the bones in the lower part of the hand and arm are already in line with each other. There's little flex or give because the hand sits right on the end of the forearm bone. This allows maximum power to transfer to the target.

This is not to say that closed-fist punches have no use. When you do use

Is the Groin an Ideal Target?

One myth that needs to be dispelled is the effectiveness of a single strike to the groin. Typically, we've been conditioned through TV and movies to think that one shot to this area will instantly incapacitate an assailant. This is usually emphasized as an option for women in "street" self-defense classes. Unfortunately, this is a dangerous fallacy.

Over and over, in police reports and testimony from average civilians, we have found that most often all a strike to the groin does to an enraged or crack-addicted thug is anger him in a really big way. So much so, in fact, that what might have been a quick hit-and-run mugging can turn into a psychotic bloodbath. Granted, if you're simply being harassed by a nonserious, sober pest, a kick to the groin will leave him gasping and doubled over after about a five-second delay. Under adrenaline, however, this target has little stopping power unless it is accompanied by a barrage of other strikes. This is why we emphasize going straight for the throat and especially the eyes in a preemptive strike. Or you can strike these areas immediately after a strike to the groin with the hand or knee, if that's what's available. Remember, though, that in all these scenarios, all you have to do is poke a 300-pound sumo wrestler in the eye with your thumb or finger, and the fight is essentially over before it starts. You can now run away or attack at will if necessary. Even here, however, you should always learn to use multiple strikes, because you can never rely on only one "magic" blow.

them, target the soft areas of the body: the nose, ribs, kidneys, and the like. When delivering them, keep the hand loose and relaxed. When you strike, tighten the hand on contact as if grabbing a bar and then instantly relax it. This creates a snapping or slashing effect on the opponent's body. But you need to understand that the strike has limitations. If you're still not convinced, slam your palm into a brick wall. Sure it hurts. But would you want to repeat that with your fist? A punch to the skull would have a similar effect. Unlike in the movies, when you punch someone in the head, it's your hand that breaks. Save shots to the skull for open-handed strikes, which have the ability to deter your attacker by snapping the neck back with a whiplash-like action.

Knee Strikes

Keep your knee strikes low, using them on your attacker's thighs, hips, sides of the knee joints, tailbone, abdomen, or groin. Use a convulsive action, to drive the knee forward as if you are coughing. This contracts the stomach explosively pulling in the stomach muscles and adding speed to your knee strike. But don't jump up to knee-strike someone in the head, like you see in the movies, unless you want to get slammed to the ground. Instead, if you have to knee-strike someone in the head, bring his head down to your knee.

Kicks and Stomps

Practice low kicking without chambering, or setting up. Chambering is a martial arts term for the practice of first raising the knee high before driving the kick out. We consider this motion a big time-waster that merely serves to announce your intention to kick.

You should be able to deliver a kick without telegraphing your intention to your opponent. If you think you need to chamber to get power, remember this: The kick is useless if you can't get it off the floor in time to take advantage of an opening. It's better to deliver short, snappy, crushing, stomping, or stubbing kicks with the point of your shoes or the edge of your sole or heel, than to thrust out a big, looping, flat sidekick like you see in the movies. Such big kicks are easy to block and may only push the attacker back, giving him a chance to regroup. Your most practical kick could well turn out to be a crushing stomp on the toes. Deliver your kicks quickly, economically, and loosely as if kicking a soccer ball or merely taking a step.

Unless you're attacked in the shower or on the beach, you'll never need to kick barefoot. Wearing sturdy shoes changes the dynamics of your kicks and effectively puts a hammer at the end of your feet. You should always practice with them on.

When do you kick? In terms of the interview scenario, kicking has limited usefulness because usually the person is on you in an instant if you do so. If you watch ultimate fights on TV, the first kick against an onrushing attacker is usually absorbed or deflected and the fight goes right to the ground. This is why your kicks need to be low and short and delivered in a sneaky manner without the chambering mentioned earlier. If you're only being harassed and your opponent wants to spar, just walk away, keeping an eye on him. If he then approaches you, you can turn to him and employ the stomping drop-step kick. If you're just beyond arm's length, stomp with your lead leg right where it is or move it forward a few inches, instantly bringing your rear leg forward to kick. If the attacker is farther away (because you tried to back away first and he moved

Learning how to make a proper fist takes a lot of practice and is actually difficult to execute in a panic, compared to a palm strike.

Understand that most men have an almost sixth sense when it comes to getting hit in the groin. Remember that this strike has little effect if not aided by the element of surprise and accompanied by other strikes.

FIGURE 2.7

toward you) then make up the distance by first stepping forward with your rear leg and stomping with it as it lands. Immediately follow that stomp with a low kick with the other leg. In either case, deliver the whole stomp-step-kick at high speed to your attacker's shins; there should only be a split second between the stomp-step and the kick. It should look like you're kicking a field goal that gets stopped by whatever target it strikes (figures 2.7a and 2.7b).

The stomp part of the kick is important because it gains power from the ground and also stabilizes you on slippery surfaces, such as water, ice, blood, or oil. In many instances, police officers and bar bouncers who have used this strategy have proven its effectiveness. Don't, however, stomp at an angle or you may slip. Your lower leg must hit the ground at 90 degrees.

Do the stomp as if your lead leg had been kicked out from beneath you and your weight collapsed downward as you recovered your footing. This "intentional stumbling" forces you to involve your complete body mass whether you want to or not. The momentum the stomp generates then drives the kick. Thus, if you weigh 110 pounds, your kick has more than 110 pounds of force behind it— because momentum is mass times velocity. When you're within arm's length of your attacker, use a lead leg stomp to close the distance and add power to a chop, spear, or chin jab. This adds significantly more force than you could generate with pure muscular arm strength. Not using pure muscular power also helps you remain loose and therefore less likely to be seriously injured in the fight.

Close Combat Drills

Now that you have a basic understanding of predator methodology and a vocabulary of basic strikes, we can begin to speak the language of close combat and combine these strikes into drills. Be aware that many of the following drills are completely different from what you may be used to doing in classical martial arts. In addition, they may seem sadistic, but this is necessary to train you for reality. (Note: We've provided a method for structuring all the drills in this book into a regular training regimen on page 204.)

Visualize your attacker as clearly as you can. This mental component of training is often neglected, but it is vital for programming your nervous system and fright reaction for danger. Although it's important to perform these drills seriously and realistically, maintain an attitude of play and improvisation at all times. As we get further into the methods discussed in part II, it's important to not only keep your movements free but also your mind.

The first drills are so simple you may overlook them. Neglecting them, however, could create the biggest gap in your self-defense, which is learning to overcome the paralysis of fear (refer to "Lightning Strikes Twice," page 32).

Run and Scream

After awareness, your first line of defense is to run, run, run. Get used to the idea. Then, if you must, you'll fight and will be prepared to do so. This drill teaches you to channel and focus your fear, allowing you to run or successfully mount a counterattack.

1. Go into a room, close all the windows and doors, and turn off all the lights.

2. Close your eyes.

3. Stand completely relaxed and slowly breathe through your nose deep into your belly.

4. Visualize tension leaving through your exhalation and the power of the sun entering through your inhalation, flooding every cell of your body. Do this for a full five minutes.

5. Now imagine that the most depraved criminal you can think of is about to attack and psychotically torture the person who depends on you most, the person you're closest to in the world. But first, he's going to torture and kill you. Not if you can help it.

6. Take all your fear, frustration, and helplessness, and crush it deep into your stomach. Take all the wrongs and humiliations that have been dealt you in life, all the anger and blind rage, and set it to burning. Ignite it with your sense of justice.

7. From the pit of your gut, drive the fire into your feet and then let it roar back up through your legs, hips, chest, and out your hands and mouth in the loudest, deepest animal scream your diaphragm can handle. We call this the "warrior cry." You may have to yell into a pillow or wait until you're alone in the house. But you need to release the potential paralysis that can occur in a moment of crisis—and become familiar with it. You need to know that you can explode and deliver the goods when you're terrified and your family depends on it.

8. Do this once a week to sharpen this skill even after you've become proficient at everything else in this book.

In our society we are conditioned to be polite, to listen, obey, and behave. The psychopathic criminal knows this. He relies on your tendency to be socially correct. You need to relearn what an animal knows to do at the first sign of danger. It runs for its life!

Not in every instance, but often enough, there is a moment of suspicion before violence or an actual abduction takes place. If you question the victims of violent crime you will find that nearly all of them had an inkling beforehand that something was just not right. At this first inkling of danger is when you run, not after. Forget about being polite to a suspicious stranger. Your personal safety is your first responsibility.

Fright Reaction I

In some segments of society today, individuals (especially teenage girls) have separated themselves from their basic instincts. Due perhaps to the inundation of popcorn violence in film and television, there seems to be a widespread blasé attitude among young people when they are first presented with simulated assault drills. In short, many are desensitized to violence. Unless they've been actual victims, kids are hip, cool, detached, and nonchalant, as the teen culture has taught them to be. It's almost like their instinct for self-preservation has been drained out of them. Nothing could be more dangerous. (There are political and sociological implications to this also, but we won't go into that.) This drill helps you channel fear-generated adrenaline into defensive reaction instead of frozen terror.

1. Find a partner to perform this drill with.
2. Stand quietly with your eyes closed and your arms at your sides. Relax and quiet your mind. Tune into the sensation of air moving over your skin.
3. Now, have your partner touch you, as gently as a fly, somewhere around your head (it may kind of remind you of annoying mosquitoes on a hot summer night.)
4. The instant you feel anything, drop explosively into the fright reaction— lower your center of gravity, widen your stance, bring your hands up around your face and sink your head low between your shoulders.
5. Have your partner make the touch lighter and lighter (thus making you more sensitive) as he goes for annoying areas like your eyelids, ears, and hair.
6. React as early and as quickly as you can, each time returning to the starting position with your eyes closed and arms relaxed at your sides.
7. Do this drill 30 or 40 times per session, and you'll begin to feel very jumpy. In a dark alley or other remote location, this feeling is exactly what you want.

Your partner should try to get his touching hand out of the way as fast as he can while you try to keep it off you. However, you're not trying to grab or hit him directly, you're simply reacting reflexively without thought or plan (which would slow you down). The key is to develop your reflexive sensitivity so that, in a blind attack, your whole body begins to move as early as possible.

Fright Reaction II

This fright reaction drill and those that follow it are vital for understanding that fear is good when used to your advantage. This drill helps you channel your fear-generated adrenaline into defensive reaction instead of frozen terror.

1. Find a partner to perform this drill with.
2. Stand quietly with your eyes closed and your arms at your sides. Relax and quiet your mind. Tune in to the sensation of air moving over your skin.
3. Spin around several times and then walk, keeping your eyes closed.
4. Within a few steps, your partner will shove you forcefully with a padded shield (available at martial arts stores). The shove should come from an indiscriminate angle.
5. At the first contact, open your eyes and go into the fright reaction.
6. Your balance, of course, will be totally blown. Regain your balance by bending your knees and widening your stance, thus lowering your center of gravity.

Fright Reaction III

This modification of the previous two fright reaction drills takes your skills a step further.

1. Find a partner to perform this drill with.
2. Stand quietly with your eyes closed and your arms at your sides. Relax and quiet your mind. Tune in to the sensation of air moving over your skin.
3. Now spin around several times, keeping your eyes closed, and walk.
4. Within a few steps, your partner will shove you forcefully with a padded shield. The shove should come from an indiscriminate angle.
5. From whatever position you end up in, open your eyes and launch yourself into the shield with straight alternating palm strikes.
6. Step forward with each strike. Nothing fancy here—simply drive forward as fast and straight as you can.
7. Scream like a banshee on each strike.
8. Keep advancing on the target, but don't get so close that you cramp the full extension of your arms. (This is a common fault of beginners—they wind up pitty-patting the shield with just their hands because their elbows remain bent at less than 90 degrees).
9. Turn your back and shoulders into each strike, so that your trunk and hips (rather than just the unbending action of your elbows) are driving your arms out. Ideally, you should also step in with each strike. Hit as fast and hard as you can.
10. After four or five shots, run away.

Interview

This drill incorporates the personal comfort zone and the Jack Benny stance. It is so simple you might think it's silly, but it's important to practice because, unfortunately, when in danger, most people who don't practice react to the wrong stimuli at the wrong time.

Remember that the interview, as opposed to a blind attack, involves a short period of time in which the assailant is sizing you up. Having been selected at all is the first stage. You may discourage the assailant from selecting you as a target if you appear to be aware of your surroundings, but don't count on it. For whatever reason, there's someone almost in your face, and he's an uninvited and dangerous intruder.

In chapter 1 you established your personal comfort zone (see page 8). If he makes a move that crosses this boundary with either a touch or strike, or the content of the conversation begins to set off alarm bells in your stomach (that's your good friend Mr. Adrenaline ready to help you), you must strike like lightning, stopping only when you can run.

Now since your first contact with this person is verbal, and you probably will be surprised, you might feel a slight fright reaction coming on. However, the interview stimulus is still not so dangerous that you'll just go off, as you would in a blind attack, so you instead raise your arm by assuming the Jack Benny stance (page 16) or a similar nonthreatening posture. This is not so unnatural, because touching your face nervously and shrinking away sideways slightly is a sign of fear and discomfort. If you think standing tall with your chest out is going to discourage a predator, remember, he's already picked you out. Short of your turning into Superman, he's going to go through with whatever he's got in mind. It's better now to appear weaker, so that he lets down his guard slightly.

This drill helps you practice delineating your comfort zone, shrinking away, and deciding to avoid petty squabbles. By doing these three things you give the enemy every opportunity to change his mind. If he enters your zone, he will have to deal with a wild animal. He has made your choice for you.

1. Find a partner to perform this drill with. Have your partner hold a "focus glove" (available at martial arts stores) with two eyes drawn on it.

2. Spin around in circles with your eyes closed, and then stop and walk.

3. Open your eyes when your partner, holding the focus glove, stops you with a verbal interview.

   • If your partner says "Come with me" or "Get in the car," run away immediately.

   • If your partner starts with some seemingly innocuous chatter like, "You got change?" "You got the time?" or "How do you get to . . . ?" say "no" and keep on walking but be alert for a rear or side attack from the assailant or an accomplice.

   • For the purposes of this drill, respond the same as in "Fright Reaction III" (page 29). If, however, after opening your eyes you see that your escape is blocked by a wall, furniture, or other objects, then immediately adopt the Jack Benny stance and back away slowly as far as you can. Backing away is important to justify what is to follow. (By the way, a scam artist, kidnapper, or rapist will often address you with reassuring conversation. Don't be taken in; it's meant to lower your guard before he gets physical.)

4. Somewhere in the conversation, your partner should reach for you or, to make it more belligerent, he should strike at you. If someone physically enters your personal comfort zone under these circumstances, attack the attacker right now with everything you've got.

5. Stomp-step, and strike with your lead hand, using a chin jab.

6. Spear straight for the eyes (on the focus glove) or chop to the front or side of the focus glove throat (the wrist of the gloved hand). Make sure both your hands come out almost simultaneously, with the closer one hitting first.

7. Without pausing, continue ripping at the focus gloves' eyes or slam the glove with palm heels, driving your partner back, screaming from the gut the whole time. Keep your arms pumping like a jackhammer, driving with your legs and powering your arms with your back and waist. If you're clawing at the eyes like an insane alley cat, try to actually rip the leather from the skin of the glove.

8. Hit 5 to 10 times and then run away. Keep in mind that when your partner reaches or strikes at you, his hand will be deflected incidentally by the curve of your arm as you go straight toward your target, like water is deflected by the hull of a boat. This holds true for your other arm also, in case he strikes with his other hand, which will happen half the time. Remember, it's a waste to block the attacker's hand; practice to eliminate this dangerous habit.

When you are practicing this drill, remember that you should not perform the stomping first strike in isolation. It's merely the first in a series of snarling, slashing, crushing blows. In general, as initial strikes, chin jabs and eye gouges work better for smaller individuals than throat chops. However, if you do practice eye strikes, train yourself mentally to spear right through the eye sockets. Ghastly as this may sound, we have experience with students who trained physically to perform them, but not psychologically. In an actual fight, with their lives in peril, they had their fingers right on their attacker's eyeballs but couldn't bring themselves to drive through them. Luckily, the students were advanced enough to use other strikes and get away with their lives.

Meet Jason

Besides being used in *Halloween*, a goalie's mask taped to a focus glove is an excellent training aid for practicing eye-gouging.

1. Have your partner wear a focus glove with a goalie's mask taped to it.

2. Practice eye-gouging through the holes of the goalie mask. Learn to deliver the gouges one right after the other like an enraged alley cat.

3. Have your partner keep the target moving.

4. Try it with your back to the glove, so that when you turn, you have to find it and hit without pausing.

5. Alternate eye gouges with palm strikes, driving in with full extension and body weight. What you will find is that palm strikes and eye gouges actually blend together because the fingers of a palm strike tend to drift into the eyes anyway, while the heel of your hand collapses into a palm strike during an eye gouge.

Surviving Rape

Rape is horrible enough. However, many women can live through a rape and recover psychologically. The problem is that there's no guarantee the monster will stop with just rape. Often, the rape is followed by torture and murder. What you need to know is that most rapes are committed without a weapon. So chances are you won't have to deal with that factor. With most rapes, there are slim windows of opportunity where the rapist is vulnerable. You need to seize those opportunities like a cornered wildcat, because your life may depend on it.

If the attack is going down and you haven't been able to escape, you could appear to submit slightly to get to those moments of vulnerability. If the rapist is armed with a gun or a knife and you are in a standing position, you can use the strategies outlined in this chapter and chapter 10. If, however, you are in a prone position, you could wait for the attacker to put down the weapon for a second while he undoes his pants. You could be just a little difficult to handle so he is taken off guard giving you the opportunity to attack him in the eyes. When his pants are down, submit momentarily and bite or crush his testicles. Immediately get up and launch into eye and throat strikes and then run.

Another strategy that could cause your assailant to reconsider is to pick up the knife or weapon your attacker puts down and plunge it into his neck. If the rapist is bare-handed and pulls you from behind, respond as in "Fright Reaction II" (page 29). If you go to the ground, the strategies on ground fighting in chapter 10 will be useful.

 # LIGHTNING STRIKES TWICE

John Perkins

At one of my classes I was told a story by a group of female students. They related that they knew of a woman who had been raped and beaten by an unknown assailant. As part of her recovery she was advised to take up a "martial art." She did just that. She attended one of the major karate "mills" and trained for four years, receiving a first and then a second degree black belt. She was good at both forms and sparring, and was in great physical shape.

One evening, she and a female coworker were the last to leave their office when suddenly out of a utility closet appeared a man holding a short stick in his hand. He was about 5 feet, 10 inches tall and approximately 180 pounds. He stated to the women that he did not wish to hurt them and was only interested in robbing the office. He then instructed both women to take off their clothes and go inside the utility closet until he left.

While both women were naked inside the closet, the monster jumped in, beat, and then raped them. Despite all her training, the woman with a second degree black belt could not fight back because she had never been taught how to deal with paralyzing fear. She is still under psychiatric care today.

I know that this is an extreme example of not receiving the right psychological as well as physical training. And truthfully, it may have been the first trauma that made the woman a victim twice. But when you are face-to-face with a psychotic criminal bent on a mission, you have to be charged with the survival energy and mind-set of a cornered sewer rat.

How does a "civilized" person prepare for these life-and-death struggles? By practicing guided chaos. Consider the following case.

COURTHOUSE FRENZY

John Perkins

Just one of the many documented cases of the use of the Jack Benny illustrates its usefulness. With only a few classes of close combat under her belt, a smallish woman was in a New York courthouse, entering an elevator. Just before the doors closed, a huge 300-pound man rushed in and immediately hit the button for the basement. Ironically, he was a paroled rapist wandering the halls of the courthouse, looking for a victim.

As he turned to face the diminutive woman, she cowered (she was terrified) and put her hands up to her mouth in horror (a modified Jack Benny stance). This put the giant more at ease. Smelling her fear, he lowered his hands, brought his face closer and opened his eyes wide, practically salivating at the prospect of easy prey. The woman's hands suddenly exploded straight out, her fingers stabbing deep into his eye sockets. The man screamed in pain, and she continued to hit and kick him while she simultaneously hit every button with her elbow. The elevator stopped and the doors opened six inches too low. The man fell out, tripping on the floor, while she continued to kick and pound his head. When security arrived on the scene, they pulled her off him, thinking it was a domestic fight. The man was severely hurt, with a torn retina among his injuries.

Gang Attack I

Ideally, you will have five training partners for this drill. This drill trains peripheral awareness and your ability to react and move powerfully in random directions.

1. Have four individuals arrange themselves in a circle facing you, the "victim." They should each be holding kicking shields (available at martial arts supplies stores). Have the fifth individual stand outside the circle and act as an instigator.

2. Face the instigator with your eyes closed.

3. The instigator preselects an attacker from the circle by pointing to him.

4. Now open your eyes. The instigator will engage you in conversation. The content need not be hostile. In fact, he should pick a subject that you become involved in and have to think about. For example, how to fix a car or bake a cake. The point is for the instigator to create an innocuous mental distraction (something scam artists do well).

5. Somewhere in the midst of this exchange, the preselected attacker simultaneously yells and charges at you.

6. Whip around to face the attacker, scream, stomp-step, and chop with the hand closest to the attacker, and palm-strike with the other.

This drill brings up an interesting point. In a multiple attack situation, if you're standing still and focusing on one stranger's spiel, you're a sitting duck. So, when engaged in conversation with someone who makes you uncomfortable, even if you think it's rude, look around (without turning your head), and keep your hands and feet moving, as if you're a nervous commuter waiting for a train. The slightest shift in body position can be enough to keep a lunging attacker from getting a perfect fix on you. This has been especially useful for cops when questioning a suspect on the street. Very often he has unseen friends nearby. Don't become hypnotized or be made unaware by a stranger's chatter.

Anywhere Strikes I

If you surveyed 100 martial arts books, chances are not one of them would train you the way this drill does. This extremely vital exercise will build your ability to hit randomly, freely, and powerfully from any angle without plan. This will come into focus with guided chaos in part II, but for now, you can start training your nervous system to simply react and recognize bizarre openings without interference from your brain dictating the angle or type of strike.

1. Choose a target such as a hanging heavy bag (available at most sporting goods stores), tree, or basement support pole.

2. Take any strike, let's say a chop, and begin hitting the target slowly using only one hand.

3. Practice turning your body behind every strike, so you're generating more energy than you can by only unbending the elbow. Drive from your feet, through your legs, and turn your hips. Unwind your back and align your shoulder so that you have one continuous, uninterrupted chain of power coming up from the floor and into your hand on every chop.

4. Now, begin to change the angle of delivery so that the pattern of strikes moves around like the hands of a clock. You will see that the mechanics of the strikes change as you go beyond the range of a specific joint. For example, with your right arm at about one o'clock (figure 2.8a), you begin to look like a very nasty waiter delivering a bowl of soup. At about four o'clock,

FIGURE 2.8

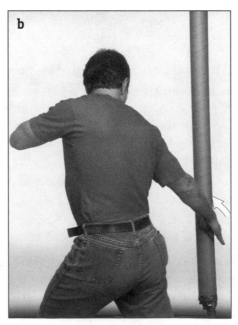

the chop becomes a ridgehand to the thigh or groin (figure 2.8b). At seven, it becomes a chop again (figure 2.8c).

5. Work around the clock three times with about 60 strikes, moving slowly and concentrating on delivering each chop with your full body weight.

6. Switch hands and go around the other way.

Anywhere Strikes II

You have to practice spontaneity to be spontaneous. Get loose and let fly.

1. Perform the previous drill, "Anywhere Strikes I," but this time, add speed and rhythm, using fast-paced music as your guide.

2. Despite the increase in speed, be sure your feet move and readjust for maximum power delivery with each strike.

3. Try a different weapon, such as your elbow.

4. When you hit, retract the strike faster than it goes out, so you're bouncing your shots off the target.

Anywhere Strikes III

We cannot emphasize enough that it's best to have no preconceived plan of what you're going to strike with. The crazier you get, the better. This drill takes "Anywhere Strikes I" and "II" one step further to sharpen your ability to deliver spontaneous, random strikes.

1. Perform "Anywhere Strikes II," but now use both hands, and strike with no pattern whatsoever. Let your mind go blank and hit with totally random chops and ridgehands. Don't plan; just let them come out however your imagination makes them, the moment they're delivered.

2. Double and triple up occasionally on the same strike to the same spot. For many people accustomed to rigid, classical self-defense training, hitting this randomly presents a problem, because they want to work like a boxer, in fixed combinations. You must, however, forget about looking cool and just let the strikes flow. With time, you'll have no idea what you're doing, nor should you. And if you don't know what you're doing, heaven knows your opponent won't have a clue.

3. Apply this entire method of practice to any weapon. With the elbow, you will find that you can deliver certain angles with a spearing action, rather than a bludgeon. Try head-butting from every conceivable angle; just don't knock yourself out—butt against a heavy bag! Remember to use your forehead just below the hairline.

4. After trying each different strike solo, mix them up. Creativity is the key. Add your shoulders. How many different ways can you hit with them? It's up to you to find out. Add your knees and feet. Remember to use the principles described earlier in this chapter regarding close combat strikes. The idea is not to hit hard (although you can go for full power later). The idea is to develop familiarity with the motion of random hitting, so that no matter what position you find yourself in, you can deliver with power and balance.

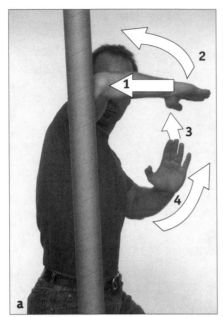

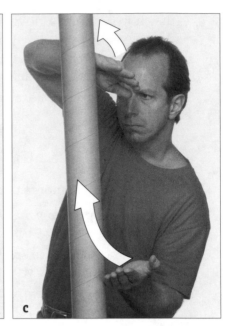

FIGURE 2.9

After a while, you'll notice something interesting. You'll see that certain strikes flow right into others, within the same movement. For example, a right back-handed elbow strike to the head flows nonstop into a right backhanded chop to the head (figure 2.9a), which in the same full-body turn a millisecond later flows into a left inside palm strike, followed by a left inside elbow (figure 2.9b). This has all occurred within one whole-body, step-and-turn movement to the right. Your arms are merely acting like the teeth of a rotary blade and your waist like the drive shaft. This multihitting principle, discussed in chapter 8, is extremely effective when combined with the other guided chaos principles you will learn in parts II and III.

To continue with this example, after your body has completed the ape-like or pendulum-like swing of blows to the right, it can immediately unleash another similar barrage of blows as it swings back to the left. Using the anywhere principle, you can also direct this swinging vertically or diagonally. For example, merely change the angle of your waist and back and the position of your feet, and the blows serve to knock the assailant's head skyward in one direction and into the ground in the other (figure 2.9c). As you can see, practicing this drill adds a vital attribute to your self-defense skills.

Mexican Hat Dance

This drill teaches how kicks are actually used combatively while moving around your attacker. The silly name applies to a maneuver that's no laughing matter if you're the "dance" partner. If you have one or more opponents, an effective tactic is to go into a wild, rapid, foot-stomping dance as if you were trying to crush 50 beer cans in five seconds and then kick them into hockey goals. You won't believe how fast people back up to avoid getting their toes smashed, only to get their shins kicked. Since they can't find a place to put their feet down, their balance is upset and this creates openings for you to run or attack further. Your foot is effectively bouncing or ricocheting from stomp to kick to stomp to kick, gaining speed and energy from each impact like a Ping-Pong ball. In short, learn to instantaneously switch feet as you stomp so you look like you're doing a Mexican hat dance. This is not simply a technique but a way of moving. If you want your kicks to look like Jean-Claude Van Damme's, this isn't for you. If you want to cause great havoc and survive an attack, it is.

1. Find a target such as a low, heavy bag or large tree.

2. Bounce or ping-pong your foot between the ground and the target as if you were trying to stomp 50 cockroaches and kick 50 soccer balls in five seconds. The ground itself is a target because you are simulating crushing toes and insteps with your heel.

3. Drop your body weight like a loose sack of potatoes every time your foot hits the ground and pick up speed as your foot ricochets back up to a low, short, shin kick, front kick, or roundhouse kick. Relaxation is the key, not muscular exertion.

4. Start delivering knee strikes with a convulsive action, as if on every strike you were coughing or sneezing violently. This causes your back and stomach muscles to pull your legs up at reflex speed (as fast as your nervous system can operate).

5. Be sure you bounce between strikes from, for example, a knee to the thigh or a heel stomp to the toes, scraping the shins along the way.

Gang Attack II

This drill simulates actual upright fighting conditions very closely. Be warned, however, this particular drill is exhausting; do it at maximum speed and intensity for no longer than 10 to 15 seconds at a time. Make sure you're in good physical condition first. This drill also requires a heavy bag.

1. Find four or more partners, three of them each with their own large kicking shield. Have the fourth person stand by the room light switch and rapidly flick the lights on and off (mostly off).

2. Close your eyes and spin.

3. Have two of your partners slam you with their shields while the third throws several loose shields at your feet, trying to trip you. Not surprisingly, this is very disorienting.

4. At first contact, in an instant, you open your eyes, regain your balance, find the heavy bag, and attack it.

5. Simultaneously avoid and attack the partners holding shields, but focus on the hanging heavy bag as your primary target.

6. Continue stomping, both to get your balance and to crush the loose kicking shields on the floor as if they were the attacker's feet. Because of the flashing lights, you will need to keep reorienting yourself; at the same time, try to keep the heavy bag between you and the nearest shield-carrying attacker. Just go nuts. Have no plan. Simply be fast, loose, balanced, and relaxed. Scream on every blow.

7. As with the anywhere striking drills, insert as many strikes as randomly as possible within your flow of movement. As you move in, elbows follow palm strikes, head butts follow elbows, knees follow both, and biting

follows clawing. However, this is not a rule. In a real fight, remember, there are no rules. Spontaneity is king. Move with your whole body.

If you do this drill several times a week, the results will be incredible. What you will find is that, just like in a real fight, all "techniques" and "planned counters" will go right out the window. The way to get better is by becoming looser, quicker, and better balanced and by not fighting your body's natural motion. Classical purists will be uncomfortable with this training and will make all kinds of excuses about why they can't get their "stuff" off. As you learn the guided chaos principles in parts II and III, however, you'll become more creative, efficient, and lethal with "Gang Attack II."

While knives and guns can enter into close combat, most assaults take place without a weapon, and if you have a weapon, you still need hand-to-hand combat skills to create enough room to get it out. For this reason we present these basic hand-to-hand close combat principles and skills in isolation from weapons in this chapter. We specifically address how to deal effectively with knife and gun attacks in chapter 10. We've chosen not to include them in this chapter because they introduce higher levels of sensitivity and awareness that you will gain with the principles and exercises presented in parts II and III of this book.

If you never do anything but study and practice the skills and strategies presented in this chapter, you will become quite formidable to an attacker. However, what if you become the victim of someone possessing the same or similarly devastating skills? This was the problem confronting John Perkins when he was a child. His father and uncles who were training him to be a warrior were all highly proficient in fighting arts similar to close combat. In addition to having these warrior skills, John's father could punch a hole in a Philco refrigerator, and his uncle could lift the front end of a Buick. This is why the guided chaos principles were devised—to give you a fighting chance against the physical monsters of the world and the most advanced practitioners of other martial arts. The material coming up in parts II and III is radically different from anything else you may have ever encountered.

Preventing Common Mistakes

➤➤ Trust your instincts early on. Run from danger.

➤➤ When protecting your personal comfort zone, don't block or reach for the attacker's hand. Go straight for his eyes and throat. Deflect and strike in one motion with the arc of your arm and shoulder, your head tucked low.

➤➤ Stand sideways in the Jack Benny stance. Beginners usually stand square to their opponents, creating a much larger target area.

➤➤ When practicing multiple palm strikes, don't crimp or overextend your elbow. Drive with your legs, hips, back, and shoulders.

➤➤ Don't forget to breathe, scream, and run.

PART TWO

GUIDED CHAOS BODY AND MIND PRINCIPLES

The main concept underlying guided chaos is this: Why train patterned movements when every real fight is comprised of unpatterned movements? Throughout a lifetime of fighting, and as a forensic scientist reconstructing homicides for the police, John Perkins has meticulously analyzed the movement dynamics of horrific life-and-death struggles. Unlike fight scenes in movies, these are far from choreographed. Through research and plenty of savage "hands-on" experience, he's concluded that the main thing all melees have in common is utter chaos and mayhem. Any system of self-defense training that doesn't appreciate this fully misses the point. In our methodology, you endeavor to become a master of mayhem and unpremeditated motion; in short, you learn to master guided chaos. How do you do this?

In most classical martial arts schools, you're taught from the outside-in. They tell you "This is what you're supposed to do against 'such-and-such.'" They give you choreographed moves to deal with every kind of attack. They impose form upon function, as if you were preparing to learn the tango. Eventually, after decades of external practice, what you're supposed to achieve is an internal state of balance, relaxation, and sensitivity—what some people would call "chi." What they don't tell you is that brawls aren't ballets. Your attacker is not going to dance the same steps as you.

In addition, to their credit, many of the newer, more innovative styles try to borrow techniques from other disciplines. Like adding spokes to a wheel, they try to make their styles well-rounded, complete, and natural. There is, however, a potential trap in this: if the techniques are never integrated subconsciously and absorbed, all you'll have are a million defensive moves waiting for a million matching attacks. When the spit hits the fan, will you pick the right one? And should this even be a job for the brain to handle at that instant? The last thing you want to do is lock up your brain with calculations and defense formulas during a fight.

Guided chaos bypasses this neural traffic jam entirely by teaching principles of effective combat through play and experimentation, so you can quickly absorb information subconsciously. When you were a child, you learned to walk and talk not from a textbook, but by natural trial and error. Similarly, guided chaos will teach you to defend yourself using your own instincts, through maximization of your human physical attributes.

It has been said that there are many paths up the mountain, but from the top everything looks the same. Similarly, after 30 years of tai chi (if your patience holds out) or taekwondo (if your body holds out), what you might finally begin to develop after endless, arduous hours of memorization, imitation, sweat, and "perfect" execution, are the four pillars of combat that everything else rests on: looseness, body unity, balance, and sensitivity. Well here's a wild idea: Why not train these principles first?

Don't misunderstand us. High quality classical training turns out superb fighters. But in parts II and III we present a realistic approach to self-defense, an approach that stresses principles, not techniques. The reason we harp so much on principles is that they're easier to apply to a lot of different situations in a pinch. In this methodology, you still train hard, just different. With guided chaos principles, you train like a jazz musician improvising on a theme, letting it flow and evolve with the rhythm and energy of the music. A martial artist learning only forms and techniques is akin to a jazz musician practicing only scales—he'll never be able to "jam" with confidence.

> Guided chaos does not train technique. It trains "response-ability."

The Language of Combat

Combat, as opposed to a sparring match with rules, is not like a song you know, with a beginning, middle, and end. Extending the improvisational jazz analogy, no one, not even the musician, knows exactly where the song will go or how it will get there. Yet, there's a method to the madness. The musician who is more relaxed, adaptable, and loose with her talent, balanced with her instrument, sensitive to the flow of notes, and able to put her whole body and soul into the groove will make the better music.

In terms of self-defense, training guided chaos will hypertune your balance, allowing you to hit with power from any position. It also allows you to get your entire body mass behind every blow—what we call body unity. This is impossible unless you also train supreme looseness in all your muscles and joints so you can achieve angles of attack and defense most people would think impossible. Developing this kind of looseness makes you as hard to hit as water, but as nasty as a bullwhip on offense. When you combine these attributes with highly trained sensitivity, you are able to detect the slightest change in your opponent's attack—often before he changes anything. This allows you to reflect and amplify his own energy back at him with devastating consequences. None of these principles will work unless you employ them simultaneously. Though training them does not involve specific techniques, concentrating on these principles will make you the better fighter.

To get this "formless" art down on paper, we have had to compromise somewhat, reducing movements that characterize guided chaos to general principles that follow natural laws and human anatomy, instead of forcing the body into a "classical box." The principles provide guidelines, while the actual execution and shape of the movements are determined by you and your experiences. We have given these principles—and the typical movements that arise out of employing them—names as a matter of convenience. You should know, however that John Perkins's best student, who's lethal beyond comprehension, employs all these principles masterfully, yet has no names for most of them. He believes some things are better left unspoken, undefined, and "unintellectualized." His advice to other students while training is to "Stop thinking!"

Your Anatomy and Motion

Your training in looseness, body unity, balance, and sensitivity takes advantage of a natural resource: your body. We all share certain physical attributes that guided chaos capitalizes on. In guided chaos, as stated earlier, we emphasize natural movement—motion that best suits the anatomical structure of whatever living thing we're talking about. Apes, who structurally resemble us most, have no claws, horns, or giant canine teeth. What we have in common are rope-like appendages that can grab, strike, rip, tear, crush, hammer, and strangle. Watch films of apes fighting. Without knives or guns, they achieve a ferocious lethality that involves no poses, X-blocks, reverse punches, or spinning-wheel kicks. They have a loose, powerful, "heavy" way of moving that employs their entire bodies as coiled, whipping bludgeons. Any movement that goes against these attributes is unnatural motion.

The power in guided chaos comes from perfectly balanced mechanical alignment, not raw muscular strength. Think of your bones as a collection of levers. With a lever, you can multiply your strength many times and move objects far larger and heavier than your own body. However, a lever is useless if it is not positioned properly. The same holds true for your bones as leverage applies to striking, balancing, yielding, or using any other combative motions.

For this reason when defending yourself and fighting back, you need to relax your muscles and suspend your body from your skeletal structure as much as possible. Like any bludgeoning weapon or striking tool (e.g., an ax or a hammer), once it's in motion, additional muscular input will not enhance its impact significantly. The looser the swing, the more the implement will make the most efficient use of its own mass.

To understand your muscles, think of them not so much as power plants, but as giant elastic fibers, anchored to your bones by cables. When properly conditioned, these "fibers" allow the body to articulate, react, and change with lightning speed.

However, when you are conditioned to fight with constant maximum contraction (using all your strength), your muscles lose their elastic properties and cause the joints to seize up, like the pistons of an automobile engine with dirty oil. Mobility, articulation, and speed are severely compromised. This is the last thing you want to happen in a fight to the death. What does this teach us? Change the oil in your car and train in a loose, relaxed manner.

Now you may say "I know where this is going, because I do train to have a loose, snappy jab." This represents a limited understanding of what we mean by looseness (see chapter 3). Even if your punches are loose, you may tighten your whole body dramatically to initiate them, creating a rigid platform to launch them from. This is not the ideal. You will be learning to initiate strikes using your own body's momentum and that of your opponent's. You can only do this with supreme relaxation and looseness.

The human body is over 70 percent water. Make use of this fact. Water is heavy, dense, and infinitely malleable. A drop of water can stick to your skin and follow your every motion (sensitivity). Bundles of energy can cause water to gather into an ocean wave that hits like a ton (body unity), yet splits easily when you dive through it (looseness). In an unconfined state, water has great mass yet no fixed center of gravity and is therefore impossible to pin down (balance). These are the qualities (and not those of mechanical robots) the principles in part II will help you apply to your fighting.

CHAPTER THREE

LOOSENESS

The best defense for any type of strike—fist, kick, or gunshot—is to not be there when the strike arrives. This is a central tenet of guided chaos, but you cannot accomplish it without looseness—the ability to change direction with any part of your body with the tiniest impetus, with no conscious thought or physical restriction. It requires becoming relaxed, reactive, rooted, and yielding.

Relaxed Looseness

We have found that muscular tension is so deeply ingrained in many people that they are astonished to learn that it isn't natural. Watch the way animals fight, especially apes, who most resemble us anatomically. They are living embodiments of loose, powerful ferocity. In the heat of battle and at extreme speed, common alley cats bend and arch away from strikes like rubber, yet their teeth and claws are always readily positioned and in their attacker's face.

Animals don't need to make a moral or strategic choice when challenged. It's simply fight

or flight for them. In contrast, the frozen terror and indecision humans experience during combat is actually a combination of

1. the brain searching its memory for appropriate physical defense responses, and
2. the body's execution of those responses with muscular tension because it has been trained that way.

The result impedes all movement. Tension lengthens your reaction time and cuts down your speed and power. It also makes your body easier to break. Thus, it is self-defeating to practice striking and blocking with full-force muscular contractions as if you were performing a 300-pound bench press. Ironically, practicing with such muscular tension is an error found in virtually all classical hard-style martial arts training.

You can't achieve looseness without relaxation, and as most top-level sport training research reveals, relaxation aids physical and mental performance. Later in this chapter, we introduce drills to help you develop your ability to stay loose. It is important that you practice these drills with full seriousness, because reacting with tension, especially in a life-or-death situation, is a very hard habit to break. In addition, physical tension encourages mental tension, which narrows your awareness dangerously.

In an effort to stabilize and strengthen our motions, we regularly use muscle groups that in fact interfere with the motion we are trying to perform. That is, the muscles tend to work against one another. When the muscles work against each other, the body has a tendency to drag. For example, if you extend your arm to strike and you exert strong muscular force, you are restraining your joints. You begin to involve other muscles (called antagonistic muscles) to overcome this drag, so you strain even harder. This creates a vicious cycle. The more force you use, the tighter your joints, the less relaxed you are, and the slower you respond to your opponent's moves.

No matter how hard you think you're punching, you're not punching nearly as hard as you could be if you loosened your muscles and thereby limited the interaction with and among other muscle groups. This is what you'll endeavor to do with the drills and principles of guided chaos in this book. By remaining loose and pliable at all times, you automatically remove the resistance created by your antagonistic muscles when you strike or are struck. This allows you to hit with uninhibited power as well as to absorb the strike of a stronger adversary. In a nutshell, you'll do this by using your muscles as little as possible and relying on momentum, relaxation, and a concept you'll learn more thoroughly in chapter 4—body unity.

All muscular movement is controlled by the mind. A loose, relaxed mind creates a loose, relaxed body—it's that simple. Relax the mind, and the body will relax. To relax your mind, you'll need to put your brain on autopilot. It must remain focused and aware, yet placid. To do this, you need to relieve your brain of the job of thinking while fighting and train it to simply sense instead.

When you practice patterned movements, you expect your opponent to move in a certain way. Trust us: unlike in the movies, he rarely does. Your brain, shocked at this discovery, may temporarily freeze, putting the brakes on your muscles and nervous system and increasing the strength you need to apply, which makes the situation worse.

Reactive Looseness

Being loose also means never being static. As long as you're either receiving energy (yielding) or transmitting energy (striking), you're in a continuous state of movement and flow. This characteristic of looseness is important to remember. In a fight there is always enough energy coming from the opponent to propel you into a constant flow of motion. As soon as you stop, the opponent gets a fix on you. These behaviors obstruct the flow of energy:

- When you think, you stop.
- When you pose, you stop.
- When you strain or grapple, you stop.
- When you execute a technique, you stop (because you're thinking).

You will learn to develop your looseness so that any input of energy from your opponent causes your entire body to respond, like the ripples caused by a leaf falling into a lake or the swing of a pendulum set into perpetual motion.

You can only be hurt or killed if you can be hit. You must be able to disappear from where your attacker wants you to be and reappear where he doesn't want or expect you to be. You must become like a phantom or mongoose. The mongoose is one of the only creatures that can stand directly in front of a poisonous snake and avoid being bit. It pops up and strikes from seemingly impossible angles. Learn to hit and articulate your body to strike wherever and whenever.

Avoid, however, the limp-noodle looseness characteristic of many tai chi practitioners who lack true combat training. Their intention is sincere, since extreme looseness does protect from hard impacts. Unfortunately, it can also leave you in a position in which you can't get out of your own way to deliver a counterattack. The problem is threefold in that extreme looseness

1. can leave you unprotected if you don't keep some part of your body between your opponent's weapon and its target (more on this in chapter 7),
2. has no power if it's not connected to the ground (see "Rooted Looseness," next section), and
3. can get your limbs twisted into positions it's impossible to launch a counterattack from (you can actually wind up blocking yourself).

Instead of just limp looseness, you want the kind of steel-spring looseness that's exceptionally flexible and reactive, yet able to slice your attacker to ribbons on the rebound. This kind of resilient energy has a name in tai chi: peng ching. It is often unfamiliar or overlooked, yet ironically, it's critical to making looseness a combative attribute.

You must develop reactive looseness and extend it throughout your entire body. Don't limit it to only your arms.

Rooted Looseness

The other factor for making looseness powerful and combative is your root, your ability to transfer energy from your foot to any external body part through a balanced connection to the ground (see also chapter 5 for more on rooting as it applies to balance). If you're unbalanced, you have no root. If you're stiff, you have no root. If you carry your body weight too high, you have no root.

To understand looseness without a root, imagine that your entire body is a "whip": limp and flexible—just a hanging rope. Your root (foot) is the handle of the whip. Your hand is the tip. When you learn to drop (chapter 6) and create an instant explosion of energy that bounces off the ground back up into your legs and body, it's your root that anchors and cracks the whip, even if the root or drop is just for a split second.

Imagine if, when someone cracked a real whip, he let go of the handle precisely at the moment of impact. The wave-like power of the whip would completely disintegrate and hit you with all the force of overcooked spaghetti. It's the anchoring action of the handle that roots the transfer of power to the tip. Beginning students tend to limit their looseness to their arms. Think of it this way: the crack of the whip has more power if the wave of looseness is allowed to traverse its entire length before reaching the tip. Limiting looseness to only your arms or shoulders or even your hips is akin to grabbing the whip in the middle and trying to snap it hard.

Looseness anchors at the foot, like holding the handle of the whip anchors the rope. The hand is like the tip of the rope. The power of your strikes is directly related to how much body mass you can get moving loosely. When doing the "Psycho-Chimp" and other looseness drills (pages 54 through 64), remember that you should initiate all your movement with stepping, dropping, or transferring weight in your feet and lower legs.

What does a strong root feel like? You can create an exaggerated sense of rooting when you do a dance that involves swinging your partner around, like the jitterbug or hustle. You counterbalance your partner's swinging body weight by

Great ocean waves build because they have an entire hemisphere to traverse. The action of the wind and currents increases the flow of energy over time and distance. This is why you don't get nine-foot breakers in ponds.

firmly anchoring your feet. At that moment, you feel like your feet are nailed to the floor. When you release, letting them go into a spin or whatever, you feel a tremendous uncorking of energy. You need to develop that same rooted sensation in your feet throughout the entire range of your own combative movements. We'll work on developing this sensation of suspending and releasing in the more advanced drills in chapter 6.

Yielding, Looseness, and Pocketing

Achieving looseness requires your body to become totally receptive and yielding, to challenge no one (see chapter 1), and to assume that everyone is stronger than you are. This is not "wimping out," but is actually tactically superior in that it will help you survive a strike. The principle of yielding, however, does not mean you become a punching bag or a leaf blowing in the wind. To learn yielding you adopt the fluid nature of water. Water is never stopped, just redirected. If you plunge your fist into water, the water moves out of the way and engulfs your arm all at the same time. It avoids you, yet sticks to you. (Think how this applies to grappling.) You also cannot compress water. No matter how hard or softly you squeeze it, it instantly moves to an area of lower pressure. Nothing is as soft as water, yet, if it's completely contained, it can be as hard as stone. It is at once extremely mobile and heavy. It can wash away whole towns and mountains. Your body is 70 percent water. Why fight nature? Use it.

Looseness enables you to achieve entry angles of attack and defense that would otherwise be totally unavailable to you.

To be loose, move your arms and body with the fluid nature of two king cobras—yielding, expanding, contracting, sliding, redirecting, engulfing, and nullifying. Just as the head of a serpent is always moving into position to strike, so should your hands always be seeking a path to destroy. If a python meets a stone head-on in its path, does it try to smash through it? Of course not. The snake isn't anatomically constructed to slam through rock. When its sensitive tongue encounters an obstacle, its entire body moves to accommodate it. It effortlessly, gently writhes around and past it. Yet, when necessary, it can crush the life out of its prey. Likewise, you are never blocked, merely redirected to a more advantageous position from which to strike or avoid an attack.

Reality is not a movie. You can't withstand a barrage of blows like Clint Eastwood in an old western barroom brawl and remain standing. When an elbow is slammed into your neck, your neck breaks. When a fist is buried deep into your kidneys, you land in the hospital. Tightening your neck muscles won't stop a chop to the throat nor will closing your eyelids stop an eye gouge. It's simply a joke to think the ability to do 500 sit-ups will protect your midsection. What muscles protect your ribcage?

To apply the principle of yielding to your body's survival chances, you have to do something called pocketing. The whole concept of pocketing is very, very simple. Remove the target, and the target only, so the rest of you can remain close. That is, get the part of the body that's about to be hit out of the way of an opponent's strike by becoming sensitive to his intentions and relaxing the muscles. For example, if the target is your stomach, make it concave so it shrinks away from the blow, but leave the rest of your body relatively where it is so you can counterattack simultaneously.

If your opponent's intended target suddenly becomes even one inch further away than he expects, you will lessen the impact significantly. Whatever the target, pull it away, as if the opponent's fist were covered with a deadly virus. Get the imagery? Don't let him even touch you with it. Self-defense is not about how "tough" you are. It's about survival.

Accordingly, in practicing the drills in this chapter, you will learn to modify your whole body's shape like rubber so it molds to avoid blows. Your head will yield like a jack-in-the-box, and your midsection will stretch like Silly Putty. Paradoxically, you will later discover that yielding can also put you in prime positions to attack from. Yielding invites the attacker in closer until, like a Venus's-flytrap, you strike.

Yielding is a kinesthetic response to stimuli. As soon as you feel so much as a hair of your body becoming compressed from an attacker or even the intent of an attack, you should already be moving. How do you know which part of you to yield? This is not something a rigid technique can teach. Rather you will learn to use your awareness (see chapter 1) and hone your sensitivity (chapter 6). Like radar, you will learn to interpret the incoming attack's direction and speed before the strike makes contact.

If you loosen your body to avoid a strike to the point where you can loosen no more, then you must step to a new root point. If you've exceeded your pocketing space limit, step in closer to the attacker either directly or to his side. In either case the step should put you in a more advantageous position from which to deliver the coupe de grace. How do you know when to step? When you feel that you're losing your balance from excessive pressure. We discuss balance in more detail in chapter 5. For now, know that even if losing balance is a by-product of your own rigidity, don't be too proud. Cut your losses and move. Don't get in the habit of challenging your opponent or you will fall into the trap of strength contests and ever-increasing rigidity. You will also get pummeled.

The following are a few examples of the principle of yielding. Understand these are only a few of many thousands of possible movements, which are only limited by your imagination. Master the principle, not the technique. The movements will vary from opponent to opponent due to different body types, physical abilities, and so on.

> Yielding has a strange influence on your opponent. He expects to make contact and finds nothing. He will often fall over himself as if drawn by some invisible magnet.

> The first law of war is the preservation of yourself and the destruction of your enemy.

Yielding a Strike

B is dealing with an attacker, A, who is trying to strike him in the chest or face. Rather than try to take the blow straight-on, B yields, or contorts his body, to redirect the force of the strike, thus avoiding it (figure 3.1a). If B attempts to block the strike straight-on, he must meet that force with equal or greater force. The strike may get through in some fashion. It will either go through his block or it will knock his own hand into his body, thus allowing time for A to gain an advantage over him. Or, if B's blocking arm is rigid, his whole body will also be rigid, allowing a well-trained opponent to move him and throw a quick

FIGURE 3.1

FIGURE 3.1

secondary strike. However, by redirecting the strike, turning his body, and pocketing the target area (figure 3.1b), B can control the direction of A's force with little or no effort.

For your opponent to hit you with power, you must "cooperate" a certain amount. Typically, you harden your body and gird yourself against impacts. You try to be tougher than your attacker. You thus become a rigid bull's-eye, basically a deer caught in the headlights. By yielding, however, you become uncooperative with your attacker. When a person throws a strike at you, there is a certain expectation that you will be there when the strike lands. This gives his mind and body a point of reference from which to balance. Because most people, including fighters, never train to develop dynamic balance, they need the resistance of your body to maintain their own balance and stay in the fight. By taking away their reference points, you take away their balance, however slightly. If you have balance and your opponent doesn't, no matter how hard he can punch or kick, he can't strike with effective power. When his energy is neither rooted nor focused, his energy is negated.

Spike-in-the-Sponge

When you are pushed or hit, you should imagine yourself as a sponge. No matter how hard you hit a sponge, it always returns to its original shape. Now, imagine yourself as a sponge with a steel spike in its center. Notice how by

FIGURE 3.2

falling into the pocket made by B's collapsing chest, A walks into B's elbow (figure 3.2). He has been impaled by the spike-in-the-sponge, a key example of the guided chaos principle of pocketing.

Your vitals are the sponge, and your weapons (hands, elbows, and so on) are the spikes. The harder the opponent hits you or the more force he exerts against you, the more damage he does to himself. This is why some people who can break boards, bats, and bricks cannot fight to save their lives. They don't understand the dynamics and chaos of combat. The human body is not like a brick. It flexes, moves its position, and fights back. There's a night-and-day difference between striking objects and hitting people. Besides, do you really have time to focus all your power into one killing blow when you're attacked? Do you think he'll stand there and wait for it, like in the movies? There are other ways of becoming powerful.

Being extremely loose and pliable leads to being extremely hard and powerful for the split second of impact. This is the same principle behind the power of a whip—or a wrecking ball.

Let your body remain as supple as a blade of grass, yet as rooted as an oak.

Pressure Responses

The following are some simple examples of what we mean by responding loosely. Remember, these are not techniques. When your body becomes familiar with the principle and you develop the feel that characterizes looseness, you will spontaneously invent your own movements.

Down Pressure on Your Arm

A's arm exerts down pressure on B's forearm at close range. B yields the forearm downward, simultaneously rolling the elbow of the same arm up and over, striking the head or shoulder or spearing straight into the gut (figure 3.3a). A's down pressure results in a seesaw action in B, using no strength whatsoever. The whole body rises and falls with the rise and fall of the elbow, and it's all started with the impetus of A's down pressure.

Another example of a loose response to down pressure is remarkably simple. Nevertheless, it would be impossible to perform with a tight body. B, yielding to A's down pressure, simply punches down into the top of A's groin (figure 3.3b), bounces off, and up-elbows into A's jaw (figure 3.3c).

You can see that this bouncing strike principle becomes effective for delivering many strikes within one motion. You won't, however, have the required

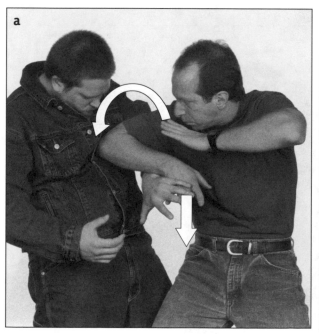
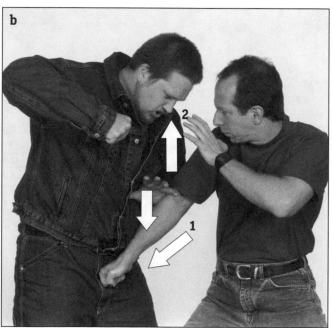

FIGURE 3.3

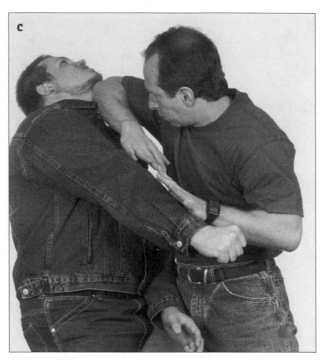
FIGURE 3.3

springiness unless you're loose. Another possible movement is B drops the down-pressured arm and turns his whole body away like a windmill, driving his opposite elbow into A's face.

You may say to yourself "How am I going to remember all these moves?" We can't stress enough, if you're loose and sensitive and have learned and practiced applying the principles, you won't have to. You'll just fall into them and say: "Oh! Look what I just did!" or "He made me do it!" and you will be right. Techniques will emerge from the flow, not vice versa. In classical training, you practice 100 techniques and hope they'll work just like they did in class if reality rears its ugly head. Or you learn one technique, perfect it, and hope to apply it to every situation you run across. This isn't practical. Would you bring a screwdriver to a job that requires a hammer?

Up Pressure on Your Arm

B can simply slide in with a horizontal chop to the face (figure 3.4a) or he can punch down by simply rolling his elbow up in a yielding response to A's rising pressure into the crook of his arm, thus giving room to drive his fist in (figure 3.4b). Or, B circles over and underneath in yielding to A's up pressure and drives a spear hand up into A's throat (figure 3.4c). Or, A's up pressure on B's forearm causes B to simply rotate his shoulder, raising into an up-elbow strike under A's arm and up into his chin (figure 3.4d). The possibilities are endless, but they're all created by looseness.

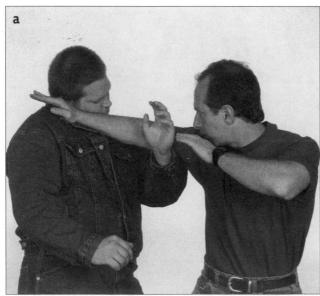
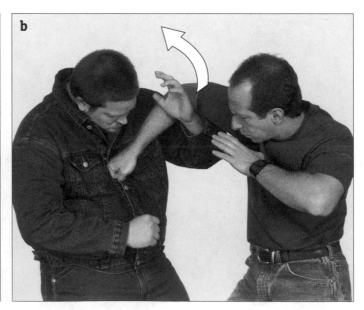
FIGURE 3.4

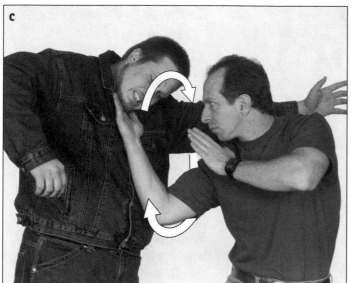 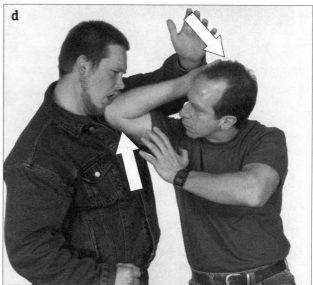

FIGURE 3.4

Inward Pressure on Your Arm

A pushes in against B's arms to collapse them (figure 3.5a). B lets A's hands go where they want to, which is right at B's throat, except that B won't be there when they arrive. Because of body unity, when B yields to A's pressure, his entire body pivots out of the way and to the side of A. This actually brings B in closer where he can easily pivot like a windmill into an elbow strike to A's head (figure 3.5b).

In doing this, B has yielded his hands and forearms inward and rolled his elbow up, over, and down on A's head or shoulder joint. B has actually sucked A into the spike-in-the-sponge. Remember, with proper looseness, all these motions have a flip-floppy kind of feel, as if you were a drunken puppet.

 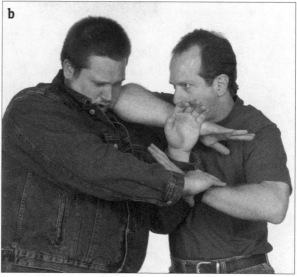

FIGURE 3.5

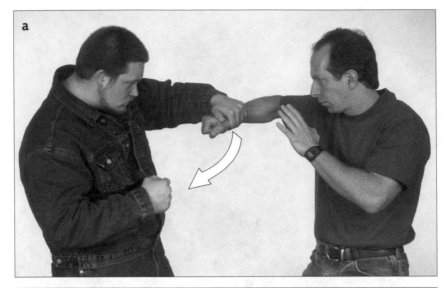

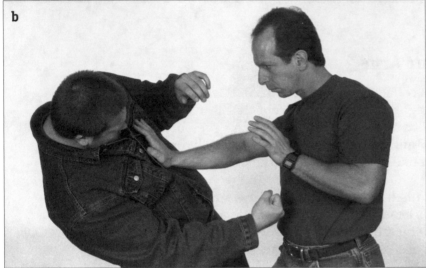

FIGURE 3.6

Outward Pressure on Your Arm

Very often, in an attempt to control his victim's arms, an attacker will actually pull them into his midsection to smother them. In addition, sometimes an attempt to block a strike downward winds up pulling the strike in. If you're loose and sensitive enough, you flow with this energy and actually augment it by striking him in the same direction he's pulling you. For example, B is now counterattacking by punching at A's throat. A, panicking, attempts to smother the blows by pulling them into his chest (figure 3.6a). B, by being loose and sensitive, detects this change and flows with it by stepping in and augmenting A's directional energy, striking to the chest with the palm (figure 3.6b).

Elbow Pressure

B is in a right lead, standing a little too sideways, so A pushes against B's right elbow to keep him from turning back (figure 3.7a). Instead of resisting, B loosens the right shoulder completely and lets it go, yielding and turning away with A's push just enough to release the pressure (figure 3.7b). The speed with which B yields is directly proportional to the amount of force A exerts on the elbow. In fact, B reacts to this touch on his elbow the same way as if he had been touched with a red-hot frying pan. Notice also that A's pushing hand has inadvertently fallen into B's other hand. With a spring-like action, B's whole body has jerked away—perhaps only one inch—and then bounces back in with a loose, smashing chop to the throat (figure 3.7c).

These are all examples of what you can accomplish with looseness. If they seem absurdly simple, it's because they are. If you're wondering if they work, they do. If you haven't trained yourself to be loose, however, even if you're highly trained in other ways, you won't be able to perform them. Here are some drills to develop your ability to be loose.

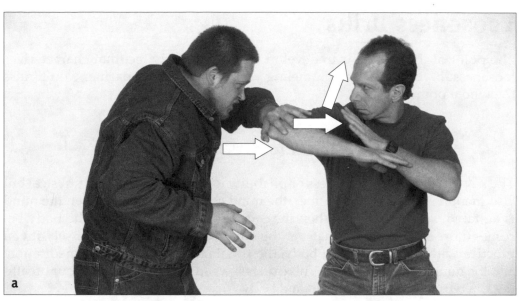

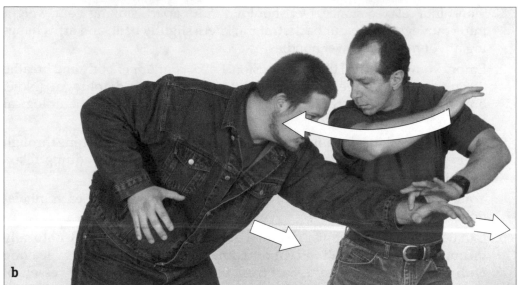

FIGURE 3.7

53

Looseness Drills

The point of these drills is to develop the overall body feel that characterizes looseness. If you focus on pummeling your target or your partner, you'll miss the whole point.

Relaxed Breathing

The key to developing looseness or pliability is relaxation, not only physical but also mental relaxation. Remember, the mind controls the body. When the mind is agitated, so is the body. When the mind is calm and focused, the body becomes more responsive to whatever the mind wishes it to do. Conversely, if you practice with a loose, relaxed body, the training acts as a moving meditation, and the mind becomes relaxed. This drill helps you focus on relaxing your breathing, thereby relaxing your mind and body.

1. Stand in a relaxed stance, feet shoulder-width apart, sinking your weight into your legs. Keep your back straight, knees slightly bent, and arms hanging at your sides like wet noodles.

2. Empty your mind of all the day's tension. Relax your upper body and breathe through your nose deep into your belly, loosening your diaphragm. (Note: breathing high in the chest, the way most people do, creates neurological tension.)

3. Imagine your skin is inhaling also, absorbing fresh air and sunshine through every pore like a sponge. Feel this absorbed air and energy adding relaxation to your body and your limply hanging arms.

4. Your stomach appears to actually expand like a balloon with each inhalation of fresh, soothing air.

5. Exhale by releasing your expanded stomach so air flows out naturally through your nose (don't force it out). Imagine all negative energy leaving with your expended breath. Feel fresh blood pumping into the vessels of your arms adding weight and liquid relaxation.

6. Feel the movement of air across your skin. Imagine a gentle breeze swaying your body like a blade of grass.

Fold Like a Napkin

This kind of looseness is not combative because you are not going to fall off your feet in a fight. However, because the concept of completely relaxing local target areas of your body is so alien, we are going for total surrender in this drill.

1. Stand with your eyes closed.

2. Have one partner stand behind you and one in front.

3. Have your partners take turns slowly pushing you.

4. Let your body be so relaxed that as soon as you're pushed, you fold like a napkin and fall totally limp into the arms of the other partner. Let yourself go completely (obviously you'll need partners you can trust).

Dead-Fish Arms

So how do you know if you are relaxed? Try this.

1. Stand with your arms hanging at your sides.

2. Have another person take your arms by the wrists and raise them outward for you. You'll be amazed how difficult this is for most people. They try to raise their arms themselves. They simply can't "let go."

3. Your elbows should hang loosely below your wrists and shoulders (since this is the "folding point" of the limb).

4. If your partner were to suddenly release your wrists, your arms should flop to your sides like two dead fish.

5. Now have your partner place his hands under your armpits and push straight up. Most people will be immovable, because their shoulders are locked to their chests. If you are truly loose, your shoulders will rise independent of the rest of your body, as if you were shrugging.

6. When the upward pressure is released, your arms should flop down like two heavy, wet noodles.

Weaving Python

The sort of body isolation and pliability you demonstrate with this drill is vital to your survival. You must assume that every person who attacks you is far stronger than you, deadly serious, and can hurt you wherever he strikes.

1. Stand with your arms hanging at your sides.

2. Have your partner place one hand about six inches away from the center of your chest, palm in. His other hand should be six inches away from the center of your back, also palm in.

3. Without moving your feet or raising or turning your body, expand your chest directly outward so you can touch his hand. This requires you to throw your shoulders and arms back, loosen your stomach and pectoral muscles, and bend your knees further to sink your weight backward into your hips and buttocks. This is a compensating move to keep you from falling on your face.

4. Now, reverse the movement and touch his rear hand with the center of your back. You will have to cave in your chest and throw your shoulders and arms forward, loosening your back muscles. You'll also have to rotate your pelvis down and forward and sink your weight into your knees to avoid falling backward.

5. Now, in one loose, continuous movement, like a python weaving backward and forward, touch one hand and then the other repeatedly. Keep this motion completely horizontal. Your head should remain the same height above the floor. Your knees should remain bent and your feet flat on the floor.

What is the point of all this? If the two palms were knives, it would be immediately apparent.

The Hula

You simply want to keep your weight low and balanced, like a downhill skier or a middle linebacker, rather than high and precarious like a ballet dancer. This drill encourages you to keep your rootedness mobile, like that of a big jungle cat or a tank on ball bearings.

1. Stand with your arms hanging at your sides.
2. Imagine that the air has weight, like seawater. Feel the currents drift across your skin. Feel that your arms, indeed your whole body, could easily float in the air through no effort of its own. Imagine, however, that your pelvis is attached by a steel cable to a 500-pound weight hanging below you.
3. Now gently raise your arms in front of you, about as high and wide as your shoulders. Help to raise them by straightening your knees slightly. While doing this, use only enough strength to keep them up. Keep your upper and lower arms totally flaccid without any muscular tension whatsoever.
4. Practice raising your arms up and down, back and forth, in a super-slow, graceful manner like a drunken hula dancer, keeping your feet well-rooted to the ground. As if your whole body is moving in a current of water, your legs, hips, back, and shoulders drift with your arms as they move. Breathe slowly and deeply into your belly at the same time.
5. Perform the above while walking around slowly with the knees bent like an ice skater or Groucho Marx.

At first your arms may feel unnatural and heavy, but as you become more proficient at this exercise, you will notice your arms beginning to feel weightless. Develop the sensation that your arms are suspended on a cushion of air, so light and responsive that a fly landing on them would cause them to move. Apply this sensation to your whole body. This is what it feels like to be loose. Remember, though, that a 500-pound weight is keeping your pelvis anchored low to the ground. Although your hips and knees can sway with the current easily, you are rooted to the ground through your feet like an oak tree. A common mistake, however, is to glue your feet to the ground and refuse to move them, even if you're losing your balance. This is both unnecessary and dangerous.

Turning

Perform this simple movement in a dream-like, meditative manner, as if driven by ocean waves. Breathe deep into your belly. If some part of your body were to hit a pole as it moves, it should wrap around the pole like a heavy sausage chain.

1. Start by standing relaxed, with your knees bent deeply and feet a little wider than your shoulders. Use only enough muscle to completely shift your weight from one leg to the other.
2. Empty your entire body of muscular tension as if you were asleep or drunk. Imagine your arms, shoulders, back, chest, waist, and hips are simply dead meat hanging from your skeleton.

3. As you slowly shift your weight completely from foot to foot without rising or leaning, initiate a slow, twisting motion. Keep your whole body fairly low.

4. As you increase the twisting motion, let your arms leave your sides and begin limply swinging in the air from the centripetal force. At the end of each weight shift, they wrap around your body one way and then unwrap as you shift to the other leg (figure 3.8). Don't make your arms move. This is critical. Let the momentum of your body dictate their entire motion.

5. Increase the twisting slowly until, with your knees bent, your shoulders turn almost 90 degrees beyond your feet.

6. At the end of each turn, your hips should be above the foot toward which you have turned. Thus, your hips travel a linear distance that is as far as your stance is wide. At no point in this exercise should your body rise. Keep your knees bent deeply.

FIGURE 3.8

Swimming

Now instead of just drifting with the waves, you will begin to glide and swim through them. The swimming analogy is useful in correcting an error often seen in beginning students of guided chaos. When blocking, beginners often actually pull a strike into the body in an effort to smother it. However, if you do this against a more experienced student or opponent, he will "push your pull" (see chapter 6) and use your energy to catapult his strike into you. In other words, when you pull his arm in, he'll add to your pulling energy by beating your energy back to its source—you—and actually strike with both, like a rubber band. When you swim, as you pull your arm back, do you pull the water into your chest? Of course not. You pull and then push the water past you. You do the same with an opponent's strike when you employ the swimming motion. This drill develops your ability to use your pulling energy to push your opponent's strike past you.

1. Do a swimming crawl stroke through the air as if it were made of water. Loosely articulate your shoulders, back, and waist to get the maximum extension; keep your body low with the knees bent (figure 3.9a) but don't lean.

2. Step forward with each stroke, with the leg opposite the arm you're using.

FIGURE 3.9

3. Turn your feet as you accommodate the extra reach required to make the motion. Reach as far as you can with each stroke, but without leaning.

4. However, keep the path your arms take as economical as possible. In other words, don't windmill them. Try to cut through the "water" with a flat stroke; move your body and arms with as little resistance, or "splash," and as much efficiency as you can.

5. As they retract, sweep your hands down a few inches away from your pectorals and make tight circles as they extend back out. Once again, make your shoulders do the circling so your hands don't take on a wide, windmill-like path.

It's a lot harder to move a flat surface broadside through water than if you turn it edge-wise. So, too, a wild, sloppy stroke will slow you down as you try to swim. The application is that in combat you should "swim" through your opponent's defenses and knife through his resistance, rather than challenging it head-on.

For example, if an opponent exerts down pressure on your arm, yield with it and swim out of it, circling your arm down and then over for a dropping palm strike to the neck or a spear hand to the eyes. This is yielding with the same arm. As your arm circles down, the tight arc it makes across your pectorals will serve to cover you as it yields. If your whole body yields, it turns away like a propeller on one side and crashes in with borrowed energy on the opposite side (figure 3.9b). This is not something you plan, it just happens, because you're loose and without a thought, like a drunken puppet.

If your opponent is applying up pressure against your arm, guess what? That's right—backstroke out of it. As the pressured side of your body yields and turns away from the force, the other side turns in and delivers a devastating rising spear hand to the throat (figure 3.9c). Practice swimming backward and forward and at different angles.

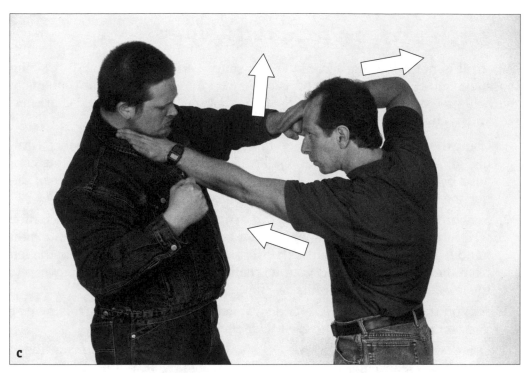

FIGURE 3.9

Swimming Sidestroke

Exactly as the name implies, practice doing the sidestroke. As with all swimming movements, fully turn and extend your back and shoulders (figure 3.10). It helps to step forward with each stroke, with the leg opposite the arm you're using. This helps to get your entire body weight moving behind each movement. This motion is useful for warding off strikes to your side, as from multiple attackers.

FIGURE 3.10

Solo Contact Flow

This drill is not a fighting technique. It's simply an exercise for emphasizing looseness and full body weight transfer. As you understand the movements in this drill you can begin performing the more random movements that characterize guided chaos any way you choose.

1. Using the same, slow, relaxed side-to-side swaying motion used in the "Turning" drill (pages 56-57), make small circles—no wider than the perimeter of your body—in front of your body with your hands and arms. (When deflecting strikes, it's a waste to protect empty space.)

2. Synchronize the movement of your arms with the flowing, side-to-side weight transfer from leg to leg, so that as you move to the left, your right hand is pushing the air across the front of your body and down to the left from the top of its arc, and your left hand is doing a backhanded sweep to the left along the bottom of its arc (figure 3.11a).

3. As you transfer your weight and sway back to the right, the arms reverse and complete the other halves of their circles (figure 3.11b).

4. Drive with the legs as you flow loosely with your upper body from side to side. Make believe the air you're pushing weighs 1,000 pounds, but use absolutely no tension.

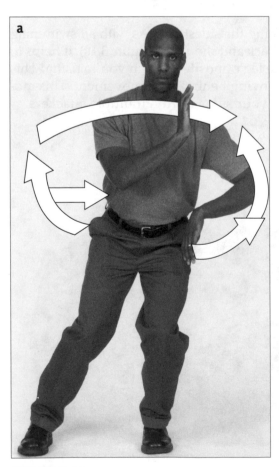 

FIGURE 3.11

Sticks of Death

This drill requires great looseness, balance, and sensitivity so that you don't swing wildly at the sticks but instead glance off them as you use pocketing to avoid contact.

1. Your partner stands with two four-foot-long padded sticks behind a heavy bag or padded dummy, holding the weapons like cue sticks against the dummy.

2. Stand three feet away from your partner. Your partner should randomly poke the sticks at you.

3. Evade and redirect the sticks, sliding through them while simultaneously attacking the dummy's eyes and throat with both hands (figure 3.12). (Refer back to the Jack Benny stance in chapter 2.) The object is to get in to biting range, while simultaneously remaining unavailable to the sticks.

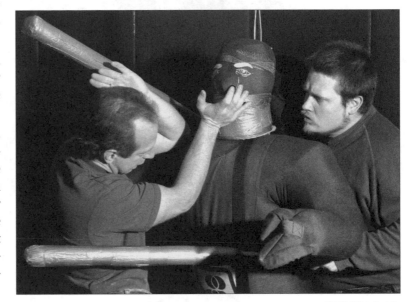

FIGURE 3.12

Sticky Fingers

Maybe this should be called "Stinky Fingers." All kidding aside, your sense of smell is a superb example of heightened sensitivity in that it forces you to extend your awareness out beyond your skin. This drill is vital in overcoming the deeply ingrained, macho habit of overcoming strength with strength by trying to withstand incoming blows.

1. Have someone try to poke you randomly with both hands at ever-increasing speed anywhere on your body.

2. You can't back up, and you can't block. It's like when you were five years old, and your older brother tried to tickle you to exhaustion.

3. It helps to imagine some vile substance on the tips of his fingers to aid in your pocketing reaction. Revulsion is a good source of yielding energy. Some people put on old clothes and try to dot each other with paint.

Small Circle Dance

This may qualify as the strangest looking of all the drills. At all times while performing this, stay balanced, no matter how wild it gets. Try it with music. If you start looking like Elvis on acid you're on the right track. This drill helps develop

FIGURE 3.13

your ability to hit with several parts of your body simultaneously, without direct control from your rational brain.

1. Start with one part of your body, say, your hand, and begin making small, loose circles in the air with it.

2. Begin making circles in the opposite direction with your other hand. This trains your brain to handle various parts of your body in motion simultaneously. From here it gets crazy.

3. Begin making circles with one elbow, then add the other (in the opposite direction).

4. Start circling with your knees. Add your hips, your head, back, buttocks, and shoulders. In short, try it with as many parts of your body as you can manage, loosely, simultaneously, and in complete balance (figure 3.13).

What is the point of all this silliness? Looseness. Police reports show time and again that when a car full of people crashes, it's the drunken passengers, ironically, who walk away. They're too crocked to panic, and their bodies stay loose on impact.

Psycho-Chimp

Second only to the previous drill in terms of wackiness, this exercise will have a very liberating result on your looseness and savagery.

1. Begin with a relaxed stance, feet about shoulder-width apart, knees slightly bent and loose, arms outstretched to the left. Your arms should feel like dead weight, with what seem like the finest strings barely holding them up by the wrists.

2. With a strong, dropping motion of your knees, let your arms fall and swing to the right, using only the turning momentum of your body, drive of your legs, and weight of your arms to propel them. Without pause, drop and swing them back in the other direction.

3. Don't stop. As you continue to do this, your arms should maintain complete, dead-weight relaxation. They will begin to take on snapping, chaotic trajectories that get wilder and wilder.

4. Drop on each motion, like cracking a whip, with your entire body (the whip) and your connection with the ground (the handle). Step around as you drop.

5. Increase the speed gradually until you're going as fast as you can, and you

begin to look like a psycho-chimp. Be free, but try not to hit yourself!

6. While maintaining looseness, merely modify your arms' trajectories (using your body's momentum, not your arm muscles) so they don't swing behind your body, which would be wasteful movement.

7. Pocket and yield your body severely to keep you from hitting yourself and to create more room for your arms to move. At the same time, modify the wildness so it occurs mostly in front of you.

8. Now, without stopping this swinging, dervish-like craziness, merely recognize the inherent strikes within the flow, without forcing them. Without much plan, have the snapping motions turn into chops, spears, uppercuts, and other strikes we don't have names for.

If the wave-like energy you're creating is properly guided by your whole body weight, the power, speed, and savagery of your movement will be plainly evident. If your arms encounter each other, they will whip and coil like live snakes, yet avoid entangling each other because of your looseness.

Notice that as the arc of some whipping movements tighten, their speed increases. We call this slingshotting, a method for increasing the power behind strikes. For example, the arm after connecting with a loose, rising backhand strike to the chin will increase in speed greatly if its arc tightens as it loops all the way around into a hook punch to the ribs. This is akin to the speed of a spinning figure skater increasing as she pulls in her arms.

Circle Clap

This drill is very important for developing a feeling of explosiveness at high speed while maintaining muscular relaxation.

1. Clap your hands as fast as you can. Your clapping speed and endurance will be dictated exclusively by your ability to relax your muscles.

2. Simultaneously, move your hands above your head and make a wide circle, down to your waist, back above your head, and in and out.

3. Now circle them side to side. Clap at any angle you can think of. Do it on one leg and with your eyes closed as you twist and turn your body into bizarre contortions. Try generating the power for the claps not in your arms, but in a vibration that wells up from your legs into your hips. Think of your whole body as spasming with your arms loosely attached. You will probably find that your hands are most comfortable about two inches apart.

5. When tension overcomes motion, stop, breathe, and visualize your exhalation spreading relaxation throughout your arms. Start again.

The reason you make the circles is that you want to maintain the relaxation no matter what your position. What is the application? Later, you will learn to deliver blows with no windup or room to move. In a fight, most people's muscles clamp up with supreme adrenaline-fired exertion. This renders the person frozen with tension as he fights the movements of his own body. With the "Circle Clap" drill, you reprogram your nervous system to tense only in tiny microbursts separated by total relaxation. This allows you to change direction at any time and thus flow with the fight.

Split-Brain Air-Writing

Since you are learning to fight spontaneously with total freedom, your nervous system needs to be able to keep pace with your increasing sensitivity in order to handle uncoordinated motion with different parts of your body simultaneously. This bizarre exercise helps you to develop a loose, relaxed brain.

1. With your right hand, write the letter "B" in the air. At the same time, write the same letter with your left hand, but flipped, as if it were a mirror image. Do a few more letters.

2. Now it gets fun. Simultaneously, write a different letter with each hand. Start at the same time and end at the same time with each hand.

It's not easy. Do a few of these until your head hurts and then stop. If you do this a little every day, the brain begins to adjust, and your fighting will become freer. Fighting multiple opponents requires just this kind of split-brain awareness.

Learning guided chaos is more like having an "aha!" experience than studying for a black belt exam. Sudden realizations of how all the principles come together will happen with increasing frequency. As such, even though we've only gone through some drills to encourage looseness, you will be using what you've learned in this chapter to develop the principles explained in the remaining chapters of part II: body unity (chapter 4), balance (chapter 5), and sensitivity (chapter 6). It's important, therefore, to come back to these drills and imbue them with your heightened understanding as you advance. Moreover, many of the drills you will perform in upcoming chapters will continue to train and hone your looseness as well.

Preventing Common Mistakes

➤ Maintain a strong root at all times while doing looseness drills. The tendency is to stumble around with your new-found looseness like a drunkard.

➤ Step to a new root point only when your balance is overchallenged.

➤ Keep your feet connected to the ground like the roots of an oak, while everything from your ankles up should be like ribbons of spring steel. Even so, you're not glued to the ground. You should be able to glide to a new root point as easily and powerfully as a jungle cat.

➤ In solo contact flow, make sure your arms move in sync with your body.

➤ In other words, as you transfer weight to your right leg, your left hand sweeps to the right and down in an arc in front of your chin. It should have all your mass behind it. If your right hand swept to the left as your body moved to the right, all your momentum would be dissipated.

➤ Be aware that looseness doesn't mean you become a helpless noodle. In chapter 7 you will learn to move in ways that help you instead of hurt you as you remain loose.

CHAPTER FOUR

BODY UNITY

Body unity is a necessary foundation for balance and a source of power for looseness. Simply put, body unity means that if any part of your body moves, no matter how slightly, then the rest of it moves also. If you weigh 180 pounds, then every movement, even a finger strike, should have at least 180 pounds of momentum behind it. (We say "at least" because the phenomenon of dropping energy that you will learn fully in chapter 6 will increase this amount.)

We're not talking mysterious secrets to achieve body unity. In almost any sport, you've got to get your body behind the ball. Top athletes, with little strain, are able to do this with grace, balance, power, and accuracy. Their body unity is manifested by a perfect, relaxed, mechanical alignment of all the skeletal joints. This is vital. Without it, you cannot develop relaxed power.

The movements in fighting, however, are far more varied and anarchic than in sports. There are millions of tiny differences in the way tennis players serve, but the parameters and the end result are always the same: they must stand behind the baseline, toss the ball vertically, and hit it into a box. A street brawl has

no such rules. Therefore, you must really understand what's going on behind attributes such as body unity, balance, looseness, and sensitivity in order to apply them to a situation of total chaos.

In Eastern martial thought, the terms are different, but the goals are the same. The esoteric tai chi term for perfect alignment is translated as "moving the chi like a thread through the nine pearls." The nine pearls are the joints of the body: the ankle, knee, hip, waist, spine, shoulder, elbow, wrist, and fist. If we take out the obscure symbolism, what we're left with is simple physics. Chi, is "threaded" through the joints, with each alignment augmenting and reinforcing the others with a smooth, unkinked flow of power from the floor to the hand (or whatever weapon you're using). "Great," you say, "but what is chi?" The simplest definition of chi is "energy." We bring up the mysterious subject of chi here because it directly relates to all our principles, especially body unity, with its concept of delivering the most power with the greatest efficiency. But to speak of chi, we must first explain the concept of internal energy.

Internal Energy

One way of differentiating the styles of martial arts is to divide them into two categories depending on whether the source and application of available energy is "external" or "internal." In an external art, the source of power is almost purely muscular; strength and speed are emphasized through learning and repeatedly executing fixed drills in unvarying patterns. The full-power muscular contractions that are characteristic of external-style arts are typically marked by a battle cry, or kiai. External-style arts place a substantial amount of stress on your tissues, as is evidenced by the high incidence of tendon, ligament, and muscle injuries in external-style schools. These injuries often occur without even making contact with an adversary. Ideally, after decades of training (if his or her body holds out), the external-style martial artist sometimes develops an easy, effortless grace that requires little muscular exertion. This begs the question "Since this is what you're really after, why not learn grace from the beginning?" This is what we do in guided chaos by developing and training the attributes of body unity, balance, looseness, and sensitivity.

Although our approach is different from all the others, you could consider guided chaos one of the internal-style arts, along with the more traditional Chinese styles of tai chi, hsing I, and bagua. In an internal-style art, the mind and nervous system are relaxed and amplified with both static and moving meditation exercises. Internal-style energy methods emphasize perfect, relaxed mechanical alignment of the bones and tendons to achieve the most efficient application of energy while using the least muscular force. It's the same with body unity. Your body, even if you're a small person, has significant mass irrespective of its inherent strength. In other words, even if you can't punch your way out of a paper bag, if you simply dropped the dead weight of your body on another individual, the force generated would be substantial, especially if the contact point was something hard, like an elbow.

The goal in using your internal energy is to have the entire mass of your body perfectly aligned with all the bones in your body so that this mass is behind every movement. This way you can strike, block, and so forth, and still maintain muscular relaxation because you are not forcing the motion but remaining loose. An example of perfect misalignment would be trying to push a car with your feet pointing in opposite directions, standing sideways, your head near your knees, using the backs of your fingertips. Even if you can bench-press 400 pounds, if you are positioned this way, the car is not going to move, and you'll probably break your hands, too. "So," you might ask, "wouldn't the ideal combination be perfect alignment with massive muscular strength?" Yes, if you're pushing a car, because in such a case, the goal is to move one object (the car) in space from point A to point B in a straight line. You can commit all your force to one direction, because you're not expecting the car to suddenly jump up and down or sideways. Unfortunately we're talking about combat, where there are no rules and where everything changes, including force, speed, angle of attack, opponents, weapons, and traction—millisecond by millisecond. In the famous film *Enter the Dragon*, a bad guy tries to impress Bruce Lee with his power by breaking boards with his hand. Bruce, unimpressed, remains calm and says enigmatically "Boards don't hit back!" In short, your assailant is not going to stand still while you take your best shot.

Body unity does not mean "body rigidity." Effective, combative body unity requires the ability to change direction effortlessly and instantaneously. You cannot respond to change if all your force is committed to one direction.

When the muscles of your arm strain to do heavy work, the triceps and biceps oppose each other to stabilize the joint. These muscles have what is called an "antagonistic relationship." This hinders either one from accomplishing their respective tasks: extending and contracting the elbow joint. Using intense muscular effort anywhere in your body activates antagonistic muscles, making you rigid, hard, slow, and unresponsive—just what you don't want to be when fighting for your life. Most people (and many trained martial artists) get very hung up on this because they think pure strength is the end-all of fighting. Unfortunately, the simple reality is this: No matter how strong you are, there's always someone stronger.

Internal energy, however, is more than just perfect alignment, more than just having a long lever to, say, pry loose a boulder. Cultivating internal energy involves developing an explosive nervous system as a conduit for chi. You can achieve this through the unique principle of dropping (introduced in chapter 2 and detailed within the context of guided chaos in chapter 6). "Chi?" you ask, "Isn't that the supernatural force you see in movies that can hit people without physical contact?" Let's look at this concept more closely.

Chi

There are many intriguing accounts of the much-sought-after phenomenon of projecting chi outside your body without actual physical contact as a source of self-defense. While decades of day-long meditation may or may not actually make this possible, this expectation continues to foster the image of your being able to develop superhuman powers with an average body. This only adds to the mystery, confusion, and eventual frustration over how to make ordinary self-defense work for you and not get caught up in the illusion of becoming Chuck Norris or Luke Skywalker overnight. You may think no one could be quite this gullible, but this expectation lives in many dedicated tai chi practitioners, as a longed-for end result of their training. However, there is a danger in anticipating the long-term development of an almost unattainable weapon when the short-term prospect of taking your life in your hands could be a much closer reality.

Since we've never seen a demonstration of chi projection (and some of us have spent large sums of money in China looking for it; see page 68), we can only speak of chi as it has been defined in other classic literature and experienced by us. Chi is not a myth. Nor is it mystical. The simplest definition of chi is "life energy." In classic Chinese literature this energy can take many forms, which we won't go into here. For self-defense purposes, let's simply call it "internally applied grace and balance." A close reading of classic Chinese texts will yield a definition that can be understood in a firm, scientific light. *The Tai Chi Boxing Chronicle* by Kuo Lien-Ying (1994) defines chi as the "circulating point of finesse within the body." What's unclear in the English translation is that chi is not some indefinable, supernatural force (although it can appear so), it's merely a code word for describing multiple, simultaneous attributes. Even the English word finesse can be hard to define. But don't worry, you won't need a crystal ball to get it. Diligently practicing and applying all the principles of guided chaos will develop chi in you to the extent that others will not understand how you're doing what you're doing to them.

In Search of Chi Projection

A group of John Perkins's friends spent thousands of dollars on a trip to China where they were invited by a particular school to witness a demonstration of authentic chi projection. When they finally met with the masters of this school, they were told they could not have it demonstrated on them because it would kill them. The masters performed great pushing and throwing techniques, but not one would demonstrate chi projection.

Another analogy for the flow of energy, or chi, through a unified body is to visualize your tendons and bones as a garden hose with water rushing through them. If the joints or muscles are not loosely, gracefully, and mechanically aligned, the "hose" becomes kinked, and the "water" does not flow. When you apply body unity to the definition of chi as a "circulating point of finesse," you can see that this implies that chi also embodies automatic physical awareness and skill—awareness of your own body's position and movement as well as your opponent's. This kinesthetic awareness requires a foundation of balance and sensitivity, which you will learn to develop in upcoming chapters.

Where is this "rushing water," or chi, supposed to come from? It comes from a relaxed, unified body that knows how to react instantly to outside force. Outside force generated by your attacker should compress your whole body like a spring, provoking a reaction: absorptive, yielding, and collecting of energy on the side of your body in contact with your opponent, and explosive, steel-spring-like releasing of the accumulated energy on the opposite (striking) side. When you're balanced, some part of your body will be rooting the energy (absorbing the energy in your feet like a coiled spring), and another body part—the hand, elbow, or other foot—delivering it.

Viewed from the outside, unified body movement is often undetectable, because it might involve only internal energy changes or slight muscle and joint realignments. As you move toward mastery of this methodology, your large body movements and circular redirections of strikes will become more and more economical. The sensation of body unity becomes obvious only to yourself or the person you are hitting. At this point, the energy is truly internal, and you may seem to move hardly at all. This occurs, for example, when some part of your body (like an elbow) is in contact with your opponent's trunk. Using dropping energy and body unity, you can achieve (with apologies to Bruce Lee's one-inch punch) a no-inch punch, that can either send your attacker flying or cause internal damage, depending on how you deliver it. And this is with no winding up. To summarize, when you move to strike, your opponent should always feel as if he's getting hit with an object that weighs at least as much as your entire body, even if it's only your finger.

There is a more common term for body unity—grace. When a person moves with grace, he or she epitomizes coordination, finesse, balance, power, and body unity all coming together as one. In fact, maybe we could call grace a mystical Western technique!

Enhance body unity when striking by training so that when your knee stops bending (when dropping or stepping), your hand stops moving also. This prevents you from leaning or overcommitting and ensures full body mass behind every strike. Another way to enhance body unity is to experience every strike you deliver as pressure building in your feet.

TALES OF CHI

John Perkins

While teaching in a New York City school in 1980, I saw a demonstration given by a group of Japanese martial artists who claimed some amazing powers. I observed one practitioner kicking to the throats of three others who were kneeling, without inflicting injury. I thought there must be something in the way the kick was performed and absorbed that would be significant.

The problem arose when these practitioners stated that no one could hurt them, because they covered themselves with a protective shield of energy. Although they did not specifically call this energy chi, that was the implication. Demonstrations such as this are typical of those who claim to have supernatural chi. I then requested if I could simply poke the kneeling men in the trachea with my index finger. They looked at me with contempt but would not allow an "unbeliever" to try it out. Later, when I engaged in some not-so-gentle kumite (free sparring) I found them susceptible to being thrown, pushed, and struck.

Now I'm not saying that chi flow or iron-shirt techniques don't exist. In fact, I've seen ordinary people struck many times with bludgeons (including blackjacks and nightsticks) and have even broken my own heavyweight police baton over a few heads without stopping the attackers. I have seen other authentic demonstrations, but they have always involved some kind of absorption of energy. I have also seen many fakers, who used tricks analogous to those used in professional wrestling.

Yes, the professional boxer or highly skilled martial arts practitioner can toughen his or her body to what seems a supernatural degree. But as far as projecting a shield of energy around the body, all I can say is, try this acid test: ask the claimant if he would allow you to poke him in the eye. See if he can bounce your finger off with pure energy.

Body Unity Drills

Body unity drills focus on training you to move with the intent of driving a thousand pounds but not the strength. In other words, you position your body to overcome that degree of resistance, but actually use only enough muscular strength to move the weight of your own flesh. Why? Because you want to avoid the tightness that comes from straining. As you learned in chapter 3, you need to remain loose enough to react instantly to a change in your attacker's energy so that then you can take advantage of your superior body position and amplify your opponent's energy to use against him.

Body Writing

Many beginners have a lot of trouble understanding the concept of body unity. They wave their arms around as if they were disembodied serpents. This exercise may help you begin to feel what body unity is.

1. Stand facing a wall and raise your arm as if to write on a blackboard (if you've got a real blackboard, use it).
2. With your right hand, sign your name in big letters at least three feet high. Notice your wrist and elbow do all the work.
3. Now do it again, but this time, lock your wrist, arm, elbow, and shoulder so they are absolutely immobile. So how are you supposed to write? By stepping, sinking, and turning your body from the waist down, you actually write with your legs.
4. Do the same thing with your other hand.
5. Repeat this drill, writing the whole alphabet, until you can achieve the same fluidity in your "body writing" as you have writing the normal way.

Granted, body unity should also involve free movement of your hand, wrist, elbow, and shoulder, but most people can do this after a short while anyway. It's the foot, leg, hip, waist, trunk, and back involvement that eludes most beginners. That's why it's helpful to do this drill, writing the whole alphabet, until you can achieve the same fluidity as you'd have writing the normal way.

Starting the Mower

This drill involves another visualization of another common movement. It requires you to follow the principle of positioning your body to do 1,000 pounds of work with none of the exertion.

1. Imagine you're starting the world's most stubborn lawn mower.
2. Without using any strength or tension, stand with your feet wide, bend your knees, turn, and reach deeply to your left or right and loosely "grab" the mower's starter "cord." Keep your head and back relatively perpendicular to the ground. Turn as far as you can, shifting your weight to your forward leg (figure 4.1a).
3. Moving slowly and loosely, breathing deeply, begin to pull until you have shifted all your weight to your rear leg. Your elbow should be behind you and your pulling hand, near your shoulder (figure 4.1b).
4. Slowly reverse the movement, pushing the cord back to its source, while aligning your body as if the cord is pushing against your hand.
5. Repeat several times, moving as slowly as possible with zero muscular tension. This is not an isometric exercise, however, so don't "flex" while doing it.

Opening the Door

No, this is not some mysterious drill from Outer Mongolia. Anytime you open a door and walk through it, you have an opportunity to practice body unity. This works best on spring-loaded doors that close on their own.

FIGURE 4.1

1. When you open a door, don't lean or stretch to reach the knob. Walk up to it so that your arm, elbow, and shoulder remain in a low, relaxed position.

2. To open the door, don't yank with the biceps or shoulder. Step away from the door and rotate your body and feet to generate the necessary torque, so you use only minimal finger strength to hold it (pull with your legs, not your hand). If you examine this motion, with the exception of your hand position, you'll see that we're asking you to move with the same mechanics you'd use if the door weighed 500 pounds.

3. As you walk through the door, stay as close to it as possible. Release your arm and swing it through, yielding your upper body so the door won't touch any part of you.

4. As you swing your arm through, bring it up at the same time in an answer-the-phone motion to keep the door off you, yet whisker close (figure 4.2a).

5. The "phone" should transition in one smooth movement into a reverse rocker (discussed in detail in chapter 7, pages 165-166) with your elbow or finger-tips until you're clear of the door (figure 4.2b). Your fingertips should touch the door as lightly as a feather. This movement acts as a check to be sure the door (or an attacker's strike) is clear or, at least, is not about to swing back on you. You can do this slowly to accentuate the feeling of powering the door with your whole body or at normal speed.

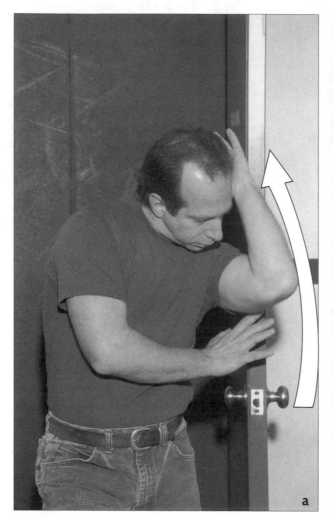 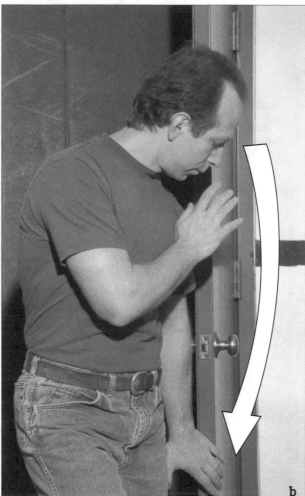

FIGURE 4.2

Preventing Common Mistakes

➤➤ While performing "Body Writing" or any other body unity drills, the object is not to move your whole body together as one rigid object, like a statue. Instead, move your body as one unit in the same loose way the entire length of a whip lends its power to the snap of its tip.

➤➤ "Starting the Mower" is not a tension exercise. Remember, move with the intent of moving 1,000 pounds but not the strength.

CHAPTER FIVE

BALANCE

Now when most people think of balance, they may imagine a tightrope walker or something similar. This type of balance is one-dimensional. The rope is always the balance point. In a fight, your balance point is always changing. Your foot positions move constantly, or you may be against a wall, on one knee, or on your back (yes, you still have to be balanced, even on your back), but even this is not the only kind of balance we're going to be talking about or having you practice.

Body unity and looseness are both fundamental components of balance, in that they help develop grace as well as the ability to deliver tremendous energy by loosely controlling your body's mass. In guided chaos, we're not talking about developing everyday balance, but hyperbalance, balance on steroids, balance that is fundamentally different in two unique ways:

1. It's dynamic. You can attack and defend in body positions and angles that other people just don't have, because they don't learn and practice them. You can't train hyperbalance with a fixed drill or static exercise, because all fights are chaotic; any

attempt to adopt a "stance," form, or technique under duress will meet with catastrophe. This is a fact and, as explained in the introduction, is born out by police reports (and anyone, for that matter, who's been in a fight for his or her life). Balance must be dynamic.

2. It's cumulative. You must first feel a sense of balance in each individual part of your body in order to then get each part to act collectively in a powerful manner. Imagine each bone as a scale, or better yet, a seesaw. If your attacker pushes down on one end of your forearm, let's say the hand, the other end of the forearm (the elbow) should swing up and hit him in the jaw. Its power is augmented by all the other bones in your body through body unity. Thus, balance also refers to the position of each bone in relation to the position of every other bone. It also refers to the ability of each bone (and the heavy connected flesh) to deliver its delicately balanced momentum to each succeeding bone in turn.

To understand this further, imagine every one of your bones as a "sledgehammer," finely balanced on the end of every other bone and connected by "ball bearings" like a big chain. The ball bearings are all the joints in your fingers, hands, wrists, upper and lower arms, and shoulders and every vertebra in your back and every joint in your hips and legs. Your job is to whip them so that their individual momentum is cumulative like a big wave. When the bones move counter to each other, there's no body unity, and they detract from the total amount of momentum, even if they're all loose. It would be like five people grabbing a whip at different points along its length and attempting to snap their individual sections with force.

With the progressive drills provided in this chapter, you will train your body to balance so that every part of it is counterbalanced and influenced by every other part, so that if one part moves, even the slightest bit, every other part moves also. For example, think about when you pass through a subway turnstile. If you walk through one slowly, the other side simultaneously rotates behind you. If you were to run through, the back side would whip around and smack you in the rear violently. This is also a simple example of yin-yang energy transformation. Briefly, yin and yang are two Chinese Taoist terms that define opposite energy states (e.g., hard and soft, or attacking and yielding). The side of the turnstile that moves away when you hit it is receiving energy and is thus in a yin state. The part of the turnstile that swings around and hits you in the rear is transmitting energy and is thus in a yang state. Understand that the balanced looseness of a turnstile happens in a single horizontal plane. Your joints are infinitely more mobile, moving in directions multiplied geometrically by all your other joints and by how each one influences the other. Now you can see why we talked so much about internal energy in the previous chapter: balance is the axle that the wheel of internal energy turns around; external energy actually disrupts the individual and collective balance of your bones by committing you to full-force movements in one direction.

When your body has momentum, it has latent energy without the input of muscular force. Guided chaos makes extensive use of this. But to generate momentum and get it to go where you want, you have to be both balanced and loose. The total momentum of a guided chaos strike will come from the weight of all the flesh and bones in motion, not a continuous muscular contraction. This allows for two different kinds of loose, powerful strikes:

1. Whipping strikes. When it's used correctly, a whip conducts its energy instantly from the handle to the tip where it is amplified and focused. The tip can cut like a knife or smash like a wrecking ball depending on how it's delivered and how much mass it has. This occurs even though every point of the whip's length is totally soft and flexible. If it strikes a solid object, like an iron pipe, the whip merely wraps around it. Every point of its length has a balanced energy relationship with every other, like a visible sine wave. This whipping motion is also perfectly suited for the human body to deliver strikes with.

2. Jackhammer strikes. In addition to circular whipping blows, balance and body unity can manifest in loose, linear pile-driver-like strikes. As explained in chapter 4, having a relaxed body allows you to drive from your feet through your hands with uninhibited power. This is why each bone must be balanced in relation to every other bone. If the bones are not lined up,

Balance acts as the axis between yin and yang, soft and hard, force and yielding, push and pull, and attack and defense, allowing for one to flow into the other, with no discernible interruption, so one becomes indistinguishable from the other.

however, energy will be frittered away into space. Whipping and jackhammer strikes will both be augmented by dropping energy (chapter 6, page 96).

Your Balance Foundation

In guided chaos you're going to be moving your body's mass so dynamically to avoid and deliver strikes that without extreme balance you'd be spending half your time on your backside. To keep your balance, you must move your body mass around your center of gravity so it's constantly counterbalanced. No matter how you bend and gyrate, if you can move a compensating amount of mass in the opposite direction from the part of your body that's avoiding a strike so your center of gravity remains directly above one or both feet, you will remain balanced.

For example, if your chest collapses to absorb a blow (see "Yielding, Looseness, and Pocketing," page 46), the target area moves outside your center of gravity. But because you're still balanced, it's possible to deliver a counterattack at the same time you're avoiding the attack. To remain balanced, your knees, hips, and shoulders need to compensate by bending forward (figure 5.1). This keeps your center of gravity in the same place and maintains your rooted connection to the ground (see the following section).

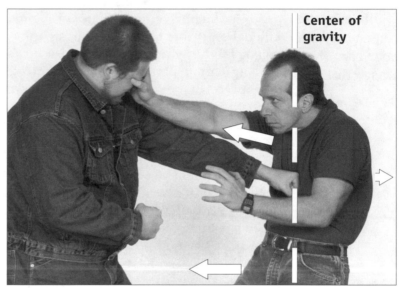

Center of gravity

FIGURE 5.1

Rooting Your Feet

Just as a building must have a firm foundation on which to stand, you must have a firm foundation from which to fight. You need to develop the surefooted balance of a cat, so that no matter which way you're pushed, you always land on your feet in a balanced and stable position to launch your attack.

When we say "root," we simply mean your body's completely relaxed, or "dead," weight sinks into your legs and distributes evenly through both feet, like the balancing of a scale, perpendicular to the ground (with no leaning or bouncing). This applies even when you are gyrating and contorting your body to avoid or deliver strikes because you are keeping your center of gravity over your feet by compensating your body mass in opposite directions. If you don't compensate, you lean—and then you fall. When you lean, you have no balance and no power.

You must not overcommit to either leg, but instead try to maintain the relationship of neutral balance—no leaning, posing, or rising onto heels or toes. When you transfer your weight for a strike, return to your neutral position in an

Fighting for your life without balance is like trying to run in quicksand: no matter how hard you try, no matter how much force you exert, the more you struggle, the faster you sink.

easy, relaxed manner, like a buoy in the ocean. This is true whether you're balancing on one or both feet.

Don't balance on one foot to satisfy some stylistic stance, however. Rather, you may have to balance on one foot when, in the course of combat, you dynamically move your entire body mass around to avoid or to deliver a strike as a sensitive response to your opponent's energy. This pouring of your loose, relaxed body from an area of high pressure to low is accomplished by dropping from a high center of gravity to a low center of gravity, on both feet or by flowing from one foot to the other. Even then, the one-legged root is achieved instantaneously, then abandoned for a new one. In other words, your feet don't need to be glued to the ground, but they must act like magnets on a metal floor that are capable of instant attraction and repulsion, as you desire. You should be so aware of your balance that you can step to a flat foot, sinking your weight into it as if you were drunk, yet glide off of it like a jaguar.

Despite rooting, your feet must be able to move to a new root point at any given moment. Trying to be tough by maintaining a static stance can get you killed. Remember that you're not stepping out of the fight, but to a more advantageous fighting position, which is often even closer to the opponent. You will actually learn to pour yourself onto him like syrup. You should be light and heavy on your feet at the same time. This creates a sensation of "relaxed springiness."

Furthermore, you want to develop a root that can't be found. Your opponent will discover that no matter where he pushes you or where you end up, you can always deliver a strike with rooted, balanced power. Whether you are on one or both legs, your feet must also be able to turn on the ground while remaining as flat as possible. This will allow you to direct the force of your strike or to maneuver your body out of the way instantaneously. A flat foot also transfers dropping power better without the flex associated with being on your toes, such as when sparring.

Bending Your Knees

Bend your knees at all times. Since the knees are attached to the largest muscles in the body (in the thighs), your knees must properly return energy without buckling, yet remain springy. The bend must be natural to allow for freedom of movement. In other words, don't use excessively low classical or posed stances that compromise your stability in any way (you martial artists know which ones we mean). If the stance wouldn't work for an NFL middle linebacker or a professional tennis player, it won't work for you in a real potential bloodbath.

Once the fight begins, the amount of knee bend can vary. Under zero pressure, always return to neutral. As you turn your body, keep your knees pressing inward slightly. Your stance becomes weak when one knee bends out further than the stance requires. It also makes it susceptible to injury and attack. Moreover, the straight leg, prevalent in many styles of martial arts, is a mechanically poor position and a bad habit to fall into. Not only does it take away from your ability to balance yourself, it also puts your leg in a position where it can easily be broken.

Balancing Your Breathing

Breathe deep into the belly through your nose using your diaphragm muscle (located under your ribcage). Your stomach should expand outward. Breathing

Develop your ability to balance as well on one leg as on both legs, not because you want to pose, but because you may inadvertently end up there. Be ready to balance and to fight on one or both knees, your back, buttocks, or any other part of your body.

Understand that when fighting, regardless of who is faster, stronger, or larger, if you have balance and your opponent doesn't, he loses, period.

high in the chest (chest breathing) tends to raise your center of gravity, disrupting your balance. Chest-breathing also neurologically increases your tension and anxiety.

Balancing Your Posture

Your posture should not resemble a West Point cadet's, but rather, an upright ape's. Your arms, when raised, should assume a relaxed, sunken position with the elbows down, as if you were riding a Harley Davidson motorcycle (figure 5.2).

Balance Drills

These exercises may seem unusual, but they have their roots in many established fighting styles, including tai chi and Native American fighting arts.

FIGURE 5.2

Ninja Walk

The key with this drill is not to build up forward momentum, where you could propel yourself from one step to another by pushing off your toes, but rather to slowly place each foot down, so you create the maximum stress, challenging your balance as you tap and change supporting legs.

1. Stand with either foot forward, hands up in a relaxed fighting position, with your knees bent, elbows down and relaxed, back straight, and head up.

2. Slowly redistribute 99 percent of your weight over your forward leg, just enough to balance on it, yet keep your rear foot flat and barely on the floor (figure 5.3a).

3. Keeping your rear leg relatively straight and the foot flat, point only the big toe of your rear leg up in the air without changing the angle of your foot. This will force you to keep your rear foot flat as you perform the following: Raise your entire body by straightening your supporting (front) leg, as if you were doing a one-legged squat. This one-legged squatting action will bring your rear foot off the ground an eighth of an inch. The purpose of raising the toe of the rear foot first is to make sure you come off the ground with a flat foot (i.e., parallel to the ground and without benefit of a heel-toe pushoff). Do this at an extremely slow speed. Do not raise your rear foot off the ground by merely curling your rear leg's knee. For the moment, your rear knee should actually remain fairly straight (figure 5.3b).

4. Once your rear foot is off the floor, bend your rear knee and point the toe of the raised foot toward the ground.

5. Tap slowly and lightly on the ground behind you twice with your toe. However, don't tap by straightening the knee of your rear leg. Rather, maintain the bend in the knee as it is. You will reach the floor with your toe by lowering your entire body with the one-legged squat performed by the front leg (figure 5.3c). Don't cheat on this or you'll defeat the purpose. Depending on how low you are, the burn in your thighs can be tremendous. You can make this harder by bending the knee of the tapping leg more and maintaining

FIGURE 5.3

78

that bend as your supporting leg's knee bends, raising and lowering your entire body. Since the tapping leg's knee is bent more, your supporting leg's knee must bend more for the tapping foot to reach the ground.

6. Slowly bring the tapping leg forward and tap lightly two times on the ground in front of you with your heel. Be sure you're tapping by sinking and squatting down on your supporting leg. Remember, do not bend the tapping leg's knee independently to make the foot reach the ground (figure 5.3d).

7. After slowly tapping twice with the heel in front of you, flatten the tapping foot, slowly placing it on the ground. Redistribute your weight so that 99 percent of it is on the new supporting leg.

8. As before, slowly raise your entire body with your new supporting leg so that your rear leg comes off the ground with the foot flat and parallel to the ground without any kind of toe pushoff.

9. Repeat this process over and over in the same fashion, alternating legs so you are "walking" forward.

One complete cycle should take no less than 40 seconds—the slower, the better.

Vacuum Walk

By doing this walk correctly, you develop tremendous balance in areas where most people don't have balance, so you will begin to glide low and powerfully on the ground like a cat. Both the "Ninja Walk" and the "Vacuum Walk" drills develop and strengthen the small muscles in the hips necessary for powerful but subtle weight shifts that occur during a fight as you constantly struggle to regain your balance and step to your new root points on uncertain ground. This walk is vital for developing the rooted, one-legged, instant balance essential to dropping in awkward positions as well as redirecting kicks or delivering multiple counterkicks "Rockette-style."

1. Begin with steps 1 through 3 of the "Ninja Walk" (page 77).

2. Once again, raise your rear foot parallel to the floor. Remember, do not raise this foot independently. Don't bring the foot in proximity to the ground by merely bending and unbending the knee of the leg that is in the air.

3. While bending the knee of your supporting leg even further so that your whole body sinks lower, bring your rear foot alongside the front supporting foot but do not put it on the ground. While doing this, maintain the bottom of the foot at an eighth of an inch above the ground and parallel to it (figure 5.4a).

4. From there, circle your raised leg from the front to the rear in the shape of an outward crescent, keeping the foot no more than an eighth of an inch off the ground at all times, as if you were vacuuming the floor.

5. Keep the bottom of the foot parallel to the floor, no matter where it moves. This requires you to constantly change the angle of your ankle as well as the bend in your supporting knee.

6. The slower you do all the movements, the better. Each foot circle should take no less than three seconds and should be no less than two feet in diameter (figure 5.4b).

7. Circle the leg slowly twice, then place it silently on the ground in front of you, redistributing all your weight onto that leg.

FIGURE 5.4

8. Repeat this process with your other leg. Continue to do this so you are slowly "walking" forward (or backward if you choose).

The foot circles force you to be sensitive to the surface of the ground as you battle in the dark or on uneven terrain. The leg muscle isolation strengthens your lower body while your upper body stays loose. If you are doing this honestly, you won't be able to perform the "Vacuum Walk" drill for more than a few minutes. Here are a few more points:

- Keep your back straight and don't lean.
- Remember to keep your head and hands up in fighting position.
- Breathe slowly, deep into your belly.

Advanced Ninja and Vacuum Walks

You can increase the difficulty of the "Vacuum Walk" by doing the following:

- Lower your supporting leg and bend the knee of your circling leg so you have to sink your whole body further down to keep your foot an eighth of an inch off the ground.
- Do both walks slowly up and down stairs. (On the "Vacuum Walk," circle behind you to avoid hitting the step in front of you.)

- Do the walks outdoors on large rocks with your eyes closed. The best place for this is a dry streambed or rocky shoreline. The mental concentration and muscular control required are considerable, but the development of your fighting root and stability will accelerate quickly.

We have found after teaching the walks to hundreds of students, that conscientiously performing these exercises alone five minutes a day for a year will effectively develop the same kind of balance and root you might get after 10 years of doing the tai chi form. This is because you're specifically working on the attributes the form is designed to develop, without spending years perfecting the exact movements. When you combine the walks with "Polishing the Sphere" (page 111) and other random-flow drills described later, you teach your nervous system to be balanced while it is becoming comfortable with spontaneous movement.

Box Step

This drill develops the box step, a key movement principle of guided chaos. With it you develop a feel for your body's equilibrium while in motion, and you learn to move your entire body in a balanced, coordinated manner, without retreating, leaning, hopping, or crossing your feet. In guided chaos, feeling where your body is and how it's balanced is more important than adopting a stance or technique. For a real-life example of how the training principles of balance and kinesthetic awareness can aid you in an attack, see "The Williams Brothers Attack" (page 86). This drill will train you to land positioned, balanced, and ready to strike, with no extra movement, especially in the dark, against multiple opponents.

1. Mark out a box on the ground, roughly three feet by three feet.
2. Stand in an L stance, with the heel of your right (forward) foot in one corner of the box and the left (rear) foot, at about a 90-degree angle to it (figure 5.5a).
3. From there, step with your rear foot to another corner of the box, landing in an "L" but with your left foot forward.
4. Continue stepping to a new corner with your rear foot, which, when it lands, becomes the new forward foot. If your right foot is forward, stepping with your rear (left) foot to the corner on your left is the easiest. A little tougher is stepping with your rear foot to the corner directly across the box. This requires you to turn 180 degrees in the air clockwise and land facing in the direction from which you came (figure 5.5b). Most difficult is bringing your rear (left) foot all the way to the corner of the box, directly to your right. This means you have to turn your body 270 degrees in the air clockwise (figure 5.5c). As you can see, with all these movements, you never cross your feet, and you never step behind yourself.
5. Continue to do this back and forth in both directions, stepping to any corner at random without pause.
6. If you feel your weight is off when you land, you are off balance, and you need to adjust in the air. This will present a challenge with the more difficult steps. To get your feet to land properly without twisting, you will have to get your hips moving early while you're still in the air.

FIGURE 5.5   a) Starting position.   b) After 180° turn.   c) After 270° turn.

Keep in mind the importance of *how* you step:

- When you step to your new position, don't hop or jump. Glide softly and smoothly, like a cat hugging the ground (or like Groucho Marx).
- Rise as little as possible, as if at the apex of your step, you might hit your head on a very low ceiling.
- Be careful not to lean too far back or too far forward when landing in your new position.
- When you land, be sure your feet are in the final L-stance before they make contact with the ground so you don't have to readjust or twist either foot in any way.
- The new front foot should land smack in the middle of the new corner.

This is the simplest way to do the box step. Once you are capable of landing without making a sound and getting your entire body balanced and positioned without readjustment at each corner, you can begin to add some of the following drills. These drills will also apply to sensitivity and other guided chaos principles, which you will learn in later chapters.

Free-Striking Box Step

Perform the box drill, but each time you land, throw a strike. This drill trains you to land balanced and ready, to throw the strike, and to then immediately go into the next box step.

1. Begin with low kicks such as short front kicks, roundhouses, sidekicks, knees, whatever. The type of kick is not important.

2. Try the kicks using either your front or rear leg as soon as you land. This will require you to be dead center in your equilibrium, otherwise you'll lean, fall, and have no power.

3. If you do this drill with a few partners, each of them can be positioned outside a corner of the box with their own kicking shield, which you will kick after each box step (figure 5.6). Your partners will step in toward you from the opposite corners with their shields.

4. Try this using upper body strikes. Remember, the type of strike is unimportant, but you should try everything you can think of. Refer back to the "Anywhere Strikes" drills (I, II, and III) in chapter 2 (page 34) if you need some ideas. Try this exercise holding light weights or a baseball bat. Using a sledgehammer is a real challenge.

FIGURE 5.6

Battle-Ax Box Step

This drill purposely challenges your balance while teaching you to not tighten up on grabs (which is itself a unique concept; see chapter 9). The goal of this drill is to work up from using a heavy stick to a sledgehammer. The key to handling a heavy sledgehammer like a paperweight is in flowing with its momentum, rather than fighting it. This way, you make gravity and inertia your ally. This is a process of self-discovery, however. No one can teach it to you. But when you eventually get it, the application to empty-handed fighting is obvious and powerful. It means you have mastered body unity as it applies to balance.

1. Perform the "Box Step" drill without pausing between steps. As soon as you land, you begin a new step.

2. As you box-step, use a heavy stick, swinging it above your head, softly and slowly, one revolution per step (figure 5.7a). Hold the end of the stick in both hands with the least amount of tension necessary.

3. Once you get good at this, begin using a sledgehammer while you're box-stepping. This will take some practice. Number one, you must center and balance your body with the added weight. Two, you must keep your hand and arm relaxed while you hold the handle. Ultimately, you should be able to hold the sledgehammer with only the thumb and index finger of one hand. Three, you must generate the power to move the sledgehammer with the momentum of your body, not your

FIGURE 5.7

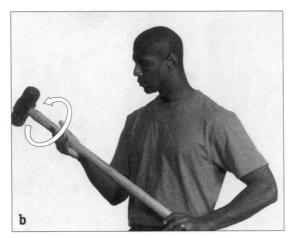

FIGURE 5.7

muscles. Obviously, you must also gently stop the hammer's motion between each step before changing the direction of the circular swing with your new step, without tightening up or throwing yourself off balance. Do this by imagining that the sledgehammer is a baby that has fallen out of the window of a speeding car, and you must catch it without causing the slightest harm.

4. During moments of weightlessness and transition between landings, try twirling it along its axis in your hand (figure 5.7b), spearing the hammer with either the handle or the head (figure 5.7a) and releasing and taking up slack by letting the hammer handle slide through your hand as you extend it. Let its momentum carry it just out to the end of the handle before, like a relaxed pendulum, you swing it back and box-step to a new position.

5. Perform this drill for 5 to 10 minutes every couple days to reap its benefits.

The "Battle-Ax Box Step" drill develops relaxation in your hands and gets you to step around and closer to your opponent to take his space (see "Taking Your Opponent's Space, chapter 7), yet avoid being hit yourself. It generates momentum for striking as a yielding response to pressure. How this applies to fighting will become more clear as you learn about developing sensitivity in chapter 6.

Whirling Dervish Box Step

The motion practiced in this drill is excellent for splitting multiple attackers if you're surrounded or for getting past your current attacker to the one behind you.

1. Box-step continuously, so that you are whirling without pause, moving forward like a spinning running back in football, avoiding tacklers.

2. Strike as you turn, using your motion to augment the blows. For example, you're in a right lead. As you begin to box-step to the right by bringing your left foot forward, your right arm chops like a helicopter blade to the right while your left arm palm-heels straight forward.

3. As you continue to spin, this chop-palm strike com-bination comes out again every time you face in the direction of your forward movement (figure 5.8).

4. However, don't make the mistake of moving high on your toes, like a twirling ballerina. When you spin, land, and strike, your body should feel mobile but heavy, like a tumbling boulder crushing trees as it rolls. Your arms are loose like flexible steel whips.

Try this exercise on uneven, rocky, or slippery terrain; fights rarely take place on favorable ground so to train on flat, even martial arts school floors is deceiving as such surfaces don't challenge your balance. Indoors, you can tune up your balance by doing this drill over platforms such as those used in aerobic step training. Then do it with your eyes closed. How do you keep from stumbling? Practice. This is why this is such an important balance drill. The chaos of a fight is no different. Keep in mind that all your movements should be free, loose, relaxed, and heavy.

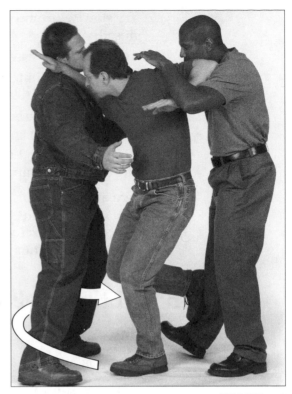

FIGURE 5.8

Wood-Surfing

The benefits of doing this drill daily for a few minutes are substantial. You build up tremendous strength and sensitivity in all the tiny foot and lower leg muscles. At the same time, you form new neural connections in the motor reflex areas of your brain, areas that become vital in the chaos of a fight. This exercise makes you extremely aware of your center of gravity and of moving your body mass in opposite directions to keep it over your feet.

1. Find a board, preferably a two-by-four, cut to a length a little wider than your shoulder-width.

2. Make the board unstable, using one of many methods. The simplest is to roll up a piece of carpet and cut a pair of two-inch-diameter cylinders that you'll attach securely to the bottom of each end of the board.

3. Stand on the board with your feet about shoulder-width apart and work to balance yourself and not fall off. This is similar to Canadian log rolling.

4. If you feel yourself losing your balance, just step off the board. In this way, you teach yourself to step to a new root point without struggling excessively to stay on the board. This can be a fatal tendency in classical training, where a practitioner will strain to maintain his stance even after his balance is shot. You need to learn how to flow smoothly to a new balance point.

FIGURE 5.9

5. Try slowly turning at the waist, staying low, until your stability is compromised.

6. Twist the other way.

7. Try this while doing the various "Swimming," "Weaving Python," and "Solo Contact Flow" drills (chapter 3). Try the "Small Circle Dance" (figure 5.9).

8. Next, position the board two to three feet away from a pole or tree and slowly perform random anywhere strikes (chapter 2). Do them on one leg.

9. Vacuum-walk and ninja-walk on the board. Try the walks with your eyes closed while swimming.

There are other drills you can do while doing the "Wood-Surfing" drill that you will read about in chapter 7. For now, while balancing, visualize attack and avoidance as you move with your anywhere strikes. Eventually, you should push the envelope with your twisting and writhing to hypersensitize your balance.

THE WILLIAMS BROTHERS ATTACK

John Perkins

No match in a ring or martial arts school is as deadly as real-life armed and unarmed murder attempts by one or more would-be street assassins. Nearly all attacks on police officers are potentially lethal. Also, anyone who would attack a person in uniform knowing beforehand that he has a weapon, has to be at least slightly psychotic. But anytime a grown person assaults another person in the real world, you should consider it an execution. Why? Because you don't know what's in the mind of a stranger or mob that wants to do you harm. Will he stop at the point of rendering you unconscious or maiming or paralyzing you? Or will he stop only when you're dead? If you are a police officer armed with a handgun, any fight you lose could be your last. When you're down, your assailant(s) could take your weapon and finish you. When you're in the ring, even though there's a tiny chance you could be maimed, paralyzed, or killed, the combatants are known, there are referees, doctors, spectators, and, most important, rules.

I was walking foot patrol one weekday evening. I had just finished my "glass check." A glass check is where you look over all the churches, schools, and stores for broken glass or any other signs of forced entry. I would do this in the middle of my tour and again at the end. It was a summer night, and people were out enjoying the weather. However, some blocks in the commercial area were deserted. As I passed a gas station that was closed for the night, I noticed the outline of a man that seemed to disappear into the shadow of the building. I followed, tracking him by sound only because it was too dark to see. I had no time for my eyes to adjust to the darkness.

As I got a few feet into the rear of the garage, I could still hear the man I was following. Then, out of nowhere, I suddenly saw stars. I was struck from behind with a terrific concussion, and my head was thrown forward until it slammed into the wall of the garage. I fought to maintain consciousness, and as I did, the strangest thing seemed to be happening: heavy sandbags were being dropped on top of me from above with crushing force, and I couldn't get away. Then I realized that the sandbags were actually men jumping down on top of me. I didn't know how many there were, but I knew I might be killed.

I later found out that they had jumped off the back of a flatbed truck, which was parked in the rear. Their eyes had had time to adjust to the dark while mine hadn't. Of course, I know now that you should never follow someone into the dark, even if he isn't aware of your presence. You might surprise a gang of five men and have them attack youall at once. Later, I puzzled over why these men would continue to attack me so brutally instead of just hitting and running. Usually most thieves just take off when a cop arrives on the scene. These guys were hell-bent on destroying me. (I'll reveal why later.)

They were all dropping on me, and I was getting pummeled from all directions in the dark. Luckily at that time I knew how to yield with punches, and even back then, I had the rudiments of what was to become the box step and contact flow programmed inside me. My balance training came into play in the biggest way. My gun was unavailable to me at this point, due to the retention device I used and the barrage of blows I had to contend with. Under the worst conditions, in the dark on uncertain ground, with an unknown number of attackers coming from all directions, it was my ability to retain my balance in the midst of chaos that kept me from going down.

My return attack was explosive and devastating. I struck outward with palm-heel, hammer-fist, and side-of-hand strikes (the whirling dervish box step), while at the same time, I began stomping blindly and with full force (the Mexican hat dance). This seemed to free up my left side so I could get to my nightstick. As I drew the stick with my left hand from the ring on the left side of my gun belt, I remembered to grab it in an underhand position so I could strike with the tip of the handle as I drew it straight upward and forward. This first blow hit pay dirt. I felt the impact, catching one of the attackers solidly in the jaw. Once I got my nightstick into action, I was able to hit with more power. If I wasn't already used to getting hit and yielding prior to this melee, that first kick to the back of my head would have finished me. Maybe they would've been merciful and just left me there, but my survival response was in full swing, and swing, swing, swing is what I did with the nightstick (the battle-ax box step).

Training took over when the assailants seemed to rain down from the sky. I remembered to flow with the blows and made myself a moving target by swaying and striking all at once. Dropping my weight also saved me at the onset of the attack. By dropping into my blows and stomping my feet, I kept my balance and my footing and attacked simultaneously. It was fortuitous that I knew how to hit with my bare hands hard enough so I could finally get to my night stick. I was also lucky that only one of the assailants had a weapon. This was a wrench about a foot long, but I don't think he was able to hit me solidly with it because there was such ferocious and wild movement in all directions. He also may have been afraid to hit one of his accomplices.

As I was delivering mostly two-handed jabs and butt strikes with my stick, I was perplexed as to why these guys kept on attacking. I knew they were getting seriously injured, but they just kept at me. I finally finished off the last attacker with a blow to the nose with the side of my stick. My sight was getting sharper, and when I finally took out my flashlight, I saw the mess around me. The groaning was loud. I couldn't believe I was able to hold onto my stick with all the blood on it. The solution to the mystery as to why they never ran off after ambushing me was that three of them were brothers, and the other three were friends. They weren't about to leave someone behind.

Preventing Common Mistakes

➤ Keep your head up while ninja-walking and vacuum-walking. Don't lean.

➤ Don't tap the floor in the ninja walk by bending the knee of your tapping leg. Raise and lower your whole body by bending your supporting leg.

➤ Don't hop while box-stepping. Glide.

➤ Don't twist your foot into position when you land in the box step. It should already be there.

CHAPTER SIX

SENSITIVITY:
THE WAY OF ENERGY

Sensitivity, looseness, body unity, and balance are the "big four" of our guided chaos methodology. They all work together. Aside from the other important subprinciples in this book, if even one of these four is missing from the mix, you have nothing. Although we've mentioned sensitivity before, we've held off explaining it completely until now because the depth and power of this principle would be meaningless without first understanding the other three. It is also the prime mover of all the other principles.

Simply put, sensitivity is the ability to detect and create changes in energy, whether in type, amount, or direction, and to do so without conscious thought. This requires using a part of your brain and nervous system that you never have to think about. Something that is actually faster and more sensitive than good old hand-eye coordination: your sense of touch.

As you probably know, hand-eye coordination is the skill you use to whack a baseball, catch a pass, or block a punch. In terms of response time in an attack, however, it's too slow. What are we talking about? For the answer, we need to conduct a little experiment.

Get into a traditional boxer's stance, with your hands up and about 6 to 12 inches apart. Have your training partner pick a mutually agreed-on spot on your chest that he will try and touch. Your job is to block him. Your partner should stand the same distance away that he would be if he were sparring with you. He, of course, should move as fast as possible to touch that spot, and you should move as quickly as you can to block it (figure 6.1).

Guess what? Even though you know where he's going, if he's reasonably fast, you can almost never block him, try as you might. Any form of fighting that relies on hand-eye coordination exclusively for self-defense is

FIGURE 6.1

at an inherent disadvantage. Think about this carefully. This includes almost all styles of fighting (especially sparring) that rely on distance, space, and visual timing; however, there are some notable exceptions. The following styles have a distinct fighting advantage, because they all to some greater or lesser degree address the subject of sensitivity: wrestling, wing chun, judo, aikido, ultimate fighting, and the tactile, internal "soft" martial arts styles such as tai chi, bagua, hsing I, and ki chuan do (the art that guided chaos is drawn from). All these styles involve constant close physical contact with your opponent. The difference is that in guided chaos, we put a premium on developing sensitivity first and last, and through a different training protocol than other styles.

Sensing Energy

Our focus in this book is on fighting to save your life, not fooling around. This may dictate some notable philosophical alterations in your self-defense strategy. It also bodes well for maintaining a personal philosophy of nonviolence. Why? Because, unless you're cornered, if you have enough space to spar, you have enough space to run. Typically, if your attacker stays at a sparring distance, he's not really serious about hurting you. Real mayhem begins only once you are in close physical contact with your attacker. This is where most of the damage is dished out and, coincidentally, where most traditional training breaks down.

This is because in a controlled environment like sparring or boxing, there are rules that govern the action. Strikes come at a cadence of one, retract, one, retract, and so on. Even in a flurry, each strike is separate from the one before and the one after. Strikes to the back of the head are prohibited. And how do most flurries end? With a clinch. And the fight stops. This is not reality.

Let's return to the previous experiment, but with a slight modification. Set up like before, only this time, gently rest your fingertips on your partner's hands, as if you were playing an expensive piano. Close your eyes, take a slow, deep breath, and try to completely relax your muscles. Clear your mind and think of nothing. All you want to do is react to the slightest change in pressure against your fingertips and nothing else. You might think "This is ridiculous. What fight looks like this?" But consider the fact that no real fight begins, nobody is hurting anybody, until you actually make skin contact. Until you reach that point, remember, running away is your first and best option. When both of you come close enough so that with arms fully extended you only touch at the fingertips, tactile sensitivity begins.

Now, moving as explosively as he can, have your partner again try and touch the spot on your chest. Keep your eyes closed. (What? You've never been attacked in the dark?) With practice, if you can relax enough, you'll find that he can't do it, not even once.

No amount of practice will enable you to stop him if you break off tactile contact and rely solely on hand-eye coordination. Why? Because the attacker is always one step ahead of you in terms of nerve impulses. When you use tactile sensitivity, however, you're relying on your sense of touch, which is hardwired into the primitive centers of your brain. You're bypassing the whole hand-eye coordination system wherein you see the punch, the image is sent to your brain, and your brain processes it, calculates an interception angle, and sends a signal to your muscles to carry out the response. With tactile sensitivity, you react at a gross animal level, the same way a cat responds to an attack, antennas on a garden snail retract from touch, or your eyelids respond to dust. There's no middleman. This is what you're going to learn and practice to defend yourself.

Tactile Sensitivity and Sticking

In guided chaos, tactile sensitivity is concerned with achieving constant contact, or sticking, with your opponent with any part of your body that stands between his strike and its intended target. This could be almost anywhere, depending on the situation. Regardless, you never lose contact with him. Your skin will become your eyes. This contact should be featherlight pressure at the beginner level, progressing through body hair sensitivity, to body heat or even energy field sensitivity at the highest level.

We make the point of saying any part of your body, because different styles of fighting may use different reference points of contact exclusively. In wing chun and tai chi, the reference points tend to be the hands, wrists, forearms, and elbows. Wrestlers have an advantage because they're used to "sticking" with their entire bodies. They have developed a certain level of sensitivity over their whole skin surface. Similarly, in guided chaos, we believe the entire body is the battleground, so we teach from the beginning that the contact reference points are anywhere on the body. The difference between wrestling and guided chaos, however, is in how we respond to close contact.

The Disengagement Principle

In wrestling, most training is focused on overpowering your opponent (although the best wrestlers have developed an elusive, slippery quality). In guided chaos, by contrast, we stress sensitivity and loose, balanced responsiveness over your entire body, first and last. Everything else is of less importance. With increasing sensitivity, you actually react subconsciously to your opponent's intentions of movement before he moves because his energy precedes him. How do you do this? By attempting a paradox: You want to be as disengaged as possible from your opponent, yet still be engaged.

We call this the disengagement principle. You stay as close to him as you can without actually exerting any pressure. To paraphrase a tai chi principle, when an attacker strikes, he should never reach you, but when he retreats, he can never get away from you. You are flowing with him, following his every move, while you simultaneously mount your attacks. There's a great advantage to this.

With increasing sensitivity, you eliminate the middleman of your reactive intellectual mind, which acts as a "drag" on your response time.

When you are involved in a death match with someone twice your strength, you will fail if you attempt to engage him, that is, to match his strength. As we've reminded you, no matter how strong you are, there's always someone stronger. This is true whether you can do 200 knuckle push-ups or break two bricks in the air. When you attempt to overpower a stronger opponent, your antagonistic muscles come into play as you strain to vanquish him; you become rigid, hard, and inflexible, and you are likely to be crushed or snapped like a dry twig. In addition, by resisting forcefully, you actually present your opponent with a road map of your intentions.

To survive the onslaught of a more powerful opponent, you need to be so light, soft, flexible, and sensitive, that to your opponent, you feel like a phantom or a cloud, dissolving like the liquid-metal Terminator, materializing only for the millisecond needed for your strike's impact. You should be like a wet dishrag that is soft and malleable until it's whipped and snapped. At the point of impact, the formerly limp dishrag then takes on the solidity of steel and the effectiveness of a knife.

In guided chaos we like to say you're both unavailable and unavoidable.

To use a different analogy, you should feel to your opponent like all your limbs are made of steel springs, connected by ball bearings and lubricated with super silicon. Thus, when you hit, you feel like a tire iron, but when you absorb an attack, you feel like a turnstile. You never oppose your opponent's energy: neither he nor you should feel any resistance at any time (except when pulsing, which we explain later in this chapter).

Or think of yourself as a block of ice. The enemy can either move the ice, shatter his arm, or shatter the ice. Now take that block of ice and melt it. Your opponent's job is to block all the water. The result, of course, is that he gets soaked. How do you block water? Liquids merely seek the path of least resistance. In this example, the water has both offensive and defensive attributes: it mindlessly slips through obstacles to attack, and it effortlessly "sticks" to his skin, following his every move and avoiding "harm."

Sensitivity and the disengagement principle offer you an alternative beyond yielding (see chapter 3). When you become supersensitive, you can let the opponent's energy slide right past you while still maintaining contact. This is analogous to a farmer trying to catch a greased pig. The instant your hands (or any other sticking surfaces of your body) sense a rise in incoming force, they simply let the offending limb slip by. By keeping your body loose and yielding, you ensure that the target won't be there when the strike arrives. Meanwhile, your hands are still in contact with his arms, but further up and closer in. This offers an opportunity to either move in to yet a closer reference point on his body or to strike.

Comparing a fight with skiing down a mogul-filled trail that's as steep as a wall at 20 miles per hour can help you grasp the need for the sensitivity principle. Skiing the bumps can feel like being a passenger in a multiple car wreck. In fact, it feels like you're being assaulted. Now, the sport of skiing is jam-packed with techniques. However, as you're flying down a hill, if you keep your head down and try to concentrate on the correct technique for the bump that's directly beneath you, the one that's slamming your knees into your face, you will never be able to deal with the 200 more bumps coming up that are about to break you in half. If your brain is turned inward and focused on technique, you won't be getting the whole picture. You need to look outward and focus on the run ahead of you. Otherwise your nervous system will be overwhelmed by the deliberations of your brain, instead of being allowed to focus on feeling the terrain. It's the same with fighting. Sensitivity means to lose yourself and follow the opponent. You simply feel his motion. If you think only of what martial arts technique to use right now against his punch, you'll never feel the intent of the 200 strikes that are right behind it, and your opponent will break you into 1,000 pieces.

As is said in tai chi, you should be so sensitive and responsive that a fly landing anywhere on your body is enough to set your whole body in motion. "Well then," you may say, "to be so immaterial to my opponent, why don't I just remain completely disengaged, dancing beyond his reach?" Because then he would also be beyond your reach. Which is fine if you have the speed and space to run away. Unfortunately, if you're cornered, unless you're the Roadrunner, escape is usually unavailable. We're not talking about sparring. We're talking about life and death. You want to mold to him, to be all over him, and yet to be completely unavailable. You need to be at close range to cause damage to your assailant and yet stay alive yourself. This is attainable by learning sensitivity, not by learning technique.

You will find that as you train, your standard of what you call "grappling force" evolves. What the average person might call a light touch, you will call a hard push. This means you are developing your sensitivity. If you overcommit to a block or forced strike in which you try to blast through your opponent's defense when there is no opening, you're stuck—you can't react. You've committed yourself to one direction and can't recover in time to deal with his next strike. Because you've committed yourself, you won't recognize openings or be able to take advantage of them. This is why you stay soft—until you actually make contact with your own strike.

You're not training sensitivity to become yieldingly passive like limp spaghetti. You're developing sensitivity to change (direction, force, yin versus yang). These changes will then be amplified by you into deadly force. By being sensitive and remaining connected to your opponent, you follow his every move. When you move into some wild contortions in response to your opponent's energy, it will be impossible to deliver a rooted, powerful strike unless you also have hyperbalance that instantly readjusts with the same rapidity and fluidity as your sensitivity.

When you have developed your balance and sensitivity, you can deliver any strike from any martial art with devastating consequences. So you see, learning to punch and kick is actually the easy part. Now that you have built your foundation of looseness, body unity, and balance, you are ready to see how sensitivity can also help you create energy.

> You want to stick—but not get stuck. You stick barely enough to sense his intentions, but lightly enough to avoid entanglement or grappling. If you grapple, you're stuck.

Creating Energy

As both Eastern mystics and contemporary physicists will tell you, everything is comprised of energy. A punch, pull, kick, or block is an embodiment of bioelectric synaptic energy. Even the opponent's intent is latent, or potential, energy. Your nervous system is both a receptor and initiator of kinetic energy. This receiving and initiating of kinetic energy is enhanced by heightened sensitivity.

In guided chaos we propose to become experts at raw movement, or energy, both in its delivery and reception. The principle of sensitivity has the effect of liberating you from concentrating on obscure techniques and configurations, allowing you to focus on feel. Feel is subconscious, and you are the only one who can develop it. Once you have it, the type of strike you use or that is used against you is irrelevant. Your feel will dictate what is appropriate, not your brain (thinking brain, that is).

Yin-Yang Generator

As you learned in chapter 5, the principal of yin and yang delineates the universe in terms of opposites that can either be sharply separated or intermixed. Hard and soft, up and down, in and out, push and pull, attack and yield—these qualities need to be understood separately yet blended and applied simultaneously at all times to achieve the unmatched power that is available to the practitioner of an "internal" art. There are many more qualities defining yin and yang, including male and female, heaven and earth, hot and cold, and so on, but these are not central to our discussion. Without getting philosophical (and to avoid the often intentional mystification and confusion associated with this vital topic), simply train yourself to be aware of and do the following: Push the opponent's pulling energy and pull the opponent's pushing energy.

This has the effects of both augmenting your opponent's energy and putting it at your disposal. We can categorize the push as yang energy and the pull as yin energy. This concept is not really so esoteric. When you push a child on a playground swing, you feel the right moment. Although you don't actually pull the swing back toward you once it's in full motion, you do retreat to stay out of its way. Given the swing's full arc, a six-year-old on a swing can knock a grown man's head off if the pusher's timing is wrong. But what does this have to do with fighting? With guided chaos, we're going to turn you into a yin-yang generator.

Consider what your stereo amplifier does to the signal it receives from an old phonograph. A vinyl record's grooves consist of millions of tiny wiggles—tiny frozen waves of energy that are an exact duplicate of the music it copied. Your stereo amplifier takes these tiny waves of energy and amplifies them dramatically, but it doesn't alter the information they contain in any way. It doesn't oppose them. It follows them exactly and adds to their energy, using electricity and magnetism. Differences in volume and frequency are translated into powerful waves of magnetism that have gigantic peaks and troughs—opposites—that your speakers turn into loud, pulsing music.

These opposites are exactly analogous to the movements of your assailant as he struggles against you. You're going to follow these opposites—or yin-yang–push-pull movements—and amplify them. Using your loose, relaxed, balanced, body-unified connection with the ground as your "electricity," you're going to generate additional energy.

As you flow with your opponent's intention (remember, intention is a form of energy), learn to pull with one side of your body while you push with the other side. Your opponent's energy drives you like a seesaw. Your sensitivity tells you when pull becomes push. This simultaneous push-pull could be a ripping or yielding action with your left side in response to an attack and a reciprocating punch with your right side. This seesaw action can occur at any angle or along any direction. What's important is that this push-pull relationship happens simultaneously (not one then the other) and that your entire body remains relaxed and whip-like, or like a steel spring, and always perfectly balanced, like a gyroscope. The classic tai chi texts refer to this as having "one side empty, one side filled" and "not being double-weighted." The theory is, if you're pushing rigidly with your whole body displaying yang, or hard, energy, you will have no counterbalance. Hence, you would be relying exclusively on muscular force.

In accordance with the principles of body unity, do not isolate the push-pull action to just your hands. Move your entire body with this quality, even if the attack or defense is the subtlest of movements. With these principles under your direction, you will eventually be able to control your opponent without effort. Remember, you need to have superior sensitivity to detect exactly when a push becomes a pull, and vice versa. When you can do this, you are separating the yin from the yang. The drills at the end of this chapter will help you learn and practice this separation.

With a kinesthetic understanding of the yin-yang generator, you can begin to develop an explosive slingshot kind of energy that is amplified by your focused fear (taught in chapter 2, "Run and Scream" drill, page 27). In tai chi they may call this "borrowing jing," but I'd like to use a more modern explanation of this slingshot phenomenon using space-age science.

Because of the tremendous distances involved in space travel, NASA relies upon the laws of physics to generate more speed in a spacecraft than its own propulsion could ever generate. To get probes, such as Voyager or Galileo, way out into the solar system, they aim them at a nearer planet or the sun first. As the probe approaches the planet, the planet's gravity draws the ship in even faster, in effect accelerating it as it "falls" toward the planet. Then, with a slight deviation in course, the probe is directed to narrowly miss the planet, whip around it, and slingshot away at tremendous velocity. The space probe borrows the planet's gravity for energy while using none of its own. Sound familiar? This is what happens when you learn to push your opponent's pull and pull his push.

Here are some actual physical examples of yin-yang energy generation. If you think of every joint in your body as being finely balanced, a breath of air can cause it to swing one way or the other:

- A touch on your elbow rotates your fist into the opponent's face.
- A touch on your hand swings your elbow down on his neck.
- A push on one shoulder shoots your other arm out.
- A strike to your chest collapses your chest like a sponge but shoots both your arms out into his eyes.
- A slight challenge to your root shifts you onto one leg momentarily, which swings your entire body weight into the returning blow.

These changes in balance are instantaneous. The energy is delivered in the transition from one relaxed point of balance to the next. There should be no pause in the flow between them.

Don't think of these balance points as slow or weak. Turning your body into a yin-yang generator is like becoming a ferocious spring-loaded trap that instantly resets itself. Where does this explosive spring-loading come from, and how do you keep it from making you tense, causing muscular exertion? The next section provides the answer.

To become a yin-yang generator, you must learn to recognize and separate the fullness from the emptiness, the tension from the relaxation, the yin from the yang. This is so the yielding reception of your opponent's energy has someplace to go. When your balance and root are strong, this energy flows through your yielding side into your feet and bounces back out through your attacking side.

Dropping Energy

We've introduced some of the basics of dropping energy in chapter 2 (page 20), but now that you have an applied understanding of looseness, body unity, balance, and sensitivity under your belt, you will be better able to understand the full depth of dropping energy to defend yourself. Distilled from the art of ki chuan do, dropping is an instantaneous explosion or wave of energy you can use for striking, deflecting, uprooting, regaining balance, and virtually any other movement.

Simply put, dropping energy refers to a spasmodic lowering of the entire body weight into a current or new root. Whatever your body weight is, it becomes a formidable weapon when you get it moving all at once in accordance with gravity. The sensation of dropping is similar to having your legs kicked out from under you, stumbling off a curb, or falling asleep at the wheel of your car and then jerking awake. If you're a downhill skier, the sensation of dropping is like "down-unweighting," used for making the fastest possible edge change in a turn. The feeling is similar to what it feels like when you sneeze and your whole body spasms and drops. The energy is explosive, but involuntary. You want to be able to control it at will, directing it to any weapon. When fueled by your fear and permitted to flow by your relaxation, the damage dished out by dropping can be substantial.

Dropping consists of three parts that all happen simultaneously:

1. Stand with your knees slightly bent, then try to bend them more so quickly that for a split second your whole body becomes weightless, so that a slip of paper could actually be inserted between your feet and the ground. Most beginners make the mistake of actually jumping up first, which entirely misses the point.

2. Halt the drop with a snap to start the shock wave of energy. You don't want to drop more than a couple of inches at most. Think of it as snapping a wet towel or cracking a whip; you're essentially trying to "catch the bounce" your body makes as it's stopped.

3. Channel the energy through looseness (chapter 3) and body unity (chapter 4) to any weapon you desire (figure 6.2). You can just as easily drop and hit off one leg as off both legs. Don't lean, though, or your energy will be dissipated by your struggle to regain your balance .

What you achieve with dropping is creating a root no one can find. This is because your instant balance allows you to step, root, and reroot as fast as you can drop and redrop. You can switch legs and stances in one, instantaneous drop (this facilitates kicking with either leg powerfully) or drop and root on one leg. The phenomenon of instant balance occurs remarkably and instantaneously whenever you drop correctly. For example, you could be in the middle of wobbling, and a drop would probably fix it. If you're off balance, dropping tends to root you, giving you an opportunity to strike with power. Anytime you drop, you temporarily fix your balance to a spot and then almost instantly abandon it as soon as you step and drop again.

There are some vaguely similar concepts in tai chi, but they are rarely taught this way. Even so, in most cases, they don't crystallize the essence of the power of dropping and its simplicity. There are also some individuals who have discovered it on their own. The legendary boxer Jack Dempsey did a form of dropping.

In dropping you make gravity your friend. As you drop, you create a shock wave of energy that travels down your body, rebounds explosively off the ground and back up your legs to be channeled any way you desire.

Dropping is an instantaneous act of total relaxation of your whole body. Just let go. You can drop into both legs or one. You can be standing on one leg and drop into the same leg or into the other leg. It all depends on what your sensitivity and balance dictate in the fight.

And if you carefully watch films of the famous Cassius Clay–Sonny Liston fight, you will see that the infamous mystery knockout punch was actually a drop, which is why it didn't look very powerful. There was no windup: it simply wasn't needed.

Dropping as a Source of Power

There are many advantages to using dropping as a source of power:

- It requires no continuous muscle tension or great strength.
- It requires no windup or chamber.
- It's perfect for fighting nose-to-nose, where the most mayhem occurs and where there's no room to pull back and chamber a strike.
- It delivers more energy in less time.
- You can deliver it at almost any angle, including upward.
- It causes far more internal damage to the enemy.
- It extends the reach of either a punch or kick.
- It doesn't disrupt your relaxation, sensitivity, or balance; instead, it augments them.

FIGURE 6.2

Dropping actually satisfies all the requirements of separating the yin and the yang: it completely relaxes and collapses the body, forming a yang wave of energy that falls into the now-emptied and relaxed lower regions of the body, ricochets off the floor, shoots back up through the joints of the body, and explodes out through the strike. For the tai chi practitioners among us, dropping energy is how you "seek the straight from the circular."

The injuries you inflict as a result of a dropping strike are different from those you might inflict with a conventional strike. The opponent may not appear to move at all, but the dropping energy reverberates inside his body like an implosion. This is due to its suddenness. You want to time your strike so you halt your drop and hit simultaneously. You want your arms loose and flaccid, with no muscular tension whatsoever. Drop-striking becomes even more devastating when someone is falling into your strike because you yielded simultaneously. The effect is multiplied, depending on your opponent's falling speed.

Some manuals, like the *T'ai Chi Classics* (Liao 1990), call this type of dropping energy cold power because the explosive, snappy action generates shock waves that blast into the opponent's body, penetrating without actually moving him much. It does catastrophic internal damage, however. Contrast this with long power that is designed to project the opponent a distance away. For our purposes, we don't want to launch our attacker away, where he can regroup and attack again. Instead, we want to disable him where he stands. Remember, the way you train is the way you fight. In tai chi, if you always use long power during push hands (a tai chi training exercise), you'll probably do it in a life-and-death situation also.

If you're not balanced, dropping energy is frittered away and misdirected into space as you try to regain your balance. Correct this situation by observing the principle of body unity.

What's the logic behind dropping? When you strike an opponent, don't wind up, chamber, or draw back in any way. This is wasted motion. When you draw back to throw a punch, no matter how quick you are, you won't be able to get the strike off if your attacker is staying close to you or charging like an animal. When throwing a punch, the only motion that matters is the forward motion. Now you may be asking "If I can't wind up to strike, then how am I suppose to hit?" Yes, as with many of the principles that govern this art, not drawing back seems to be a contradiction. This is because the principle is paradoxical to everything most of us have ever been taught about punching and kicking.

If you're relaxed and balanced, you can hit with enormous power with no windup by using the principle of dropping. With a "no-inch punch," your acceleration is virtually instantaneous. This is strategically efficient for two reasons:

- If you draw back to strike, you create a natural opening for your attacker that can't be defended.
- Since you're already sticking to follow his every motion, dropping allows you to attack and defend simultaneously because you never lose contact with your opponent. For example, if your hand is already near the opponent's face and dropping would allow you to hit with effective power, why draw back only to have to bring it forward again? In fact, in the time it takes you to pull back on a strike, not only could you have thrown a strike at your opponent, but you could have struck him twice: once on the extension and once on the return.

Bruce Lee taught that punches should be felt, not seen. Whether or not he was the first to espouse this idea is unknown. Nevertheless, it's a very sound principle of fighting, which the looseness of dropping energy encourages. First, the strike is like steam—vaporous, illusive, unknown. Then it becomes like water—fluid, continuous, ever-changing. Finally, on impact, it becomes like ice—crushing, destroying. Dropping repeats the cycle over and over again.

Due to the dynamics of combat, however, it's not physically possible to drop on every single strike you deliver, because you're continually loading and reloading your body weight. However, in your practice, you should try to drop as often as you can.

Stealth Energy

Stealth energy is a term given to sensitivity so high you're in contact with your opponent's intent only. When your opponent's sensitivity is untrained, you do not appear on his "radar screen" while he is clearly on yours. Thus, his body's targets are defenseless, as if you were a stealth bomber preparing to drop its payload.

John Perkins can actually sense the heat of his attacker's skin. For most of us, this is a lofty goal, but it is definitely achievable with practice and not the stuff of legend. Training to be so light and responsive that you actually avoid bending the hairs on his arm (except when landing with a strike) is one approach. Another is to visualize that you're sticking to a fatter version of your opponent, a "Michelin Man," existing outside the skin of your enemy. This helps to keep you from "bearing down" on your opponent.

Pulsing Energy

Pulsing is any movement you make with any part of your body that adds energy to your contact. This may be a push, pull, tug, nudge, hip check, rocker (see chapter 7), or the like. For the sake of clarity, we will call all tugging and pulling actions inward pulses.

Now you may be thinking "Isn't guided chaos about not adding energy, about being unavailable and sensitive to your opponent's intentions?" That's exactly right, because the purpose of pulsing is not to overpower your opponent with a titanic push or tug-of-war pull: You're merely instigating a reaction in your opponent that you can flow off of. This is an important distinction to understand. You're not trying to engage and grapple with him. You're messing around with his balance and sensitivity, and thus trying to get him to grapple and engage you. When he does this, he uses more energy that you can turn back at him using push-pull principles. When you get him to react to a pulse, you can also lead his energy away and slide into the opening. The sensation of pulsing is very elastic and bouncy, kind of like a rubber ball bouncing rapidly between two walls or quickly tugging and releasing a bungee cord. The amount of energy imparted can be very subtle. Remember, however, that even though the pulse may be small you should still have your entire rooted body behind it. You just don't use any muscle. An inward pulse that tugs down on an opponent's arm could actually rip a tendon or cause him to stumble if it's properly rooted.

A pulse can be as light as a touch; an inward pulse, as delicate as plucking a guitar string. You then take his reactive energy and amplify it against him. This is, in effect, what you're doing when you pulse an opponent. When he reacts, he loads your spring, quite unconsciously, setting in motion a devastating slingshot or boomerang effect. In addition, by dropping as you pulse, you supercharge your next strike. To summarize, with pulsing

1. you instigate,

2. he reacts, and

3. you amplify his reaction, using the yin-yang generator principle and dropping.

The difference between the yin-yang generator principle and pulsing is that in the former you are passively following the opponent and then amplifying his energy. In pulsing you're actively provoking a reaction you then flow off of.

Up until now, the following has been a closely guarded secret, but we will now reveal it. Moe of the Three Stooges was actually an ancient guided chaos master. If you can picture him with his outstretched arm, telling Curly to "Hit this!" and see Moe's fist flying around in the opposite direction from the impact, you get the idea. The difference, to be serious, is that the wild, extreme swing Moe takes would not be in keeping with the economical tight circles that come from moving behind a guard (chapter 7).

For example, let's say you pulse an opponent's arm by pushing with your elbow (figure 6.3a). He panics, and his immediate unconscious reaction is to tense up, pushing you back. This loads your spring. Your arm and shoulder, supercharged by his energy, move in a tight circle in the opposite direction, and you palm-heel him in the face (figure 6.3b).

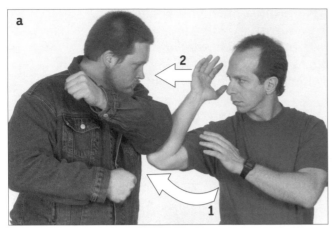

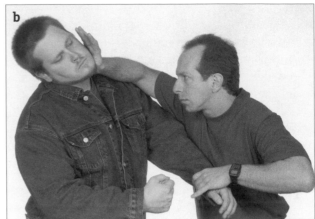

Or, suppose you inward-pulse him by tugging on his forearm with your hand (figure 6.3c). He tightens and yanks back, in effect pulling a chop into his throat (figure 6.3d). This will cause an involuntary outward deflection on his part, allowing you to pull his push. When you run this through your yin-yang generator, his attempt to block your chop to his throat gets his arm extended out, perhaps leading to a break. This little exchange, as you can see, has a Ping-Pong sort of quality, where one event (your inward pulse) starts a whole chain reaction.

Pulsing can get nasty very quickly, because once you set the chain reaction in motion, it can feel to your opponent as if he's been thrown into a giant pinball machine. If he's not sensitive, balanced, and yielding like you, it will seem that every move he makes is wrong, putting him into even more mayhem.

A pulse can also be something as simple as a hand squeeze or pinch. This could be all you need to provoke a reaction. Just remember that when you pulse, you become the spark of an energy generator. It's easy to get off balance due to the forces you'll be creating. Learning to pulse is easier than learning hyperbalance, so be sure your training emphasizes the latter. Don't cheat yourself on the basics.

By the way, a fake is actually a pulse, because, although you make no contact with it, a fake adds energy to the mix. Fakes provoke a reaction in the opponent that you can take advantage of. For example, if B fakes a chop straight into A's throat and circles into an overhand palm strike, A, moving to cut off the chop, overcommits to his centerline, leaving his outside line open to the palm strike.

FIGURE 6.3

Once you understand pulsing, you can use as much force as you want, as long as it's rooted, dropping, nonmuscular force. But it's often not necessary and sometimes wasteful. Stealth energy is of much higher value because the opponent can't even follow you. It's important to aspire to this level. Then you can sprinkle in some pulses randomly, without thought, and the combined effect will be overpowering.

Ricocheting Energy

Ricocheting occurs when you're moving at high speed and loading the spring almost instantaneously. You strike and bounce off a block into a different target, like a bullet ricocheting off concrete into an escaping felon (remember the scene from Robocop?). The point here is that the bullet changes direction without using any of its own energy, just what it receives from bouncing off the wall.

Ricocheting occurs whenever you strike some portion of his body and the resulting recoil bounces you into further strikes you augment by dropping. The potential for ricocheting is always there when you strike. The problem is, if you're not loose and sensitive to the energy, it won't happen. Remember, don't tighten up and bear down on your opponent when you strike, because this commits you to one direction only.

Sliding Energy

In the process of being as disengaged as possible yet still engaged, you attempt to slither through openings like a snake, not blast through them like a bull. This sliding energy requires great balance, sensitivity, and articulation, because you will be moving at many angles as you simultaneously stick and slide through the opponent's defenses. For example, suppose B is sticking to A's hands (figure 6.4a), and A decides to blast through B's guard to push or strike. B simply lets him go where he wants by letting A's arms slide right past his hands. By moving just his body out of the way but sticking with his hands, B remains in contact, yet makes his targets unavailable (figure 6.4b). B maintains strong structure the whole time by keeping his elbows low but does not use any force.

We also call this kind of energy forearm-surfing. Using sliding energy, treat your opponent's forearms like ocean waves and your hands as the surfers. Since you could never hope to overpower a wall of water

FIGURE 6.4

that weighs perhaps 20 tons, you have to learn to ride the wave's surface. Similarly, as your opponent's arms move, slide your hands along their surface, moving to the elbow to stop an elbow strike or to the wrist to stop a chop or punch. To maintain a balance of yin-yang energy, keep sliding back to the middle of the forearm until your opponent's energy tips you off.

A little move we call the rising ram is another example of sliding energy. While fighting A, B's lead arm winds up in an extended low position, pointing toward the ground. As B raises the arm, it is blocked by A's hand or forearm. The instant the top of B's arm contacts the bottom of A's, the relaxed rising motion of B's arm turns into a forward, sliding strike aided by dropping, turning, and stepping forward slightly. It's almost like shoving your whole arm through a greased mail slot. This is a good example of highly tuned sensitivity, because if B is tight and tries to fight upward through A's block with brute force, he'll miss the opportunity for an easy, sneaky, and decisive blow forward into A's torso. Although we've given this strike a name out of convenience, we can apply the principle behind the rising ram to almost any strike at almost any angle.

Sticking Energy

Sticking energy is an extremely subtle opposite of sliding energy. (This is not to be confused with sticking, which is simply maintaining tactile contact with the opponent.) As you let the opponent's body slide through your hands, you can at any time press into his flesh slightly with your fingers, nails, or the V formed by your thumb and forefinger. Create an extremely brief and elastic adhesion by stretching his skin. Instantaneously rebound off this into a strike or whatever. At no time do you grab onto him or squeeze with your hand in any way. This is difficult, of course, if either one of you is sweaty. Sticking energy takes a lot of practice but is extremely sneaky.

Skimming and Splashing Energy

Actually, you've already practiced skimming energy with the "Sticks of Death" drill (chapter 3, page 61). Skimming energy refers to the glancing action a strike or deflection may take, similar to a flat stone skimming the surface of a pond. Note that the stone will stop and sink rapidly if its angle is too steep. Similarly, if you become too engaged with an opponent, a skimming strike will get bogged down and will not have a clean bouncing action. If the opponent strikes to your face, skim by shooting your own strike in at an angle that glances off and deflects his attack and connects with your own simultaneously. For example, A punches at B's head. B shoots a spear hand at A's face, which deflects A's strike and skims off into A's eyes (figure 6.5). Skimming differs from ricocheting in that the strike trajectory remains relatively unchanged. It also differs from sliding energy because you are skimming past him, whereas in sliding, you allow him to slide past you.

Splashing energy is an interesting principle, in that it relates the human body to a body of water. Being mostly liquid, the body has a lot of give to it, so you must hit it differently than you would a brick. To make liquid act like a solid for a split second, you have to splash it. If you punch the surface of a pool, your hand will knife right in, but if you smack it as fast and snappy as you can with an open hand, you create much more disruption.

For various strikes, you can actually cause more trauma with a splashing action than with a strict reverse punch. You cause shock waves that travel deep into the tissue. The other advantage of splashing is that it doesn't overcommit you to the strike. Your aim is to penetrate the target to the depth of perhaps two inches and then completely relax the hand. This allows you to resume sticking to the exact spot you struck the instant after you make contact. This is an enormously important concept that keeps you balanced and ready to defend yourself further.

FIGURE 6.5

Suspending and Releasing Energy

Suspending and releasing energy is a more subtle and advanced form of pulsing. It involves the synthesis of balance and sensitivity and requires you to determine unconsciously the exact moment when the opponent is between pushing and pulling, striking and retracting, or yin and yang. In that split second of frozen time, he is suspended and helpless.

What you're doing while sticking is encouraging this suspension with the tiniest pulse so you are set up to release or catch his reaction and do with it whatever you wish. This is analogous to pushing a child on a playground swing: for that split second of suspension at the end of each arc, all the latent energy in the swing is frozen. Before it begins to move again, the swing can be moved in virtually any direction without the resistance momentum would give it. This is also like a tight end in football tearing down the field and then leaping into the air to catch a pass. Although he may weigh 220 pounds and be able to squat 500 pounds, for that suspended moment in time, a child could throw him on his head. This is when the most dangerous injuries in football occur, with very large men getting spun in the air by defensive collisions and landing on their necks.

You can create an exaggerated sense of suspending and releasing when you do a dance, like the jitterbug or the hustle, that involves swinging your partner around. You counterbalance your partner's body weight by firmly anchoring your feet. Then you release, letting him or her go into a spin or another move. You need to develop that same rooted sensation of suspending and releasing in your feet throughout the entire range of your combative movements. You let the pressure between you and your opponent build to whatever degree you want and then release it so he practically knocks himself out running into your fist.

Isolation Energy

Isolation energy is another very subtle and advanced principle. An example is placing your palm on someone's arm and being able to walk around him, rising and sinking, all without his being aware of any change in pressure or direction.

FIGURE 6.6

This kind of sensitivity allows you to confuse his nervous system and set up for strikes without triggering an alarm reaction on his part. You can use this point of contact as a fulcrum around which you may rotate to any new attack angle. For example, if your palm contacts his forearm so lightly that he can barely feel it in the heat of battle, you can move your body just enough to change your attack angle.

Here, A's forearm is in between B's palm and B's intended target, which is A's face (figure 6.6a). By using isolation energy, B is able to subtly move his upper body and shoulder just enough to create a new entry angle, allowing him to launch a chop to A's throat through this opening (figure 6.6b). Understand that this whole scenario takes place in a fraction of a second. There's no obvious posing or setting up going on.

Transfering Energy

Your sensitivity is heightened, and you're sticking, when all of a sudden, your "radar" picks up your opponent's intention to strike with his fist. Instead of only yielding or pocketing, you pass off his incoming energy to another part of

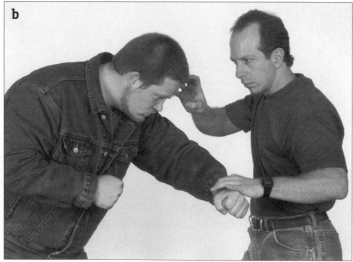

FIGURE 6.7

FIGURE 6.8

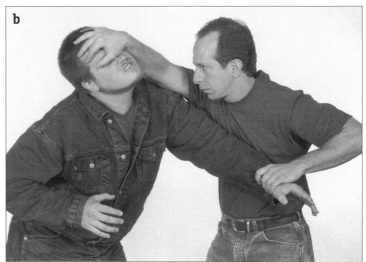

FIGURE 6.9

your body better positioned to redirect the incoming energy. We call this tool replacing, or transferring energy. For example, your hand is on his forearm (figure 6.7a). As soon as you feel his forearm tighten as preparation for a strike, pass it off, using no strength on your part, to your other hand (figure 6.7b).

This action is similar to a waterwheel passing water to the next paddle as it rotates, two gears turning with their teeth intermeshed, or simply climbing a rope, hand over hand. It's important not to grab or wrench the forearm, as this would tighten you up, destroy your sensitivity, and alert your opponent to your intention. If you're skilled enough, you can pulse, which gets him to push harder (remember the average person tightens up when pressed, in effect "fighting fire with fire"). Once he does this, you can clear or break his extended arm, opening up new angles of attack.

Since the tool-replacing described here is going from hand to hand, we like to call it passing the apples. This implies that neither hand is going to keep the "apple," you're only transferring it to its final destination. Tool replacement is a flexible and powerful principle. You can essentially tool-replace between any two parts of your body, for example, your hand to your elbow of the same arm (figure 6.8a) or the other arm (figure 6.8b), your elbow (in a rocker position; see chapter 7) to the hand of the other arm (figures 6.9a and 6.9b), or your elbow to your chest. This

FIGURE 6.10

last example is particularly interesting, because your chest, acting as a checking tool, frees both your arms up to strike (figure 6.10).

One little tip about passing from the hand to the elbow of the same arm is that since you're constantly trying to take your opponent's space, try to have the elbow reconnect further up the limb you're passing. If your left hand is on his right forearm and he's pressing hard, you can step in slightly, pocket, and pass his right arm by reconnecting to it with your elbow at a point somewhere around his triceps. With this done, his right arm is completely cleared and out of the picture, you've closed the gap, and your left hand is free to chop, spear, or claw his face. In the meantime, your right hand has "received" the apple by hyperextending his right arm.

Releasing Tension and Taking up Slack

While you're sticking to the opponent, you should let his limbs slip by while maintaining contact (sliding energy). This can be the result of a missed push or an attempt to retreat. What concerns you is when to stop giving slack and start taking up tension. Do so at a moment and from a position that is advantageous. At that point, you drop rapidly and pulse, then wait for his reaction. For example, you can be pulling a shoulder; he resists. Like a fishing reel, you release tension and let his arm slide out through your hand to his wrist. You then drop, root, and snap in for a strike.

Recognizing Energy

After reading about the different energy principles, you'll probably recognize that you've probably felt them all at one time or another already by accident. These "accidents" can be the turning point of a fight, as they can constitute the dynamics of effective self-defense. You may have deduced that they're all interrelated and seem to happen simultaneously. That's the idea. It's very hard to dissect spontaneous energy and movement. We've simply tried to define the effects of certain kinds of motion and categorize them so that as you begin to do the following drills, you'll recognize and encourage all these accidents to happen more frequently.

Sensitivity Drills

The energy drills presented later in this chapter will help you develop sensitivity simultaneously with other attributes. For now, though, here are three very odd drills that develop sensitivity exclusively. You may think they're too wacky to be any good, but that's their strength—they force you to move in ways you'd never think of, and they require great concentration.

The Coin Dance

The positions you get yourself into during this dance can be bizarre, but so are the positions you need to assume in a fight. This drill heightens your sensitivity by helping you focus on being relaxed and loose.

1. Place a penny on the tip of each index finger.
2. Have your partner carefully place the tips of his index fingers on yours, so you are holding the two coins between you.
3. Moving extremely slowly, begin to make large random circles with your arms without dropping the coins. The only things that should be holding them are the extreme tips of your index fingers. This will require both of you to forget everything else and really tune in to and follow the motion of your partner.

In the beginning, you'll drop the coin frequently. But as you learn to stay focused, loose, and relaxed, you can actually strike at each other like two sloths slugging it out. There's no leader or follower, so don't cooperate with each other. To increase the difficulty, move your arms in and out, high and low, and spin your bodies 360 degrees so, at some point, you actually have your back to your partner. Just don't drop the coins. If you have a third person available, add one more coin and join fingers so that you have three people attempting to sense the movements of each other. Also try holding the coins between your and your partners' respective elbows.

The Coin Chase

To make things wilder and faster, hold a coin between your palm and your partner's, both your and your partner's hands should stay flat at all times with no cupping. Now you can both go crazy running, spinning, jumping, and whipping your palms—but don't drop the coin. You must learn to sense your partner's movements. Yield when he pushes and follow when he retreats.

The Back Walk

This drill goes counter to most martial arts training, because you're not trying to bull or otherwise overpower your opponent. You're trying to listen to his movements with your whole body.

1. Stand back to back with your partner with your shoulder blades touching and knees slightly bent.
2. One of you becomes the leader and the other the follower. The leader tries

to disconnect from the follower (not too quickly at first or you'll both be on your backsides) by walking forward, rising, sinking, and twisting.

3. No matter what happens, maintain contact between your shoulder blades at all times.

When you get better at this, you can dispense with the leader-follower scenario and try to freely chase and avoid each other. Your job is to completely eliminate any buildup of pressure between you, so if he suddenly stops running and comes toward you, you can immediately sense the change and reverse course. At the same time, don't lose him. Beware, this puts a tremendous load on your quadriceps. Do this regularly and you'll develop legs like Arnold's.

Dropping Drills

Beginners often misinterpret dropping as simply falling or bending the knees. But the motion is more of a spasmodic jerking action similar, as we've said, to the snap of a whip. To promote this feeling, notice what your body does the next time you sneeze. Your whole body spasms and then relaxes. How do you know if you are dropping correctly? Place your palm on a brick wall about chest high with only enough pressure to bend a blade of grass. Now drop and direct the rebound energy out of your palm without ever breaking contact with the wall. If your relaxation is high and your timing is right, the shock wave that ricochets back into you will feel like it could dislocate your shoulder. If your balance is poor you will stumble backward.

The first two drills may help you approximate this snapping action. In addition, go back to the "Pyscho-Chimp" and "Circle Clap" drills in chapter 3 (pages 62 and 63) as well as the "Anywhere Strikes" drills in chapter 2 (page 34-36) and add dropping to them.

Stumble Steps

Here's an artificial way of simulating the sensation of dropping.

1. Stand with your feet shoulder-width apart, knees slightly bent.
2. Close your eyes and have a partner suddenly push you from behind with moderate force. The shove should be enough to make you stumble and lose your balance.
3. Catch yourself by landing on one or both feet as abruptly as possible. If you're standing on a wooden floor, you should actually feel it give slightly beneath you. All the dinnerware in the house should rattle. This doesn't mean you should purposely kick the floor, however. The energy comes from the sudden collecting of your balance. This, timed with a forward punch or palm strike delivered simultaneously on landing, is the essence of dropping power.
4. Try to duplicate the sensation without being pushed. Just fall forward and drop on your own.

Stair Steps

Here's another way of simulating the dropping sensation.

1. Stand at the top of a sturdy flight of stairs.

2. Balance on one leg and extend the other leg out in preparation for walking down to the next step.

3. Collapse your supporting leg abruptly as if someone had kicked out your knee. Don't try to brake yourself, just let yourself go, falling hard into the other leg as you land on the next lower step, heel first. Do not absorb the impact by bending the landing knee but actually keep it only slightly bent and immobile. You have only fallen perhaps 10 inches, but your whole body weight should hit that lower step like a ton of bricks.

4. Continue in this way down the stairs, pausing momentarily and then crashing down to the next step. This exaggerates the feeling of dropping; when you drop, however, you will sink only about an inch.

TV-Cut Drill

The beauty of the television as a training tool is that picture edits, without music or sound, have no rhythm whatsoever—as in a real fight. MTV works best because of its fast-paced programming and quick cuts. This is a highly effective drill that builds incredible quickness, looseness, relaxation, and reflexes as well as dropping ability.

1. Make sure you're thoroughly warmed up first or you can easily tear a muscle or tendon.

2. Stand in a relaxed ready position in front of the TV with the volume off.

3. Begin by performing one type of dropping strike every time the picture changes. Explode out like lightning and retract the strike even faster.

4. Once your mind and body become extremely quiet and focused, work on spontaneously changing the strikes without thought. When you can do this with no plan whatsoever and still maintain perfect balance (especially when kicking), you will have achieved an extremely high level of combativeness.

If you know when you're going to strike, you can bet your opponent knows also.

Beanbag

This drill teaches you to both drop and splash. For this drill you'll need to purchase an empty beanbag from a martial arts supplier and fill it with from 2 to 10 pounds of beans or shot.

1. Standing in a wide, loose stance, swing the beanbag from side to side like a pendulum, turning with your whole body.

2. At the end of each swing, let go, so the bag rises into the air a few inches.

3. As it descends, drop strongly, palm-strike, and snatch the bag in one move before it falls too far. After a few minutes of this, your forearm muscles will

be very fatigued, but your tendons and ligaments will get direct stimulation for growth.

4. Now try snatching the bag on the way down, continuing the downward motion of the bag uninterrupted so you can flow with it and swing it up to do another release and snatch in the other direction; your whole body should look like a pendulum. If you don't splash the bag, you'll knock it away and won't be able to stick to it for the grab.

Ball Compression

This develops the no-inch punch from extremely close range, where most fighting ends up. The beauty of these strikes is that they require no chambering or pulling back of any kind. This drill develops body unity, balance, focus, relaxation, and, most importantly, full-power dropping.

1. Take an old tennis ball and find a fat tree trunk or telephone pole.
2. Select any tool, for example, a palm strike, and place the ball in your hand against the tree (figure 6.11).
3. Orient your body using the principles of body unity into some rather strangely angled strike, such as might occur in a melee. It could even be on one leg.
4. Hold the configuration, breathe deep into your belly, and relax your entire body—muscles, joints, and mind—while palming the ball against the tree as lightly as possible.
5. Now, as if you sneezed from the soles of your feet through all the joints of your body and out your hand, drop so the tennis ball is instantaneously and explosively compressed.
6. Change the angle and location of the strike and repeat.
7. Then change the tool (the palm is the easiest; chops are a lot harder; try with the fist, elbow, shoulder, knee, and foot).

Remember to be relaxed, balanced, and sensitive when you practice this drill. If you are not completely relaxed, you will have no power. Muscle tension will have you fighting your own body's mass. Even if you are unusually strong, you will not compress the ball as much as when you drop correctly. If you aren't completely balanced, you will actually blast yourself away from the tree. If you aren't completely sensitive, the ball will shoot out of your hand due to the tree's curved surface.

FIGURE 6.11

If you practice this drill five minutes a day, you will increase the availability and effectiveness of your dropping strikes. The shock waves reverberate inside the assailant without actually moving him. Through splashing energy, they cause internal damage from their concussive force. This is effective when you're grappling with a larger opponent, especially when the strikes are slipped inside his arms and directed against the five vital zones: the eyes, throat, spine, groin, and kidneys.

Energy Drills

Energy drills help you develop a natural synthesis of all the guided chaos principles in a free-form and spontaneous manner working by yourself. While doing them, you must remain loose, unified, balanced, and sensitive to the energy, no matter how much you contort, articulate, or pocket. Perform these flow exercises with an attitude of play and improvisation. Work to develop a sensation of natural movement that is both effortless and powerful, yet virtually random, where you're both free, yet properly positioned to strike and deflect. Your movements should augment and support each other without thought as to what you're doing.

Moving spontaneously is a purely subconscious kinesthetic skill. Anyone can develop it, since it relies on mastering looseness, body unity, and balance, not mechanical techniques. The only thing you need to learn is how to develop and use your spontaneous movement so it's unified and powerful for mortal combat. Otherwise, you'll wind up looking like a puppet on angel dust. These exercises are not only an excellent form of low-impact aerobics, they're also a form of moving meditation. If you combine them with proper breathing, so that all yang, or outward, movements involve exhalation and all yin, or yielding, movements use inhalation deep into your belly, you'll achieve a level of relaxation and chi development equal to what you might find in decades of doing "forms."

Polishing the Sphere I

This drill, when done regularly, will tremendously improve your looseness and body unity resulting in greater power.

1. Breathe deeply into your belly, expelling all tension as you exhale.
2. With your shoulders relaxed and your knees slightly bent like a sleepy ape, visualize all muscular tension draining out your fingertips and into the ground. Your joints should be totally free and relaxed.
3. Imagine yourself standing inside a large glass sphere with a perimeter as far as you can comfortably reach with the palms of your outstretched arms.
4. Slowly and methodically, moving your entire body, polish the entire inside of the sphere with random circular movements in all sizes and directions. For example, you may polish a 12-inch section of the sphere in front of your face clockwise with your left hand while, with your right hand, you

polish a six-foot arc directly overhead, to your side, or underneath your feet counterclockwise. Your entire body rises, falls, and turns side to side with the circles you make, no matter how small they are. Drive with your legs to reach the perimeter of the sphere and to make the circles just as you did with body writing in chapter 4.

You don't want to stand stiff as a post with your arms rotating at the shoulders like two propellers. In baseball, you can't hit a home run swinging the bat with only your wrists. Likewise, during this drill you've got to stride, drop, and turn your feet, knees, back, hips, torso, shoulders, and arms. A tennis professional chasing down an opponent's ground stroke is not going to merely stand like a statue and flick at it with her wrist to smash it back. She has to reach, plant, drop, and align her body. When one part of you moves, your entire body must back it up.

Polishing the Sphere II

Perform "Polishing the Sphere I," but begin to polish using any and every part of your body as the polishing implement. Polish with your head, feet, back, chest, hips, buttocks, elbows, forearms, shoulders, and knees. Use everything in any order you wish. This time the perimeter of the sphere is as far away as you can comfortably reach with a maximum, balanced, full-body stretch, using whatever part of your body that's polishing. For example, by squatting with your

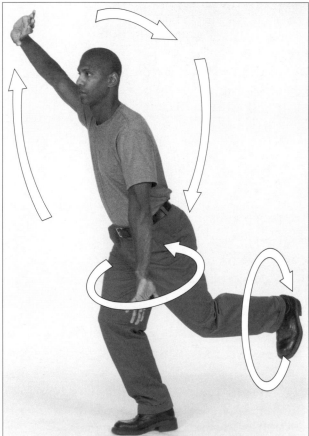

knees deeply bent and your back twisted perpendicular to the ground, you should almost be able to polish the floor with your elbow. This, then, would be the perimeter of the sphere for this implement at this angle. Use big and small circles, arcs, and brush strokes. Drive with your legs and turn with your body.

Polishing the Sphere III

Now polish as high, low, and as widely as possible while standing on one leg (figure 6.12). Close your eyes. Try using the flat of one foot to polish the sphere both in front and back of you at various heights. Ideally, you should polish using both arms and one leg simultaneously, along with as many other body parts as you can put in play. The object is to challenge your balance as drastically as possible, even if it's only your pinkies that are polishing. These motions mimic the kind of chaotic positions you might find yourself in during a fight. For the ultimate challenge, do all of this while doing the "Wood-Surfing" drill (see chapter 5).

FIGURE 6.12

Rolling the Energy Ball

Yielding and redirecting, pushing and pulling, taking and giving away, twisting and tearing all happen at the same time. This relationship of opposite energies gives enormous power to guided chaos, and you need to practice this in a completely unpatterned and nonrepetitive way. As such, rolling the energy ball helps you to develop that all-important push-pull feeling, in which your body moves with wave-like unity.

1. Imagine you have in your hands an invisible "energy ball." It has no weight, but it has a volume that can change from the size of a pea to that of a beach ball. If you roll it around in your hands, imagine it maintains its roundness with an outward pressure something like the feeling of repulsion you get when you try to bring together two magnets.

2. Take this ball in both hands and make it the size of a basketball.

3. Using the same side-to-side weight shift that you practiced in the turning drill in chapter 3 (page 56), carry the ball with your body. As you move to the right, your right arm is on top (figure 6.13a). When you reach the limit of how far you can move sideways, you roll the ball, so that as you carry it back to the left, your left arm is on top (figure 6.13b). The top arm leads with the elbow, so it helps to visualize an elbow striking with each sideways carry, as your lower hand clears, redirects, or shoves the opponent.

4. Drive your hands around the ball by turning your back and hips. Get your shoulders into it, as if the ball weighed 80 pounds, but without any tension. "Carry" the ball, by completely transferring your weight from foot to foot, but don't lean sideways as you shift from leg to leg.

FIGURE 6.13

 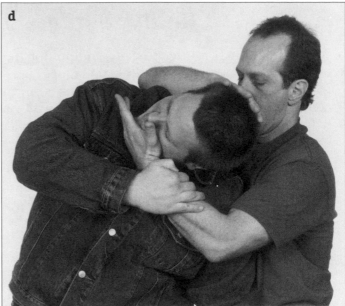

FIGURE 6.13

5. Keep your upper body perpendicular to the ground, like a buoy floating in the ocean. This emphasizes that all power comes from your legs while all the joints and muscles in your upper body remain loose, like ball bearings.

6. Now, roll it clockwise, counterclockwise, horizontally, diagonally, and all around—full arm's-length, in front of your face, in front of your stomach, by your hips, and then so close to you that you must actually pocket to get out of its way (figure 6.13c). You will find that your hands move quite unconsciously in a yin-yang relationship to each other as they roll the ball. While one moves up, the other moves down. When one moves out, the other moves in. No matter where one hand goes, the other, mirroring it, is never far behind. This is a critical relationship principle, essential to all movements in guided chaos. The application to self-defense is that while one hand strikes, the other deflects (figure 6.13d), and while one hand rips, the other hand tears.

The center of the ball is the pivot point around which your blocks and strikes effortlessly roll. It's also useful to think of whichever hand is closer to your body as the backup, or checking, hand, ready to deal with whatever gets past the front hand. Thus, the checking hand is frequently employed to pass the apples.

The ball itself represents your opponent's energy, which you never oppose. You roll around his attacking limbs and body, staying whisker-close, yet unavailable. When you combine the effect of your opponent's energy being amplified by the yin-yang generator and your body unity loosely flip-flopping your arms between their opposite positions, the end result is that your rolling hands become like the blades of a blender; anything that gets between them will get torn apart or crushed, using little of their own energy.

Washing the Body

Washing the body is one of the most important drills for developing the main four principles on your own. The goal is to turn you into a human sponge. Remember "Weaving Python" (chapter 3, page 55), where you alternately collapsed and expanded your chest and back in response to your partner's palms? Similarly, with this drill you can practice the limits of your looseness, but you'll be doing it with every part of your body and by yourself.

1. Shrink the energy ball to the size of a pea.

2. As your hands roll the pea, again notice the yin-yang relationship between their movements. Roll it between your hands, and between your hand and your forearm, elbow (figure 6.14a), shoulder, chest, waist (figure 6.14b), and head (figure 6.14c). Use the lightest pressure possible.

3. Perform this motion as if you were "washing" your hands or entire body with a slippery soap. This is where the drill becomes a little schizophrenic. As you wash, simultaneously avoid and pursue yourself. Simultaneously attack and yield by pocketing—moving those areas of your body that are being washed away from those that are doing the washing. At the same time, the attacking areas chase them. For example, as your palm washes your elbow, your elbow moves away while maintaining a featherlight pressure on your hand the whole time. Your whole body turns away with the elbow. As the elbow avoids the buildup of pressure by the hand, it tries to circle back on the hand at a different angle. Your whole body circles back with it. The hand, sensing this change, yields and moves away, while also maintaining a featherlight pressure on the elbow. Remember, due to body unity, even if you are rolling a pea with your hands, your shoulders and back rise and fall to move your hands around the pea. In addition, your feet and legs stride and reposition to get the best body unity. You want to move with the intent of driving 1,000 pounds, but not the force.

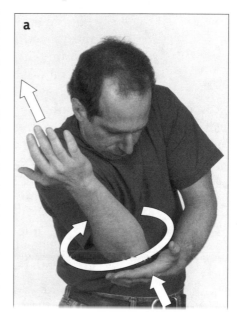

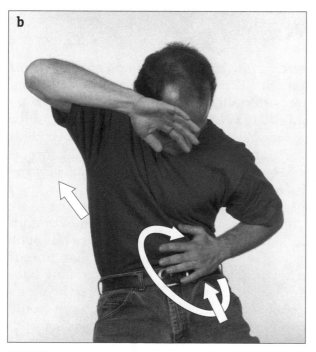

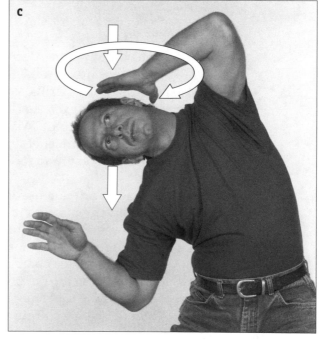

FIGURE 6.14

This will make your mechanics perfect in a real fight so for the millisecond that you drop and deliver the goods, the power will be there. Otherwise, stay completely relaxed. If your opponent resists, your mechanics will *remain* perfect as you instantly flip-flop and pull his push like a spring-loaded mousetrap.

4. Try rising and falling, carrying the pea all the way to the ground. Continue washing while lying on the ground. Wash any part of your body that could be struck or grabbed in a fight—in other words, everything. Twist and contort your whole body like a beached catfish. Rolling on and off the floor develops total looseness, grace, and balance even when ground-fighting (see chapter 10).

Along with keeping your joints as loose as ball bearings with your flesh simply hanging off your bones, the washing action embodies the principle of being as disengaged as possible yet still engaged. You roll around the pea (or in this case, your skin) with zero resistance.

You can wash (attack) your own ribs with your elbow, yield, pocket, and check or clear it with the other hand. Meanwhile, don't forget to root and pulse yourself (again, as if you're your own worst enemy), looking to create suspend-and-release situations you can simultaneously escape from. Remember, the extremes of your looseness and the rolling of your hands are actually balanced energy opposites. The ferocious power of guided chaos comes from flip-flopping between these opposite positions at a hair-trigger's notice by dropping.

Try combining all the energy drills: "Polishing the Sphere" (I, II, III), "Rolling the Energy Ball," and "Washing the Body." For the ultimate challenge, flow from one to the other while wood-surfing. In the end your nervous system won't be able to tell the difference between attacking yourself and attacking someone else. So go ahead. Beat yourself up. The benefits are immense.

The key to developing your sensitivity when training alone is to imagine that you are engaged with a real opponent.

Relationship of Human Energy to Movement (RHEM)

When you combine slow, deep breathing, the "Box Step" (chapter 5), the "Ninja Walk," and "Vacuum Walk" (chapter 5), "Polishing the Sphere" (I, II, III), and "Washing the Body" drills, you are performing the relationship of human energy to movement exercise (RHEM). RHEM looks like a tai chi form, but the methodology is different. With a form, you try to imbue patterned movements with qualities that are energetic and combative. After many years, the form is supposed to dissolve, and its essence become available to you if you get into an altercation.

RHEM is a more potent form of learning because instead of training fixed, patterned movements, you're teaching your subconscious to become comfortable with spontaneous, random motion—the kind you would use in a real fight. As we've alluded to previously, you give your nervous system what it needs from the beginning for combative development instead of programming it for hesitation. You develop creativity, governed only by guided chaos principles.

You perform the movements very slowly, doing the same things you would do in a real fight, concentrating on looseness, body unity, balance, and sensitivity. As you perform the exercises, you will cultivate chi, because you will be integrating internal energy (breathing, visualization, and calm, focused mind), with physically coordinated, balanced, and aligned body movements. You may recall that we support the definition of chi as the "circulating point of finesse in the body" (chapter 4, page 67). As such, you will derive many of the benefits of cultivating chi without locking that point of finesse into choreographed forms. Then the chi can really flow spontaneously, the way you actually need it.

1. Breathe deeply, slowly, and evenly. Continue to breathe this way throughout the entire movement, exhaling as you move outward and downward.

2. Rise high onto one leg as you inhale deeply, simultaneously raising your other knee as high as you can. As you slowly exhale, slowly step to a new root point, anywhere you like. When you get familiar with RHEM, you should slowly step to the most challenging spot you can find. There should be a long period where you're suspended and balanced on one leg before your foot actually touches the ground and settles in. Observe all the principles of weight transfer you've practiced in the "Ninja Walk" and "Vacuum Walk" drills (see chapter 5, pages 77 and 79).

3. As you inhale and rise and then exhale and step to a new root point, simultaneously and slowly do an energy drill: "Rolling the Energy Ball" (page 113), "Polishing the Sphere" (I, II, or III, pages 111-112), or "Washing the Body" (page 114). Then, as you settle into your root point, slowly perform one strike of any kind (it doesn't matter which). To maintain body unity, three things should happen simultaneously:

   - You complete the strike.
   - You finish sinking into your new root.
   - You do all this during one exhalation.

   The slower you can do all these, the better.

4. Without pause, slowly inhale deep into your belly and begin to rise high onto the toes of the new root point while doing one of the three energy drills. Suspend yourself here for a split second and then exhale, continuing one of the three drills and ending in a different strike. Don't forget to try kicks, knee strikes, elbows, and head butts—everything.

If you do this exercise every day for 15 minutes, the improvements in power, balance, and looseness will be remarkable. You will imprint your subconscious with the necessary dynamics of combat instead of fixed choreography. In addition, you'll derive all the benefits of moving meditation: inner and outer harmony, stress reduction, and low-impact aerobic conditioning.

- The rising and falling emphasizes body unity and separation of the yin and yang within dropping energy. Obviously, you don't rise this high or drop this slowly when you fight, but we want to immerse you in the sensation rather than fixate your brain on "perfect" execution.

- The rolling the ball, polishing the sphere, and washing the body movements are for programming your nervous system to become spontaneously evasive as it simultaneously attacks. This gets you as disengaged as possible, yet still engaged.

- Feel the exhalation and let the continuous, slow dropping drive you through the entire movement. Remember, gravity is your friend. Don't resist it. Learn to use it.
- Become familiar with the sensation of "swinging" your entire body's mass through every movement.
- Keep your hands in sync with your legs. When your legs stop moving, so do your hands, whatever the relationship between them.
- Throughout the entire exercise, visualize the enemy while focusing your fear, mold to him, and destroy him.
- This is not a form. Creativity is king.

Contact Flow

Let's face it. While training on your own will enhance your mastering of the principles, to get good at fighting with people, you have to either fight or train with another person. There are at least a million ways a person can move (and that's no exaggeration). You need a way to become comfortable with all of them, without memorizing any of them.

The only way you can effectively practice all the principles in this book simultaneously is in a totally unchoreographed, completely spontaneous interchange, where you can train with another person, without getting hurt. The "Contact Flow" drill is essentially free-fighting, and absolutely anything goes—except for hurting your partner. It's not about machismo. It's about energy and movement.

There's nothing highly complicated about this exercise, no obscure mystical secrets. You're simply learning how to deal with another person's motion. That's it. Now you may be saying to yourself, "If two-person training is so critical, then what value is there in training on my own?" The answer is that both types of training complement each other. Each time you train, you get a little bit better, even if you can't discern any progress in your ability immediately. When you train on your own, you not only reinforce the basic principles but also discover and develop what works for you. This allows you to bring more things to the table the next time you contact-flow with a partner. Also, if you practice diligently on your own you won't regress if you later have little access to a partner. Because you're reprogramming your neural pathways, it's important to do drills that involve the four basic principles a little bit every day. When you're alone, you can examine your development closely. But the last thing you want to do when performing contact flow is think, plan, or try to win.

Instead, simply feel. Your biggest enemy is your brain. Your subconscious, the same part of you that carries out the billions of operations that keep you alive and upright without your thinking about it, is the part of you that will be guiding your movement. By using visualization when you perform the solo drills, the principles will creep in slowly by themselves. So relax and be free. When you're done, you can analyze what you did and refer back to the book all you like. But remember, while you do this drill, empty your mind. After all, how much analyzing are you going to do during a fight? This drill helps you prepare to flow with your movements in any situation you might find yourself in.

"Contact Flow" is the most advanced of all the drills, combining everything you've learned and will learn, allowing you to continue learning. Nevertheless, it's something you practice with a partner from the very beginning; it should be the foundation of all your future training.

1. Face your partner in a basic Jack Benny stance (sideways, so you don't expose too much target area). Before beginning every "Contact Flow" drill session, note the distance between you immediately and recognize that, if he's safely beyond your personal comfort zone, you should run or back away.

2. If he's not, reach out with your sensitivity, so you make contact with his intent before you even touch him. This way, your body is already in motion by the time the action begins. Slowly reach for your opponent, both to slowly strike and stick, simultaneously. When you first approach your partner, don't be casual. You can actually begin with a slow fright reaction, chin jab, or stomp-step-kick from chapter 2. This is basic close combat. Once contact is made, however, guided chaos begins.

3. Stick to your opponent as closely as possible, but keep the contact as light as a feather, except, of course, when you're hitting or gouging him. You both want to strike each other and avoid being struck, without ever losing contact with each other, all at the same time. Twist, bend, and pocket like two weasels.

4. When moving, use whatever you want to on each other: elbows, palm strikes, chops, locks, punches, gouges, pinches, hip checks, wrestling, kicks, head butts, you name it. If you know a "technique" from some other art, try it. Interestingly, what you will find is that you will rarely be able to pull off any techniques. This is because your logical mind plans them, which not only makes you tight and slow, it practically "airmails" your intentions to your partner (that is, if he has any sensitivity). Don't cooperate. One of you is not defense and the other offense, as in some styles. There are no points, pauses, breaks, or restarting. You stop when you both feel like it. You are, in essence, fighting.

After much practice, you will plan nothing. Everything will happen seemingly by accident. You should actually have no idea what you're doing or what you'll try next. All you should be doing is developing a feel for your own and your opponent's movement.

Throughout the drill, maintain a relatively slow, constant speed, proportionate with one another. Move with your whole body with the intent of driving 1,000 pounds but not the force. Speed will come later, as you naturally learn to move in the most efficient, natural, and powerful manner you can. You'll find it's much easier for your brain to work toward developing a feel while doing "Contact Flow" than to analyze, plan, and execute prescribed techniques.

Another reason to go slowly at first is that all human beings have virtually the same top muscle speed, no matter how much it's trained. Put a straight razor in the hands of a sedentary woman and tell her you're holding her children hostage, and she'll cut you up faster than lightning, black belt or no black belt. Therefore, if you or your partner should suddenly accelerate to 10 times practice speed to "score a point," it's stupid and unrealistic. In a real psychotic bloodbath, you'll both be going at maximum adrenaline velocity anyway, which is virtually the same speed. If your partner speeds up, it's you, ironically, who'll benefit because you'll get a chance to see how calm and loose you can stay while your opponent foolishly exercises his ego and wastes his own time and energy. Moreover, if you get competitive or angry, you'll learn nothing and bring tension and rigidity to your development. The same is true in a real fight situation. If either extreme fear or anger paralyzes you, your emotions have inhibited your sensitivity. Your attacker is not a person, just energy—motion you have been training to deal with. Train for life-and-death combat, be real with yourself, and worry about looking cool later. You can actually do "Contact Flow" as fast as you want, but in the beginning, go slowly so your nervous system won't become overloaded. Keep your speeds proportionate so your subconscious can digest the kinesthetic data it's experiencing.

This same principle applies to using excessive muscular strength. We can't emphasize enough that it's senseless to get competitive and try to "score" on your opponent by overpowering him. This is not why you're training. Remember that, in reality, no matter how strong you are, there's always someone stronger, perhaps even twice as strong as you. The rampant egotism in many disciplines can't get past this. This is not to say you can't experiment with excessive speed and strength. It's just that as you get better, you won't need it, and if your partner is far more balanced, loose, and sensitive than you, you'll be annihilated, no matter how fast or strong you are.

How do you improve at this drill? There's no mystery, just lots of practice, with as many different partners as you can find. If you have friends who are schooled in different defense styles, performing "Contact Flow" with them can provide a gold mine of experience. Most schools train students to move in characteristic ways. But because *you're* not locked into any one way of moving, you react to the motion and nothing else.

Once you've finished practicing, think about what you experienced:

- How did he feel? How did you feel?
- Did you turn your brain off to avoid thinking about what you were doing?
- Did you observe the principles? Which ones?
- Did you feel rooted? Balanced? Did you step when you needed to?
- Did you challenge your opponent's strength or did you flow with him like a ghost?
- Were your mind and breathing slow, calm, and relaxed?
- Did your body have unified motion?
- Did your body feel relaxed, yet springy, like a metal whip?
- Were you leaning?
- Did you stand sideways to your opponent or did you face him squarely, creating a giant target?
- Was your sticking pressure light, like a butterfly's, or were you pushing your partner to force openings?
- Did you stick consistently without grabbing?
- Did you drop at every opportunity?
- Could you clearly separate the sensations of yin and yang in your body, so your opponent's energy was reflected and magnified back at him?
- Did you keep your elbows down?

- Did you stick with whatever part of your body was necessary or did you limit yourself by sticking only with your hands?

There's much to reflect on, including some additional principles in the following chapters that you will also apply to this drill. Just don't think while you're training. If you've read all this without actually experiencing contact flow, you may think it's wacky, New Age junk. All we can say is, try it, practice it diligently, and you'll be shocked how much faster you'll learn how to protect yourself than you would by doing 100 knuckle push-ups, board-breaking, forms, splits, sparring, and "fighting by the numbers."

Contact Flow Variations

Most beginners over-rely on their hands for sticking and sensitivity. To break this habit, perform "Contact Flow," but stick using only your elbows. You must learn that they can be as, or more, versatile than your hands. After that, try doing "Contact Flow" with just your shoulders. That's right. Stick as if you had no hands, forearms, or elbows. How much subtlety and sensitivity can you develop? Explore all the deflecting and striking angles, using only your shoulders as weapons. Note that this doesn't mean you should be shoving each other around like bulls or sumo wrestlers. Instead, your goal is to develop extreme shoulder looseness and isolation so the joints become as disembodied and articulate as your hands. They should slide and circle into attacks and deflections. To add the ultimate challenge, do "Contact Flow" with your eyes closed. After understanding and practicing the information in chapter 10, add ground fighting.

Once you become comfortable with the concept of contact flow, try it while wood-surfing. First try it with both you and your partner on boards, then with only one of you on a board and the other person standing on the ground, creating an obvious balance mismatch. This forces the person standing on the board to further develop his or her hyperbalance. This is equivalent to fighting someone on the edge of a cliff. To make it even more difficult, stand on one leg with your eyes closed.

As you contact-flow with every movement and in any position, remember to learn to feel the separation of yin and yang. What part of me is relaxed, and what part is tensed? Where is the energy building? Where does it want to go? Where am I resisting its trajectory? How can I let go enough to guide it without exertion and without planning?

Following is an example of a ferocious altercation where form went right out the window. It is the same kind of situation you may come up against some day—with one big difference. In this case, the defending parties were police officers who put their lives on the line trying to subdue the attacker without the use of lethal force. Even if they had decided the situation warranted it, the ongoing chaos would have prevented them form using their guns. Perkins was obliged not to end the fight immediately with deadly strikes to the eyes and throat, even though the opportunities were there. Remember, as a civilian, you're under no such obligation—and neither is your attacker.

MIKE THE SAILOR

John Perkins

Headquarters called us and said we had a 14B—a person with mental illness in need of assistance. The department rule on 14B calls at that time was to unload your weapon before you engaged the suspect. The reasoning for this came from years of experience. The last thing you needed was a person with an emotional disability getting your gun during a struggle. (I don't believe this is as likely today because the new holsters are much better at retaining the weapon.)

We arrived at a small apartment. My partner, myself, and two other officers began interviewing a young man and his mother. The mother was very distraught and crying. She told me they were originally from Europe and her son was a sailor. He was giving her a very hard time, and she felt he might become dangerous. He seemed pretty calm to us. The mother then revealed that her son would not take his Thorazine. Now we felt a little more uneasy.

My partner and I separated the son and his mother into different rooms. While two officers were interviewing "mom" in the kitchen, we were speaking with "Junior" in the bedroom. The young man was approximately 23 years old. He stood 5 feet, 10 inches tall and weighed 190 to 200 pounds. He was powerfully built with a great deal of natural strength. We spoke with "Mike" (a fictitious name) for a few more minutes until the mother began to yell and make a scene. My partner (who was the senior member of our radio car team) told me to keep an eye on Mike for a few seconds so he could see what was going on.

As soon as my partner left the room, Mike started chuckling. I looked at his face and saw that he was not in the same mood as before. He then stated in a thick accent that he could have easily killed my partner. I guess he wasn't impressed with the size of Bill, who was 6 feet, 5 inches tall and about 240 pounds. Maybe the outcry from Mike's mother and the fact that Bill had stood with his chest in Mike's face precipitated the change in Mike's behavior.

I looked at Mike's hands to see if he had a weapon we might have overlooked. He was bare-handed. Mike then stepped a little closer to me and stated that he knew karate. My back was facing an old wooden closet door. This door had panels three-quarters to two inches thick, made of solid maple, which is a hardwood. As he finished saying the words "I know karate," he flinched on his right side. At that point I knew he was going to try to hit me. What I didn't know was how. I jumped and yielded to my right just in time to see his right hand, with his fingers fully extended, fly past the left side of my face as he lunged forward. His outstretched hand was aimed to take out my eyes. Instead, Mike's hand struck the closet door and broke through a three-quarter-inch-thick section of wood, whereupon his pinkie came off.

When I saw this, I realized I'd have to fight for my life. As Mike pulled his hand out of the door, he spun around to find me. I had box-stepped and landed behind him. As he started to turn, I hit him on the side of his head with a right palm-heel strike. It was a solid shot. This unbalanced him for a split second and he bounced into the closet door. I knew instantly that, given the amount of force I had hit him with, he would not easily succumb to kicks and punches.

My blackjack was in my side leg pocket of my uniform pants, but before I could pull it out, he was on me. I drove him away with a dropping two-handed palm-heel shove. (I later found out from the hospital it had broken two of his ribs.) I felt the power of his body at that instant and realized that, given his mental state, I was no physical match for him. I knew that my fellow officers were only seconds away and that I had to hold out until they arrived. As I moved backward, I found that the bed was now at my right side. I dragged the bed for an instant and tried to place it between Mike and myself as I attempted to get through the doorway. Somehow I lifted the bed up and pushed it forward, sending Mike backward. At this point my buddies came crashing in behind me to get at the enraged Mike. They got around and over the bed, and with blackjacks and sticks flying, attempted to subdue him.

Mike proved to be even stronger than I imagined. With strength powered by his mental illness, he was able to disarm two of the officers and to begin kicking them and striking them with an absconded nightstick. I recognized that even if my gun was loaded, it would be too dangerous to shoot because of the chance of hitting an officer. I then leaped in, and through the barrage of hits and kicks from Mike and the officers, I got myself onto Mike's back. Just before jumping in, I made the conscious decision not to strike Mike in the eyes or throat. Mercy, and the hated paperwork I would have to do if I blinded or killed him, guided my actions. I quickly applied a "sleeper" hold, which was legal at the time. This was dangerous, because he was trying to take out my eyes with his thumb. I placed my head close to Mike's back, squeezed, and in a matter of seconds, he went limp. We then handcuffed him and tied his upper torso and arms with the bed sheet. We took Mike and his mangled hand to the hospital, where, after a long struggle, he was finally sedated and repaired.

Preventing Common Mistakes

➤ You can't be stiff and drop effectively. Dropping is a brief, instantaneous act of complete relaxation with your whole body that essentially loads your spring, so you can't be totally limp either when you rebound and strike.

➤ Pocketing requires counterbalancing other portions of your body. For example, when pocketing your chest, don't lean forward, stick out your chin, sit back on your heels, or stick out your buttocks. This can throw you off balance. Instead, drop your hips straight down and rock the bottom of your pelvis down and forward. Keep your head in line with your pelvis (unless it's your head you're pocketing). This allows you to respond quickly.

➤ When "Polishing the Sphere," you don't want to stand stiff as a post with your arms rotating at the shoulders like two propellers. As with the body unity drills in chapter 4 ("Body Writing" and "Starting the Mower," pages 69-70), you want to get your entire mass behind every nuance of the circles you make, even if they're just an inch in diameter. In other words, your entire body rises, falls, and turns side to side with the circles you make, no matter how small they are.

➤ When "Washing the Body," don't just rub yourself. You actually attempt to move those areas of your body that are being washed away from those that are doing the washing. At any time the areas that are moving away can turn around and chase the others.

➤ With all movements, keep your hands in sync with your legs. When your legs stop moving, so do your hands, whatever the relationship between them.

➤ When you do "Contact Flow," don't think, plan, or try to win.

➤ When you first approach your partner in "Contact Flow," don't be casual and don't cooperate. One person is not offense and the other defense. You're fighting. Your very first move is to simultaneously attack and avoid, as in the Jack Benny. Reach out with your sensitivity, so you make contact with his intent before you even touch him. This way, your body is already in motion by the time the action begins.

➤ Keep your elbows down (in general, not as a rule).

➤ Don't lean.

➤ Never oppose your opponent's energy: neither he nor you should feel any resistance at any time. Don't power through blocks; go around them or entice them away via pulsing.

➤ You want to stick, but not get stuck. Stick closely enough to sense his intentions, but lightly enough to avoid entanglement or grappling.

➤ You're not developing sensitivity to become yieldingly passive like limp spaghetti. You're developing sensitivity to change direction, force, and yin versus yang. You can then amplify these changes into deadly force.

PART THREE

GUIDED CHAOS FOR SUPERIOR SELF-DEFENSE

Now that you have an understanding of the fundamental principles of guided chaos, we can begin to discuss more specific strategies and tactics that will help you use the principles to move freely as well as efficiently, effectively, and combatively. Although all fights are chaotic, the human body tends to move in characteristic ways when attacking and defending. Part III addresses these tendencies by showing how the guided chaos principles flow into related subprinciples that deal effectively with the particulars of combat. We have waited until now to go into these subprinciples, because to the uninitiated, they may seem like techniques. In fact, they'd be useless unless we had first torn down any preconceptions you had of "real" self-defense, so you could see them for what they are—"snapshots" in a continuous flow. Before we explore part III's subprinciples, however, let's review the larger concepts you picked up in part II:

- The state of natural awareness is a combination of looseness, body unity, balance, and sensitivity functioning as one, not as independent parts of the whole.

- You cannot have looseness without balance. You'll simply be knocked over or twisted into a pretzel.
- You have to develop sensitivity to know when to yield or step around a strike to a new position with balance.
- When you're better balanced, your opponent can't move you, yet because of body unity, you can move him at will.
- When all four principles come together, you become an enigma. If your opponent pushes you, he finds himself off balance, pushing against nothing because you're loose and balanced, yet you're all over him constantly, sticking like jelly.
- Because you're sensitive, you've already moved as little or as much as you need to strike your opponent with deadly force from bizarre angles, seemingly out of nowhere.
- When you're sensitive, balanced, and loose, you can be as hard as you want to be and as soft—both at the same time.
- With extreme sensitivity and balance, you can move like the wind, strike with the authority of lightning, then leave like the wind. Your strikes should be felt, not seen.
- By dropping and driving from your feet through your legs, turning at the waist, and extending the power loosely through your arm, you're able to hit with immense power yet with little effort.
- You're able to do this because you have learned not to exert negative tension with antagonistic muscle groups. Without strain, power flows uninhibited.
- When attacked, you're able to negate the opponent's force by yielding and redirecting. You can even "borrow" his power and use it against him.
- In all this, you're developing your mind and body to function and fight from any and every possible angle.
- You can't fool your subconscious mind. It knows what's real and what's illusion when it comes to life-and-death struggles. Regardless of fighting style, your mind and body will move naturally, responding purely to the attacker's motion instead of following an internal script.

How is this natural motion manifested specifically? That is what we explore in part III.

CHAPTER SEVEN

Applying the Principles to Motion

The subprinciples discussed in this chapter are not some great secrets of the universe; they merely reflect the way the human body moves naturally. We emphasize natural movement because wild animals don't have a cognitive mind fighting for control over their nervous systems as we do. You can't, for example, teach a tiger to fight "better." It's always performing at maximum capacity for its species. Similarly, there are ways of attacking and defending that are naturally efficient for the human body. Part II explained these in terms of looseness, body unity, balance, and sensitivity. Now, to help you understand how to apply these principles to specific attack and defense scenarios, we have divided the material into two sections: the body as a shield and the body as a weapon.

The Body as a Shield

You've already learned in close combat that blocking as a fixed technique is wasteful, slow, and inefficient. Moreover, the understanding of skimming energy that you picked up in chapter 6 shows you that it's far better to deflect an incoming strike incidentally, on the way to delivering your own. You facilitate this by being aware of the natural deflecting attributes of positioning certain parts of your anatomy. We explore these movements and positions in the following sections.

Move Behind a Guard

In an effort to be really loose and avoid an initial strike beginners often twist themselves into

127

positions that leave them even more vulnerable. The solution is to always move behind a guard. Keep some part of your body between your opponent's weapon and its target. When you practice the "Contact Flow" drill, you learn to both stick with your opponent's every move and still keep something (something practical like a hand or elbow, not a toe or nose) in front of the nearest threatened vital area—your face, neck (front and rear), torso, and groin. You can cover your face and neck primarily with your hand (and sometimes your elbow), your torso with your elbow (and sometimes your hand), and your groin with the angle of your hips or knees. Of course, keep the area you're protecting as unexposed as possible. Remember, by standing sideways, you reduce the size of the target area. Also, turning sideways allows your lead leg to guard your groin.

"OK," you say, "so I'm loose, balanced, and sensitive, but when my opponent punches through my hand and so punches me in the face because my hand yielded like you said, I get a little confused as well as bloody. What's wrong?" The answer is so simple it may sound like a joke, but there's a principle involved: Yield in ways that are advantageous and not hurtful to you. And, of course, still maintain balance. In the previous example, by putting up your hand, you've only got it half right. Instead of yielding your deflection so your opponent's fist drives your own hand into your face, guide it ever so gently past you to either side. You only need to deflect the strike until it's one inch out of its attack path; don't overblock. You then immediately slide or skim along the arm and slam him with your own strike, maintaining contact the whole time.

Your guard is not a static thing, and your arms should still stick, following the opponent's body within the flow. Moving behind a guard also dictates that the guard—the arms in this case—move in arcs that are no wider than the perimeter of your body. Since the only thing they're protecting is you, avoid excessive movement.

If your opponent swings wildly to hit or get away from you, slide into the centerline opening this creates and attack. This is not a mental strategy. You will simply "feel" a crack in his defense and fall through it automatically, like water going through a bucket full of holes.

When do you change your guard? There's no rule; rather, it depends on how you move. By practicing the flow exercise "Rolling the Energy Ball" (page 113), you'll find that your lead hand is constantly changing into your rear checking hand, and vice versa. This is a process of discovery. In line with everything else you've learned, you'll soon see how moving behind a guard is also an offensive strategy.

Moving Behind a Guard

Simple as this sounds, when most people move, they leave vital areas wide open all the time. Now, of course, in guided chaos your arms won't be locked into "guard" positions because they'll be flowing freely with the attacker's limbs. This is simply a reference position, something you'll return to when under lower pressure. You'll see this more clearly as you read the coming sections.

1. Raise both your hands so that they're 18 inches in front of your face, palms outward and elbows down.

2. Adopt a stance about twice shoulder-width, and raise and lower your whole

body by bending your knees deeply. In addition, move sideways by shifting your weight completely from one leg to another.

3. While you do this, turn your body in the direction you're moving. You should look like a bobbing and weaving python peaking from behind your arms. The key point of this drill is that however you move, your vital areas should be covered as much as possible by whatever body part is practical. There is no rule or form to this. To keep this drill simple in the beginning, one or both palms should remain in front of your eyes and throat (facing out) in the direction you're moving, and your elbows should be within 12 inches of your kidneys. The elbow should be down with the lead arm in whatever direction you're facing.

As a variation, do the same drill but move so the elbow of your lead arm sticks out in front of your face with the arm bent and held horizontally like Count Dracula. Keep the palm of your rear hand facing forward, near your solar plexus. As you turn and face a different direction, your hands reverse, with your new lead arm doing the "Drac" elbow and the other palm guarding your solar plexus (figure 7.1). Try having your lead elbow randomly move from a vertical to a horizontal or to an inverted position (see the "Elbow Strikes" section in chapter 2, pages 22-24).

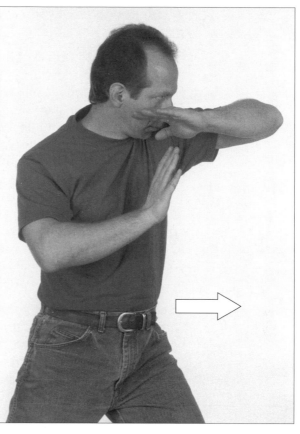

FIGURE 7.1

The Formless Stance

Don't equate "formless" with "ineffective." To generate the most power by separating the yin from the yang, your body needs to adopt a neutral position that allows it to move between extremes. Your stance, therefore, should be dictated by function. It needs to provide efficient cover as well as the ability to move freely in any direction.

NEUTRAL BALANCE.   When you stand in the formless stance, you attempt to distribute your weight evenly between both feet, creating neutral balance and thus a strong root. Since you're in constant motion, you'll never have perfect 50-50 weight distribution; however, as you fight, you'll continually attempt to revert to your neutral balance when you can to create a stronger platform. When you have neutral balance, you can move in any direction, redistribute your weight, and yield or change positions at any given time without the need to "dance on your toes." Focus on adaptability, not choreography.

YIELDING VERSUS LEANING.   Don't confuse "yielding" with "leaning." Leaning means you're committed from the start to a poor body position, which prevents you from adapting to the chaos of a fight. When you yield, even though you may be gyrating your whole body into bizarre contortions to avoid being struck solidly, you're still in balance. It doesn't matter what it looks like, as long as you can deliver an effective counterattack. This is why you need a formless stance.

COUNTERTURNING.   Through practice, you learn to move loosely in ways that help rather than hurt you. For example, when you turn, you want to be able to counterturn: pivot or swivel your waist fully around your body's vertical axis, twisting your shoulders and hips, sinking, and driving with your legs. However, you should maintain a proportionate relationship in your twisting. In other words, as you twist to the right to absorb a push to your right shoulder, your left hand comes out and hits automatically. This is like the turning of a subway turnstile. You're using your opponent's energy to launch your counterstrike.

When turning, your back foot should move more than your front. This is easy to do if you simply stand sideways, keeping your front foot pointed at your opponent. This creates a stronger platform. You can easily prove this to yourself by doing the opposite and overturning the front foot in either direction. When you overturn, your balance is carried out beyond your center of gravity and the overtwisted knee is susceptible to injury, especially if your front foot is turned out.

ELUSIVENESS.   Keep your feet as flat to the ground as possible (refer to the "Ninja Walk" and "Vacuum Walk," pages 77-79). This is easier if your lower back remains relatively straight as it comes to rest in the neutral position, because it prevents you from leaning forward on your toes or backward on your heels. Leaning is a reactive handicap common in many classical fighting stances. If you must root off one leg, keep the foot flat and drop into it, then get off it immediately.

This makes you extremely hard to pin down. Every time you drop and root, you're delivering a strike, and then you're gone. Even if your feet have only repositioned one inch, you become a ghost because your center of gravity has moved with the bounce characteristic of dropping energy. Your own strike is delivered like a slingshot, but to your opponent, you feel like a blob of mercury. You flow right through his fingers.

EFFICIENT GUARDING.   Apply the principle of moving behind a guard to your formless stance to make you hard to hit. Seek to root yourself so you face your opponent sideways and your profile becomes narrow enough to protect with one arm. Your lead hand covers your face and wards off all head shots with the palm facing out. Your lead forearm protects your chest, and your lead elbow covers your kidneys and ribs.

Try an experiment: stand sideways to your opponent with your lead elbow low and your palm facing your partner. Keep your body positioned like a fencer's with your feet in an L so your lead foot always points toward your opponent and your rear foot points to the side. Imagine that you're both boxers. Have your partner throw left and right hooks at your midsection. With the smallest rotation of your shoulders and hips, your lead elbow can easily pick them off (figure 7.2a). In fact, if you drop a little, you can actually bust his knuckles. Now have him throw left and right hooks at your head. If you're in a left lead, by turning to the right, you can ward off a left hook with your left palm (figure 7.2b). You could then chop with the same hand. Make sure your whole body turns so you have full-body unity behind the palm. If he throws a right hook, turn your upper body fully to the left and again block it with your palm (figure 7.2c). We call this a hello block; we explain it more fully later.

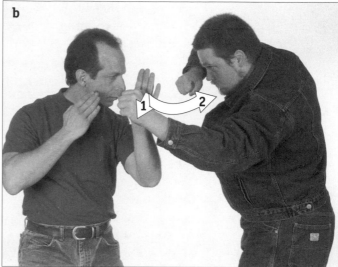

FIGURE 7.2

Each part of the arm takes care of its own region. If your opponent tries to circle you, simply pivot slightly on your front foot, keeping it pointed at him so you retain a narrow profile. He'll have to travel five times further than you to get around your lead. See how little you have to move to defend yourself? And you haven't even used the other arm! This is how efficient moving behind a guard should be (and you're not even sticking or using sensitivity at all). Every time you block with your lead elbow, your lead hand is free to immediately strike. When you block with your palm, you can easily slide your hand into his face, as long as you only protect your head and not the empty space around it.

Follow these important guidelines for creating an efficient guard:

1. Don't stand square to your opponent. It creates too much target area to defend economically. Stand sideways, behind your guard.

2. When you turn your body, turn fully so you then present your other side to your opponent. This is an example of separating the yin from the yang. Don't hang out in between; the target it creates is equivalent to the broadside of a barn. This is a common beginner's mistake.

3. If you turn your upper body only (e.g., your right hand, shoulder, and left foot are forward), you'll be poised for a split second, suspended like a wrecking ball or a rubber band before you release and fly back the other way to a normal lead. With your wound-up energy, as you return, you can deliver a strike out of both lead positions like a whip.

Remember you only need to protect yourself, not the empty space around the perimeter of your body. Don't go chasing his strikes.

Take Your Opponent's Space

Taking your opponent's space is something you try to do continuously in guided chaos. It doesn't mean, however, that you bully your opponent. That would run counter to everything we've discussed so far. What you want to do is enter, but remain unavailable. This is a paradox that may seem difficult to understand without showing some parallels in nature.

Think of water flowing out holes in a bucket. Similarly, you flow through the holes in your opponent's defense. But you'll only be able to find them if you're loose and sensitive. This means moving in where there's no pressure. If you're not loose, you may not recognize an opening even when it's right in front of your face.

For example, A is firmly controlling B's hands with his hands. He's on top of them and forcing them inside. If B isn't loose, he'll perceive that there's no way he can throw a punch at A's face because he thinks he's blocked. Typically, he'll reason the only way out is to draw his arm back. If B is loose, however, he'll sense that the hand-to-hand reference point is actually a pivot point, much like a door hinge. He'll perceive that there's actually nothing standing between his elbow and A's head—if he merely relaxes his shoulder and box-steps in on either side.

This actually brings B in closer, yet takes him away from A's hands. This is an example of taking his space. Now, suppose as B box-steps around, he's stopped by A's elbow in the side of his chest (figure 7.3a). Once again, if B is tight, he'll perceive an obstruction and (wastefully) either back off or attempt to muscle through. If, however, B is sensitive, A's elbow will feel like a red-hot poker, and B will pocket his chest out of the way, allowing him to box-step to A's rear without interference (figure 7.3b). Now that B is closer, he can drive his knee into the side of A's knee, further taking his space as well as causing significant pain.

Any time you fold a limb under pressure to bring you closer to your opponent, you're taking his space. If A pushes up on B's forearm, B merely folds in underneath with a spearing up-elbow strike, which he steps in with (figure 7.4). All B is doing is folding into an area of lower pressure that also happens to be closer to his attacker. In addition, as B steps in, he steps deep between A's legs, severely disrupting his balance and leaving him wide open for strikes, not the least of which could be a knee to the groin.

Another parallel from nature: a boa constrictor often kills animals far stronger than itself. Does it crush them with brute strength? Of course not. It loosely wraps

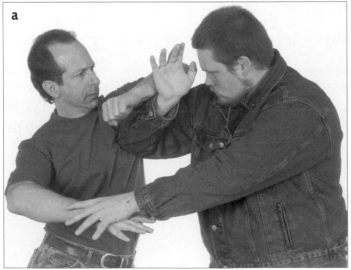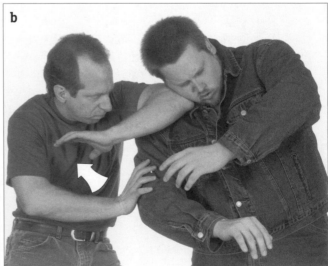

FIGURE 7.3

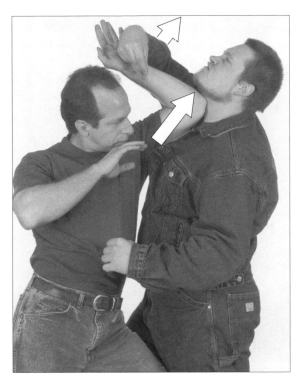

FIGURE 7.4

itself around its victim and waits for it to try and shrink out of its coils. When it does, the boa contracts a little. If the prey struggles, the boa just relaxes, using its own mass to hold its position. When the prey exhales, the boa squeezes its coils a little tighter. This goes on until the animal can no longer expand its lungs to breathe, and it suffocates. So too, you should relax, allow your opponent to panic, and guide his energy just out of your way as you slide in closer.

Overbending

In the act of yielding, don't let your elbow bend totally or you'll wind up crimping yourself. This is a mechanically weak position that your opponent can easily lock. You shouldn't need to overbend the elbow anyway, because the yielding should be taken up as your shoulder joint rotates, your trunk pockets, and your waist and feet rotate or reroot.

Riding the Harley

If you are relaxed, loose, standing formless, and aware, with your back straight, arms up, and hands facing out (on the "handlebars"), you might look like you are riding a motorcycle (although slightly sidesaddle). Most important, your elbows are down in the "home" position (see figure 5.2, page 77).

Structurally, you're stronger with your elbows near your body's center of gravity—basically a point halfway between your hip bones and below and behind your navel, with your weight sunk. (Many beginners keep their elbows aloft and flapping like bird wings.) With your elbows low and protecting your ribs, they can swing like pendulums in either direction, efficiently blocking strikes to your midsection and still leaving your hands free. This position, combined with the awareness that the elbow can stick, deflect, strike, and flow as naturally as the hand, often allows you to block a strike to your head and ribs simultaneously with only one arm. This is because when you stand with your side turned to your opponent, thus presenting a smaller target, your elbow covers your lower torso by swinging left and right (see next section), and your hand covers your head and neck area.

When your elbows come near your sides, either from pushing, pulling, or yielding to your opponent's pushing or pulling, you should get even looser than you already are so your elbows don't get trapped against your sides. Your body should turn, your sides pocket, and your shoulders articulate. As your elbows pass the home position, they gain energy from the center of gravity due to the slingshot effect of dropping.

There are a million counters possible through taking your opponent's space, but all you need to know is that if you remain loose and sensitive, you will simply flow into the openings without effort.

FIGURE 7.5

For example, B has deflected a shot to the ribs with his elbow, using a rocker motion. As his elbow swings through the home position, it gains energy like a roller coaster, shooting his arm up into a "shovel" punch (figure 7.5). It is important to feel the effect of relaxed acceleration through this movement instead of forced muscling.

The Rocker

The rocker is an effective movement that arises from combining the principles of yielding, pulsing, tool-replacing, and moving behind a guard. It also capitalizes on the elbow home position. Because of its usefulness, you'll find yourself in a rocker quite often.

With your elbows down and relaxed, your whole arm rocks from side to side from the shoulder like a pendulum, sweeping across your lower midsection. Envision your shoulder as the fulcrum and your upper and lower arm as the pendulum, roughly maintaining a V position as your elbow swings through the widest portion of an arc near your waist. This protects an area from one side of your ribcage to the other. At each end of the arc, your body turns also, so you have a pendulum swinging from a horizontally rotating base. If it swings inward, we call it a rocker. If it swings outward, we call it a reverse rocker.

Whether you do one or the other depends on the direction of the force applied to the arm. They both serve to gently lever and redirect energy away from your centerline as you yield, setting your opponent up for what may come next. If the strike to your trunk takes an inside line, the rocker uses the outer ridge of your forearm down to the elbow as a blocking surface. You pocket simultaneously, so there's little chance of getting hit (figure 7.6a). The rocker can also be a smash that destroys the attacking limb (see "Tool Destruction," page 157). If the strike to your trunk is coming from the outside, the reverse rocker deflects it, using your lower triceps area (figure 7.6b).

A variation of the reverse rocker is to use your hand as the clearing tool, bypassing your elbow entirely (figure 7.6c). This is a delicate, sensitive maneuver because your hand is structurally weak in this position. Ironically, that's its advantage. Your arm and body act as a finely balanced pendulum in this maneuver, because if your opponent exerts the slightest resistance, he loads your spring, and you can come smashing back with a variety of strikes. Furthermore, because this kind of reverse rocker is so subtle, your opponent often doesn't notice it. Using just your fingertips, you clear his arm perhaps half an inch (suspend and release) before you explode through the tiny opening straight forward with a punch to the throat or solar plexus.

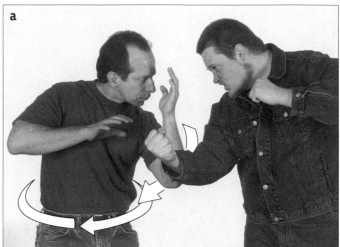

FIGURE 7.6

The rocker is a natural position if you're relaxed, loose, and rooted with your elbows down in the home position, moving behind a guard. The beauty of the rockers is in how their wedge shape works with tool replacement (see page 104). Reverse rockers are good for fending off attacks to the ribs as well as for wedges that create openings inside. Here, with A in close, B circles his elbow over A's forearm and reverse-rockers it outside slightly (figure 7.7), creating an inside line to punch through. This could be a short shot to the ribs or a punch straight down to the groin.

The rocker and reverse rocker are energy opposites: one arm rockers, deflecting an inside attack inward (yang), while the other arm reverse rockers, pulling the attack to the other arm outside (yin). You may have also noticed that if you do a rocker with one arm and a reverse rocker with the other simultaneously, you've assumed the shape of an energy ball (see "Rolling the Energy Ball," page 113), which you can roll to your advantage.

Triangle Defense

This elaborates on the principle of moving behind a guard. The name is derived from the shape created by keeping a forearm in front of your neck and head with your head tucked low behind your shoulder and your elbow always threatening to extend into your opponent's face at close range, like a spear or a spike, forming the point of a triangle or wedge. You can create the triangle by positioning your elbow either horizontally or vertically (figures 7.8, a and b), although neither position is something you should pose with. Let it do its job, and then return to the elbow home position.

FIGURE 7.7

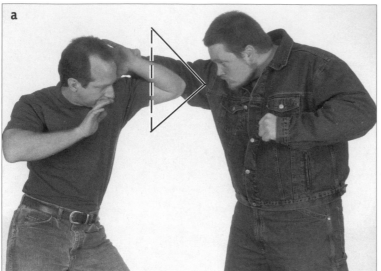
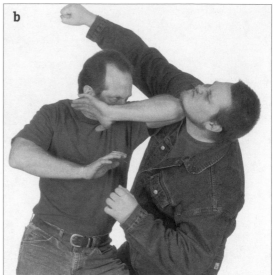

FIGURE 7.8

Standing sideways in an L position (exposing the least amount of your body to attack), think of the triangle as the prow of a ship. It easily slips through water or ice, diverting them to either side. Can you imagine a boat trying to move through the ocean broadside? Well, that's how dangerous and inefficient it is for you to stand square to your opponent.

The triangle is never static. You're constantly moving behind your guard, so the guard also moves. Usually, what your opponent feels is that he can't hit you (because you divert his attacks to either side) but he feels threatened by an elbow spear or smash to his hands or face in his centerline any time he presses you. Like a finely balanced sledgehammer, your arm can roll either way, with the elbow occupying centerline and the middle of the forearm acting like the balance point. A breath of air should be enough to set it in motion. Of course, your feet and body must move to set up the right range. Your hand should maintain light contact, while your body drives inside and your elbow folds left, right, or up underneath. You swing the triangle up when defending your throat and eyes becomes more important than guarding your kidneys with the standard elbow home position.

It's also not a bad idea to throw an up elbow every time you cross centerline when you move side to side. You can even fake the up elbow as a pulse to get a reaction, then circle over for a down-elbow strike. When combined with the hello block (see next section) and high sensitivity, the triangle makes a formidable defense.

Use your palms, edge of hands, inner and outer forearms, elbows, shoulders, and hips as primary sticking surfaces.

Hello Block

When your opponent's hands are on top of or outside yours and you feel the pressure of his hands release without his stepping back, usually it's because he intends to retract his arm and take a high outside line to attack you (like with a big ol' Hollywood roundhouse punch). If you're moving behind a guard as you stick, your hand will come up and fill the area he's vacating by the side of your face with a blocking move that looks like you're waving "hello" to someone standing on that side. In addition, after your palm blocks, you can easily slide it right into a strike to the face (figure 7.9).

Ideally, the palm intercepts his arm between the wrist and the elbow. If it checks his punch at the biceps, he may have enough leverage to blow through it. Practice turning your body toward the side the hand you're using is on to maintain strong alignment. Most important, avoid using the back of your hand to block. Face your palm outward, as if you were saying "hello" to someone on that side. This is a much stronger position structurally than the back of the hand, which can easily be bent, breaking the wrist, or merely blasted through with a strong roundhouse punch. Which would you rather catch a Nolan Ryan fastball with, your palm or the back of your hand? Which would you push a stalled car with?

FIGURE 7.9

There's also a tendency in the beginning to block hooks to your head with either a high elbow or a traditional boxer's "fist by the temple." The elbow may work, but what if your opponent's arm is longer than yours? It will just snake around your elbow and find your head anyway (figure 7.10). Furthermore, this approach leaves your kidneys wide open. The hello block prevents this situation entirely because your elbow is in the home position protecting your midsection simultaneously. It might only have to drop a few inches. The boxer's block, with the palm toward the face and only an inch away, was meant to be used only with big soft boxing gloves, which act as cushions. Without the gloves, your own hands would only serve to hit you in the head as the opponent's punch comes barreling through. Moreover, in a real-life attack there's nothing to prevent your attacker from punching you in the back of the head, a move that is illegal in boxing.

By the way, the high elbow block mentioned earlier could work very well—if it's not used as a block. Typically, blocking an overhand right with your left elbow is not tactically efficient, unless you're diving inside with it to take your opponent's space, which simultaneously deflects the blow and smashes him in the face like a spear. Following the principles of the triangle defense and taking his space if or when you feel the pressure release on the top of your arms, you simply tuck your head behind your upraised shoulder and spear your elbow straight into his face (as in figure 7.8b). In this way, you could stop an attack cold as well as be inside its arc.

The hello block and the triangle defense underscore a very important subprinciple of moving behind a guard: the guard must be structurally strong. This may sound obvious, but often even well-trained people use

FIGURE 7.10

naturally weak parts of their bodies or hold their arms in weak positions to fend off strikes. Instead of yielding, some styles train a reliance on highly developed neck muscles to protect the head and neck from impact. Others have the mistaken belief that tightly closed eyelids protect you from eye gouges. But the prime example is using the back of the hand as a blocking surface. It has no strength in this position and, in fact, is very easy to lock up and break. The back of the hand is suitable only as a sensitive antenna, and even then, you should use it only for an instant.

Hello Block–Triangle Combo

When you combine the hello block with the triangle defense, you've got two natural motions that work together to turn away most attacks. For example, A has his hands on top of and in control of B's. But as the backs of the hands are a structurally weak place for B (figure 7.11a), he needs to move them to get to better control surfaces. This is because from here A can do almost anything: punch straight to B's face, hook to B's ear, and so on. B needs to entirely cut off this whole line of attack in a way that doesn't require muscling A's hands off. By being balanced, loose, and sensitive, B can turn in either direction to take both of A's hands out of his attacking centerline and move them outside. For example, if B turns to the right, he does a hello block with his right hand and a smashing down elbow with his left (figure 7.11b)

The hello block tool replaces the sticking surface of B's right hand from the back of the hand to the palm, which forces A's left hand outside. B's down-elbow strike tool-replaces the sticking surface from the top of B's left hand to the bottom of his left elbow. This elbow comes over A's right hand and either strikes A's upper arm or the side of his face, as you can see in the picture.

What are the energies that prompted these movements, and why aren't they a technique? The elbow strike was actually motivated by a loose, seesaw response to the mere weight of A's right hand on the top of B's left. Notice, too, that turning right has brought B's left side closer to A, driving A's right arm down and

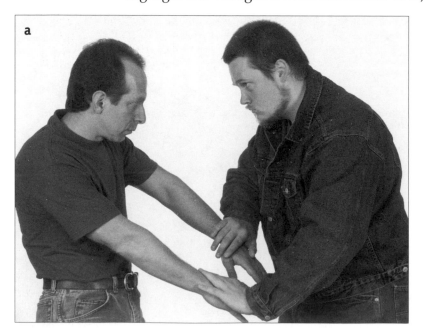

out of B's centerline. By being loose and thus turning fully, B's left elbow now occupies centerline (instead of A's arm), and his left side is facing A. Also, turning to the right has allowed B's right hand to simply yield to pressure from A's left hand and thus rise up into the hello block, keeping A's left arm outside.

All B has done is respond to stimuli. This is a different mindset from intending to pull off a flashy technique. Now for the coup de grace: following the principles of suspend and release, looseness, and multihitting, B immediately turns back to his left like a spring-loaded door hinge,

FIGURE 7.11

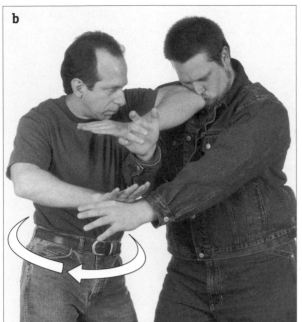

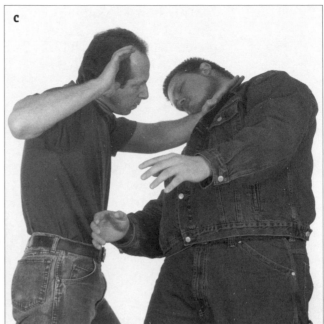

FIGURE 7.11

whereupon his left inward elbow strike turns into a left outward chop to A's throat and his right outward hello block turns into a right inward palm heel (figure 7.11c).

We have painstakingly broken this movement down so you can see the simple physics behind it. In reality, though, you shouldn't get too hung up in each part of the movement, because the whole feel of this thing is actually like a gorilla swinging his body back and forth with his arms flying. Program that into your brain instead.

Flipper

The flipper is insurance against having a wrist broken. While sticking to an opponent, if his hand slides down to yours and your hand bends downward and inward in an attempt to yield, it can be easily broken by an aikido-type wrist lock (figure 7.12a). This is an example of moving in ways that hurt rather than help you. You can prevent this potential mishap by being sensitive to the attempt and merely flipping your hand up in a hello gesture (figure 7.12b).

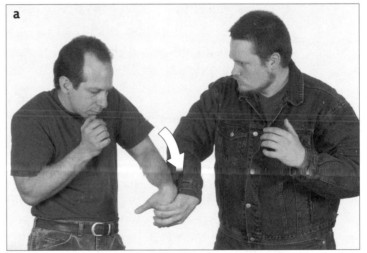

FIGURE 7.12

This stops the sliding action leading to your opponent's wrist lock and gives you yet another springboard from which to launch either a rolling elbow, triggered in a seesaw fashion by applying pressure against the flipper, or an inward pulse toward you with the back of your hand acting as a hook, which then springloads a palm strike forward in response to his resistance.

The Body as a Weapon

Without having fangs or claws, the human body nevertheless has some formidable natural weapons. Any system that minimizes their importance for some "artful" purpose does its followers a grave disservice. All of them are for close fighting, where the most damage is dished out. It's important in your training, from solo anywhere-striking to two-person contact flow, to incorporate the following weapons at all times.

- Head butts from every possible angle
- Biting (yes, you can just go through the motions with this, but it's important to visualize doing this so you won't flinch in reality)
- Heel stomps (see "Mexican Hat Dance," page 36)
- Spitting into the eyes (as a visualization, of course)
- Multihitting with the knees
- Pinching and clawing loose skin
- Eye-gouging

We apologize for the graphic nature of these suggestions, but survival is rarely pretty.

Fighting Like You Have Four Hands

You want to think of your elbows as an extra pair of hands, sensing, deflecting, and blocking in a state of constant flow and movement. Rather than using your hands exclusively to clear an opponent's arms you want to work from your elbows as much as possible. By doing this, you free up your hands while allowing yourself the same degree of control. After all, it doesn't matter whether you control a person's movements with your hands or elbows. The principle to understand is that control is control.

When extending the elbow or doing a tool replacement from the hand to the elbow, don't lean forward or hyperextend your arm to control the other person's motion. Step in. Your elbow shouldn't stretch away from your body as if it's a flapping wing. This will only place your body off balance. Remember that your elbows, no matter how loose they are, must move proportionately with the rest of your body (body unity). In other words, if you rocker your left arm to the right (inward), your hips, back, and legs turn that way also. Even though you align your body to push forcefully, you use little muscle, only the power generated by dropping. As you're moving and sensing your opponent's intentions, the motion of your body creates a moving platform that keeps your elbows in proximity to your opponent's weapons. Don't reach for them. He'll be reaching for you, and then your elbows will meet his weapons, either directly or from folding due to pressure on your hands.

Place the elbow of your rocker against your opponent's outer elbow; you don't need to use any muscular tension to do this—just rooting and body unity. This will pin his arm and prevent him from striking you with it. From here you can either push and clear with the elbow rocker, push and pass the arm to your other hand, or deflect with the elbow and slide a chop in with the same arm. You can also reach underneath your own elbow (figure 7.13a), clear, and chop (figure 7.13b).

If he offers resistance to the rocker moving inward (i.e., pushes back), simply reverse-rocker outward with your fingers, letting his resistance spring-load you. This opens an inside line you can snap back and strike through with the same or other arm. Execute this movement smoothly in one fluid motion, so to your opponent it appears seamless.

You can push from your elbows with incredible power as long as they remain close to your body. Having them near your center of gravity gives you a distinct mechanical advantage. The action of

FIGURE 7.13

the elbow can also be subtle. Depending on its position, it can lift, pull, pulse, depress, or nudge the opponent's guard sideways, creating limitless opportunities. It's up to you to explore them.

- Getting hit with an elbow is like getting hit with a baseball bat.
- Keep your elbows close to but not touching your sides when moving. This helps protect your ribs.
- This doesn't preclude you from throwing down-elbow strikes. It simply means they shouldn't resemble independent flapping wings. You should deliver the elbow strike while dropping by turning your back, shoulders, hips, and legs in proportion to the movement of your elbow.
- To loosen your elbows even more, you must loosen your shoulders. By doing this, you give your elbows an extra three to five inches in range and mobility.
- Stab the elbow against the soft parts of your opponent's body with an abrupt thrusting motion. This spearing (accompanied by dropping) feels to him like being jabbed with a crowbar and it creates openings for you by knocking the attacker back.

- Used in conjunction with taking his space and dropping, your elbow can uproot an opponent while it slashes back and forth in a rocker motion, continually moving through the home position to gain power.
- In line with the principles of the triangle defense, remember that when you're in close and sticking your elbow in your opponent's face, it should have the same sensitivity as your hand. If it's pushed or pulled, it can yield with a small circle and come right back in his face like a rubber band. You can use the elbow to pulse his arm slightly in any direction so you can move it in a small circle and wedge it into an opening from another direction. Thus, the elbow slithers in with the same sensitivity as the hand.

The best way to practice using your elbow is with the "Anywhere Strikes" drills (pages 34 to 36) against a pole and with the elbow contact-flow option. When striking a pole, also practice pulsing (inward, outward, and side to side) from every possible angle.

Open Hand Versus Fist

As you learned in chapter 2, open-handed strikes using the palm and the side of your hand are better designed than your fist for striking hard targets like heads and jaws. Try smacking an iron radiator or a brick wall with a palm strike and a chop. Hard. Now try this with a clenched fist. No? Good thinking. If you applied the same force on both strikes, then your hand would be broken.

The palm can deliver more force than a punch (fist) because there are fewer bones interspersed with tendons acting as shock absorbers. With the palm strike, you have almost a direct connection to the forearm because the hand essentially sits on top of it. A fist needs to compress through all the joints of the fingers and the hand before it can deliver a solid blow. Also, to make a proper fist, you need lots of practice. You must learn to align your wrist bones and make your hand tight, employing antagonistic muscles throughout your arm. This slows you down, decreases your sensitivity, and makes the rest of you rigid.

By considering the palm or chop your primary hand position, you're already set up properly for using skimming energy. Like a flat stone skimming the surface of a pond, the palm and chop combination skips in more easily over blocks than a fist.

You should only punch against soft targets. When striking, keep your arm and fist loose until the moment of impact. At this point, close your hand as if grabbing a bar and then instantaneously relax it. Combined with dropping, the effect of the hand's relaxing and tightening is like the crack of a whip: the fist remains fluid and loose until the wave of energy reaches it, whereupon it solidifies into steel.

Skipping Hands

As far as sensitivity goes, developing your hands by making them tough as stone also makes them dumb as a doorknob. Through skipping hands you'll be able to play the attacker's body like a piano.

When sticking with your hand, try to use two points of contact: the tips of your fingers and the heel of your palm. Think of them as having a yin-yang relationship: your fingers act as delicate probes and the heel of your palm as a structurally strong guard. When the opponent's pressure builds beyond what your fingertips can handle (which isn't much), they tool-replace to the heel of the palm of the same hand.

As you already know, the reason you stick with your fingers is so you can remain disengaged. It's easier, and you've got more clearance to throw a strike, than when your hand is clamped on his body. In addition, if your fingertips sense so much as a muscle twitching in his forearms, you'll know something's coming. It may help to think of the hand as a smaller version of the rocker: with the slightest increase in the opponent's energy, the hand rockers from the fingers to the heel of the palm, allowing his arms to be redirected. With your elbow down low in the home position and your body lining up behind it and your palm, you can exert tremendous checking power with no muscle. This is all in accordance with moving behind a guard.

From the heel of your palm, you can tool-replace back to your fingertips with a walking, or skipping, action. This allows you to alternately scoot and check along the surface of an attacking limb as you redirect it. This is a very sneaky and effective concept you should play with while doing the "Contact Flow" drill (page 118). Although a little different in principle, the effect is the same as with sliding energy, allowing the attacking limb to slide past. For example, B's fingertips are delicately poised on A's forearms with the heel of the palm barely touching. B picks up that a muscle is tensing slightly a millisecond before A launches a strike. B's fingers rocker, or "skip," to the heel position with the elbow low and supported by the alignment of your whole body and both legs (figures 7.14a and 7.14b).

This position is structurally powerful, needing little muscular exertion. This stops A's attack as well as occupies the line he was going to enter. If A attempts to slide around this, B forearm-surfs and takes his space, in effect, letting A slide into an even more disadvantageous position. B's hand actually skips, or scuttles rapidly like a crab, along the outside surface of A's arm as it "runs" from heel to fingertips, heel to fingertips, letting A's arm go by. B's

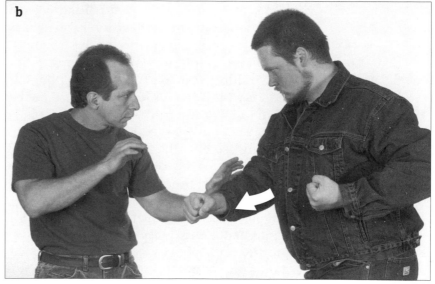

FIGURE 7.14

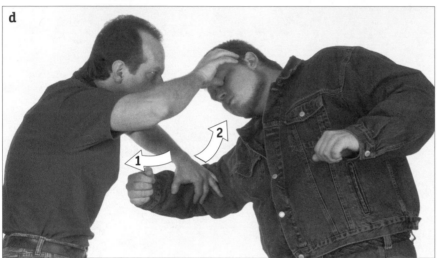

FIGURE 7.14

hand has thus skipped from an initial contact point on the forearm up to the outside of A's elbow, which is a better control point. From the palm, B can let A's elbow fall into the groove between thumb and index finger for more control (figure 7.14c). If A attempts to power through the heel of B's palm, B does a reverse rocker with the fingers, clearing A's arm in the same direction it wants to go (figure 7.14d). B slides right into a strike that A practically falls into with his chin.

Ripping and Tearing, Crushing and Breaking

In line with your understanding of looseness and separating the yin from the yang, you should be aware that learning guided chaos makes a whole different way of hitting available to you. As you become more comfortable with whipping your body around with full body unity, you'll find that strikes often come about because the attacker's body simply gets in the way. After a strike, you may find that your body's turning and contorting momentum makes your arms fly apart of their own accord. You can learn to use this by grabbing with both hands on different parts of the attacker's body. What you will find is that you begin to create situations where you're literally tearing your assailant limb from limb with virtually no muscle strength. This works best when the two areas you grab are obviously designed not to be pulled in opposite directions. For example, in the course of practicing "Contact Flow", you may find yourself pulling your partner's face to the left with your left arm in a backhanded grab (twisting his head clockwise if viewed from above) and pulling his right arm out to your right with a two-fingered grab with your right hand (perhaps because you were redirecting his punch). If this were an actual fight, you could easily see how the assailant's neck wouldn't resist this against-the-grain tearing motion for too long.

Similarly, in the process of rolling the ball, you might find yourself pushing the back of your partner's head forward to the right with your left hand while pushing his left shoulder to your left (or clockwise if viewed from above) with your right hand. You do this almost as if you were trying to make them meet in the middle. Like the previous example, if this were a real fight, the assailant's neck couldn't endure this crushing motion for more than a second or two.

THE POWER OF THE PINKIE

John Perkins

In the chaos of a fight, any part of the body can become a nasty weapon. In one incident as a police officer, I was fighting a raving man with psychiatric problems on a stairwell who had me so tied up I couldn't punch, fire my gun, or swing my nightstick. The only thing I could get free was my pinkie. This I drilled into the corner of my attacker's eye. After the man started going into convulsions, the fight was over.

Preventing Common Mistakes

➤ Being loose doesn't mean your defense should collapse like a house of cards when you yield. Train yourself to be loose and move behind a guard at all times.

➤ Moving behind a guard is not merely a defense. Remember, within the triangle principle, pressure anywhere against your hand or forearm is a stimulus for folding and striking simultaneously with the elbow like a seesaw, while, conversely, pressure on the elbow unbends it, turns your body, and drives your palm into the attacker.

➤ Don't stick with the backs of your hands. They'll be overpowered and locked, maybe broken.

➤ Don't rocker with only your elbow. It requires a loose shoulder, rotating waist, pocketing ribcage, and turning feet.

➤ Don't stand square to your opponent. It creates too much target area to defend economically. Stand sideways behind your guards. When you turn your body, box-step, and turn 180 degrees so you then present your other side to your opponent, which is now also behind a guard.

➤ When you turn, it can also be a simple twist of your upper body. Your legs can remain in a reversed stance (e.g., right hand, right elbow, and right shoulder forward with your left foot in the lead position). This is because you're here for just a split second—suspended like a rubber band or a wrecking ball—before you release and fly back the other way to a normal lead.

➤ Use yielding as an opportunity to get in, not run away. Take his space. Don't box-step to the side and away from your opponent. Box-step to the side and in or, better yet, behind the opponent to throttle him.

➤ When yielding, don't totally fold your elbow joint or you'll get your arm broken. Your yielding should be taken up by other areas of your body, like your shoulder or waist (by turning away).

CHAPTER EIGHT

ECONOMY OF MOVEMENT

In keeping with guided chaos's inverted learning structure, you'll notice each succeeding chapter in *Attack Proof* is more specific. From recognizing some of the body's natural offensive and defensive attributes in chapter 7, we move on to even more specific combat subprinciples. Though you can easily see that everything in this book is interconnected, in this chapter we attempt to point out more precisely the economic qualities of guided chaos movement that you should foster in your training. Within guided chaos exist many powerful ways to economically cover your target areas as well as to deliver the most damage with the least movement. The elbow home position and the triangle defense discussed in chapter 7 are examples of the former. In addition, you already know that chambering, or setting up, is a wasted attacking movement. We now explore many other offensive and defensive methodologies that promote efficient fighting.

Defensive Economy

To begin, let's address a commonly asked question: "How can I move with maximum looseness and not windmill wildly to take myself out of the fight?" The answer is to follow the economy of movement principle: Move your body and feet more so you have to move your arms and hands less.

When you're balanced enough to step and move your body more, you accomplish three critical goals:

1. You remove vital targets from direct attack.
2. You generate tremendous counterattacking energy through body unity.
3. You are ready to attack as your arms are close to centerline in the home position.

If you keep your body static like a statue but swing your arms independently like propellers, your balance will be off, your power weak, and your arms twisted, pinned, or generally taken out of the fight. This is even more evident when you develop looseness without moving behind a guard.

Move as little as possible. Don't block beyond the perimeter of your vital areas. Better yet, don't block even an inch beyond an imaginary cylinder formed by the width of the weapon and its attack path toward its target. In other words, if the attacker is punching at your face, you only have to be concerned with intercepting an area that is four inches wide (the diameter of his fist) and about two and a half feet long (the distance to your face). This will keep you from performing superfluous movements that will only take you out of a fight. Be sure, however, to move enough so that you can survive.

Zoning

How do cats and dogs confront danger? They either run or fight. When they fight, they dive in with their teeth for the kill. Rarely, however, do they go straight in. They penetrate at a slight angle, far enough to get past their enemy's teeth and claws, but close enough to get a death grip on their throat. They go in be-

cause backing up can be fatal. It's easy to trip and fall. When you dive in, you move in at a slight angle; we call this zoning. You can then actually avoid big looping blows as well as close-in strikes as long as you remain loose, flexible, and relaxed.

If you are fighting, it's assumed you have no other recourse. In guided chaos, you rarely back up. When you need to relieve pressure, you zone by stepping in and to your opponent's side, staying close. This is the purpose of box-stepping (page 81). By pocketing and passing the apples (pages 46 and 105) you get their energy to bypass you. Thus, you attack and defend simultaneously. This is why zoning is an economy of movement principle. When you box-step, your outside foot goes directly to the side of or behind his. You tool-replace to keep his limbs from impeding your progress. In addition, your chest or shoulder can become a checking tool replacement, leaving your arms free to hit (figure 8.1).

FIGURE 8.1

An important economy point about zoning and any other stepping move is that you should almost always be hitting simultaneously as you step. This unifies your body and power, giving the opponent more to deal with. Although in guided chaos it's a basic principle not to use two of your hands on only one of the opponent's, zoning gives you the opportunity to violate this. Usually whenever you try "two-hands-on-one" (if the other guy is sensitive enough), he will immediately hit you with his free hand. Since zoning effectively takes you out of reach of his far hand, you can safely use two-on-ones for a variety of breaks, strikes, and so forth.

Remember, if you have room to retreat, you usually have room to run.

Riding the Vortex

How would you deal with an advanced internal art practitioner who is also moving at top speed? If you attempt to stick with him directly, your nervous system will become overloaded, and you'll get sucked into his vortex of spiraling energy. Your limbs will become tense and susceptible to fakes, grabs, and other nastiness.

You'll need to become even less engaged, while still remaining in contact. Here is where you must amplify your sensitivity. To ride the vortex, imagine that your opponent is the Tasmanian Devil. As in the cartoon, his moving limbs form the surface of a spinning tornado. Even though the area between his arms is mostly air, his speed creates the illusion of solidity. As such, treat the perimeter of this tornado as you would skin. Do not attempt to penetrate it directly. Flow with it as if it were one solid object. For those spared in childhood from this Warner Brothers character, you can visualize a potter molding a vase on his rapidly spinning wheel. Without losing contact, he deftly alters the shape of his creation as it flies through his fingers. The potter is at once engaged, yet disengaged. Similarly, you can use sliding energy (page 101), forearm-surfing (page 101), releasing energy (page 103), and taking up slack (page 106) to control your opponent's motion.

The Three-Part Insurance Policy

We have broken down a typical defensive response so you can see how several things happen at once. If you're attacked down your centerline, take the following actions:

1. Yield (figure 8.2a), fold (figure 8.2b), slide (figure 8.2c), or skim (figure 8.2d) the "sticking limb."
2. Pocket the intended target area (figure 8.2e).
3. Turn your body to cut off the attack angle and channel out the attacking limb, once it's been pocketed (figure 8.2f).

It is important that you do all three things simultaneously. If your attacker is extremely large, or if he takes your space, step to a new root point and zone if you run out of turning and pocketing room.

In addition, make sure you don't trap your inside elbow as you yield and turn. Do this by rolling your elbow over so it doesn't get stuck between your chest and his arm. Pocketing the chest gives the elbow the breathing space it needs to get out. This ensures that you always have a weapon on line. You might then chop or elbow-strike with your inside arm, depending on the distance.

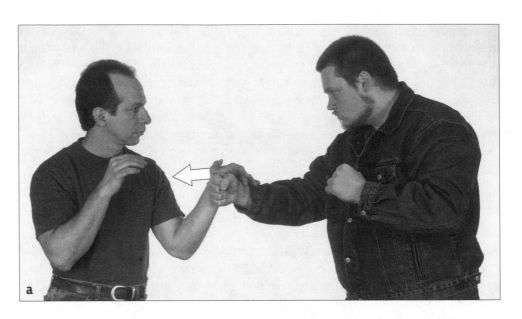

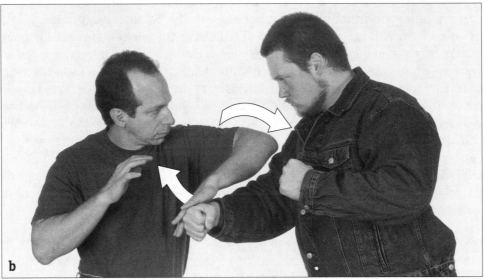

FIGURE 8.2

150

FIGURE 8.2

151

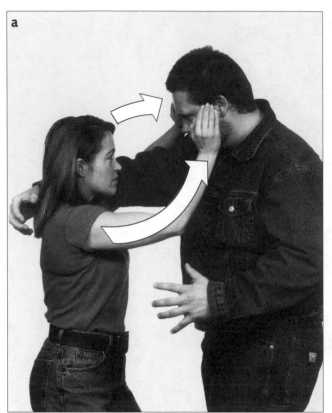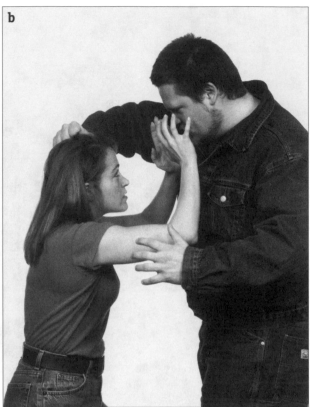

FIGURE 8.3

The Steeple

If your attacker is much taller than you and you're in close, an economical movement while skimming his blows is to steeple. Both hands shoot straight up over your head, skimming and deflecting his downward strikes inward (figure 8.3a) or outward (figure 8.3b), and clap together against his ears, possibly rupturing his eardrums. This attack is unorthodox, and you can do it without looking. Don't forget to drop on impact.

Drop to Deflect

As part of moving behind a guard, remember that most of the deadly damage an assailant can inflict is against your head, neck, solar plexus, and kidneys. As such, develop an extra sensitivity field that extends about a foot away from these areas. Remember, keep his hands off your body. A big part of this involves dropping simultaneously as you pocket and deflect an attack away from you. This is vital, because the dropping gives you power, rooting, and stability at the moment you need it most, while your looseness evades the strike. This enables you to take his space while defending and attacking simultaneously.

By dropping a split second before you yield, you create a situation in which you can loosely but powerfully deflect a strike, yet slide in and strike, all in the same motion. The yielding and articulating allows you to slither in and strike simultaneously, but it's impossible to pull this off without dropping. Dropping anchors you to your root so you avoid the floating and light-footed sensation of instability common in beginning students who are learning to yield.

Another advantage to dropping as you yield is that your explosion of energy loads your own spring, because you bounce off the attacker's strike. This acts as a pulse, which makes the attacker push even harder to knock your hands off. But it's too late for him. You pull his push and crush him or fold around and impale him (see the "Spike-in-the-Sponge", chapter 3, page 48).

As long as we're in the defensive category, it would be neglectful not to mention such martial arts fundamentals as tucking your chin (except when yielding the head) and keeping your mouth shut.

Offensive Economy

We're now in the category of economical attacking principles. The first one is unique to guided chaos, and it totally depends on your ability to develop looseness. If you refer back to the "Circle Clap" drill in chapter 3 (page 63), you'll better understand what we're going to talk about here.

Multihitting

The goal of multihitting is to insert as many strikes within one flow of movement as possible. This is tactically efficient, so you can mete out maximum damage in the least time. However, do not force superfluous or awkward blows into the mix. What you should find is that the enemy's targets are just conveniently in the way of your body as it moves from a yang state to a yin state, and vice versa. All your strikes should be empty and unformed until contact. Remember, do not clench your fist until impact. This prevents stiffness. Here are some examples of multihitting, some of which you have already practiced in your "Anywhere Strikes" (I, II, and III) drills in chapter 2 (pages 34 through 36).

- When you step straight in with a palm strike to the head or chest, continue the motion without stopping so that, immediately after contact, your elbow folds and blasts up into the attacker's chin. Obviously, you must step in and take his space simultaneously to do this.

- If you deliver a right palm strike along a more circular path (like a right hook to the head in boxing), continue rotating your body to the left, fold your elbow slightly, and slam him with a horizontal right elbow to the side of his head within the same motion.

- When you turn out with an elbow strike to the side of the head, continue turning so it becomes a chop to the same spot. This can obviously be linked with the move just described in the previous bullet.

- Explode with a palm strike to the face, and as you retract, you might claw the eyes or clear an obstructing arm.

- If you're punching into the stomach, you can slide into an uppercut.

- Using ricocheting (chapter 6), you can bounce the opponent's head between a hooked backhanded chop and an elbow from the same arm repeatedly, like a yo-yo (figure 8.4).

- If you've just punched with a right into and past the assailant's midsection so your right arm is "backhand" to the left of his body, why waste time chambering the arm to strike again? As you retract the arm, do it with a slashing backhanded chop or forearm against his side.

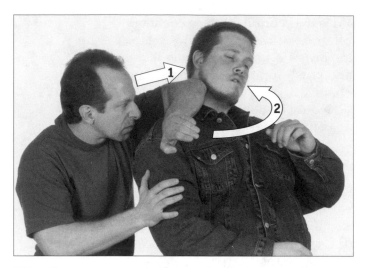

FIGURE 8.4

All strikes and blocks are merely motions within the flow. As soon as you separate them out in your brain and say, "Now I will strike," or, "Now I will block," you become rigid, slower, weaker, overcommitted, less sensitive, and less balanced.

To make things more interesting, you can combine all of these, so, for example, the palm-elbow combination happens on the way in and the elbow-chop combination happens on the way out. So with a simple, swinging yang-yin motion, you have delivered four blows with one arm in the time it takes most people to throw one.

To make things even more interesting, note that these combinations have transpired within the motion of only one side of your body. If you think of yourself as a gorilla, swinging your arms loosely from side to side, you can double the number of strikes by performing this with your right arm moving in and out, immediately followed by your left arm moving in and out and back again. That's eight strikes in the time it takes most people to launch two. Combine these with a couple of drops and your opponent will think he's in a Cuisinart. If this all sounds familiar, it's because you've already practiced a more basic version with the "Anywhere Strikes III" drill in chapter 2 (page 34).

There are an infinite number of combinations possible with multihitting, but you won't need to memorize them because your looseness and sensitivity will create them spontaneously. As we've asserted throughout this book, focus on acquiring the feel of the principles, and the strikes will arise automatically. Try to have your blows bounce from one to another, as if your opponent had fallen into a giant pinball machine. With enough looseness and dropping, you can actually ricochet repeatedly between hooks to the head and the ribs. The reason many boxers can't do this is that they're concentrating on smashing through the body rather than splashing or skimming it. Remember that a flat stone thrown too steeply into a pond will sink without bouncing across the surface. When you splash your target (chapter 6, pages 102-103), you will cause great damage without having to blast through it. This allows you to remain loose—and to multihit.

Vibrating

An extension of multihitting, vibrating occurs when you deliver no-inch punches so rapidly that the striking weapon seems to vibrate with energy. This linear ricocheting energy is like doing a drum solo or blasting with a machine gun. An example is if you bounced five palm strikes off an attacker's head or chest in one second, dropping with each shot (recall the "Circle Clap" drill, page 63). Still another example of vibrating is a movement coming from Native American martial arts called "shaking the tree." The vibrating energy spasms your entire body as you take the opponent in both hands and shake him violently. You do this loosely, powerfully, and quickly, so that at any moment you can explode off the shake into a barrage of multihitting elbows.

Taking Something With You

If your punch goes past your opponent's face (or any other part of his body), why not strike on the return (e.g., while retracting your arm as with a chop or a claw)? This concept—taking something with you—is an important economic corollary to multihitting and something you've already practiced with the swimming drills in chapter 3 (pages 57 to 59). After every strike, if possible, take a piece of the opponent with you as you retract the weapon. Here are a few examples:

- After you turn through your punch, as you pull back your arm, you might grab the back of the opponent's elbow, opening his ribs to a strike from your other arm, which is simultaneously moving toward them.
- Grab the side of his head and wrench it sideways after a palm strike (while pulling his lead arm in the opposite direction).
- Grab his wrist or some hair, pulling his head past you into an elbow smash as if you were clearing your way through bushes in the jungle.
- Palm-heel under his chin on the way up, rake his eyes, or rip at his chest hair on the way down, then spring up into another palm heel.

Typically, your opponent is still trying to push you away as you withdraw a strike, so you'll end up pulling his push. It's important to combine this with checking and passing the apples to create and briefly maintain an opening. For example, B chops at A with his right (figure 8.5a). A's block misses, but his energy continues to carry the blocking arm outward (remember, we're talking about responses that last only a few hundredths of a second). B's right arm is already retracting after the chop, but on the way back, it takes A's right hand with it, using a delicate two-fingered grab. Almost instantaneously, B's left hand or elbow checks or destroys A's right elbow to the inside, clearing the line (figure 8.5b).

Shortening the Weapon

Shortening the weapon is a subtle but powerful economic principle that affects virtually all your movement. The reason we've waited until now to explain it is that without first understanding sensitivity and looseness it would be meaningless.

You're already familiar with the concept of sensitivity and being as disengaged as possible, yet still engaged. We're now going to take it a step further to make your sensitivity more ballistic. By mixing in constant pulsing, skimming, and ricocheting energies, we now want you to experience contact with your attacker a little differently.

FIGURE 8.5

The energy behind shortening the weapon is like having to hold a hot potato in your hands and carry it from the oven to the table without dropping it on the floor. You must rapidly engage and disengage the potato to maintain control over its motion.

Imagine that your training partner's skin is red-hot. If you touch him for longer than a fraction of a second, you'll burn yourself. At the same time, remain close enough to sense his motion. This paradox sets up your nervous system for explosive movement, because you are constantly loading your own spring.

This approach trains you to instantly open new entry angles and protects you from grappling. Basically, any time you contact your opponent, you should shrink from his touch and then reacquire him, over and over at high speed. This can be extremely subtle (compare with vibrating energy and multihitting). To an observer, in fact, it might look like you've never broken contact at all. What this does, however, is keep you from becoming overly engaged with your attacker, except when you have clean openings that you skim, slide, or stealth your way through. This forces you to probe for different entry angles. It also has another dramatic effect: your opponent has a hard time getting a fix on you because you know what you're doing, but he hasn't a clue. As his frustration quickly mounts, he tries desperately to hit and grab you except that this only increases your reactivity. As his energy rises, you react as if his skin were getting hotter and hotter, which loads your spring even further. Eventually, he overcommits himself, which explodes you into action.

Consider shortening the weapon something you need to apply to all your motion. For example, B chops at A who manages to block it. When B first senses contact with the block, his nervous system should react like he just touched a red-hot frying pan (figure 8.6a). This causes him to shorten his weapon, pulling his shoulder up and back while he continues to step in (taking his opponent's space). Simultaneously, B readjusts, turning his torso and shoulder slightly and fires the same or a slightly different weapon (like a spear hand) at a slightly different angle (figure 8.6b). In the meantime, A is still reacting to the feel of the block he just made, because he expected the contact with B to be longer-lasting and more substantial. As if sucked away by a vacuum, B is no longer there. This begins to establish a pattern of overcommitment on the part of A who searches for something to get a grip on. When you throw in pulsing and dropping, shortening the weapon becomes very nasty.

When shortening the weapon, however, you're not pulling your hand back dramatically as if winding up. Instead, the shortening should be whatever the maximum range of your shoulder joint is. Shortening the

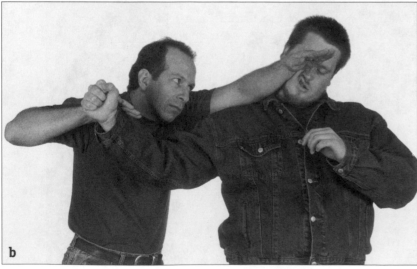

FIGURE 8.6

weapon can also be a completely internal movement, in the sense that your nerves, muscles, and tendons reverse suddenly without actually moving your arm. This makes you even harder to read. Ideally, you should be able to strike his arm with power and then instantly relax so your fingertips stick to the target with featherlight pressure, never once breaking contact (compare with splashing, pages 102-103).

An extremely important point about shortening the weapon is to never let anyone get control of your elbow. Your elbow is one of the most critical control points of your body. If your opponent possesses any sensitivity at all and gets an opportunity to grab, pull, or press it, it could put you in great peril. Therefore, at the slightest touch on your elbow, shorten the weapon and get it the heck out of there immediately.

By the way, you can take advantage of the reverse scenario: take control of his body while forearm-surfing to slide to the back of his elbow. With just two fingers, you can pinch the joint, wait for him to panic, and either pass his arm off to your other hand or hit directly with the same hand.

It is vital in guided chaos to develop a full, isolated range of motion for every possible angle in the shoulder joint so that you look like you are shrugging up, down, backward, and forward. When you accomplish this, your hands can be in contact with your opponent's limbs and remain relatively motionless, yet have a multitude of different attack angles available because of the dynamic, isolated movement of your shoulders. For example, B is in contact with A, whose arm is in the way of a direct strike. B raises his whole shoulder joint while leaving the rest of his body still so that a new angle opens up, which he can strike through. Practice shortening the weapon with the "Row the Boat" drill (page 159) and the "Contact Flow" shoulder option drill (chapter 6, page 121).

Attacking the Attacker

To attack the attacker you must get past his guard as efficiently as possible, clearing a line of entry to his vital areas. You already know you should never force your way in, nor forcibly move a block to get to a vital area, because it's typically a waste of energy against a stronger opponent. Instead, use as much of the opponent's energy and as little of your own as possible. When your guided chaos skills become highly honed, you'll be able to use stealth energy and ghost your way in virtually untouched. Until then you can clear the line with skills you already know like passing the apples, pulsing, and taking something with you. In this section, you'll learn a few more ways to clear the line.

Tool Destruction

While this initially sounds like you're forcing your way in, the reality of tool destruction in guided chaos is that you're actually going to be using your attacker's energy. You're already familiar with tool destruction if you've used rockers to smash incoming punches with your elbow. Since rockers involve a loose turning of your body like a turnstile, it's the force of the incoming strike that does the damage. A rocker performing a tool destruction is initiated like a see-saw by your sensitivity. For example, your fingertips, perched on the arm of the attacker, sense the intention of a strike. As it comes, your arm folds rapidly at the elbow into a rocker as your midsection pockets and turns. Instead of the rocker simply redirecting, the rapid folding of your elbow caused by the incoming force of the opponent's blow smashes the rocker elbow into his arm. The power is augmented by the turning and dropping of your whole body. This has a popping quality, quick as lightning, while your rear hand accepts the passed apple (the attacker's fist) and clears it. The ricochet off the destruction immediately launches you into further strikes with both hands. Note that this can't be done if you linger or grapple with the opponent's arm in any way. (Note that tool destruction also appears in chapter 9 as a sensitive reaction to grabs.)

Checking

Checking refers to a short, snappy pulse that pops an opponent's tool slightly off line. Usually done with the palm, checking can be used to initiate an attack, create an opening, maintain an opening (by knocking an arm out of the way), or ensure that an opponent's attack, like an elbow to your stomach, never reaches its target. This is merely a safeguard you can combine with pocketing. Checking and its more aggressive cousin, tool destruction, are both far more effective with dropping.

Don't overcommit with a follow-through motion in a check or tool destruction. Splash his striking arm and shorten your weapon, so you can take his space without being thrown off balance. Your splashing hand penetrates only a maximum of a few inches beyond the point of contact. If your check or tool destruction knocks the opponent's arms away and wide, you still need to be sure he's not going to come back and nail you as you step in to take his space. If you pass the apple by guiding his arm and elbow past you, a check with your other hand makes sure his arm stays out of your line for the split second you need to enter and attack. Palm-strike or splash the elbow and dive through the opening into another strike. Just remember whenever you enter to get as close to your opponent as possible.

Dog-Dig Entry

The dog-dig entry qualifies as one of the simplest and most effective entries you can do. Skip in and kick the assailant's shins while rapidly rolling your hands in a dog-paddling or dog-digging motion. Similar to a swimming sidestroke entry, you smack his lead hand out of the way and either gouge out his eyes, chin-jab his head, or spear his throat repeatedly like a buzz saw.

If he resists the first clearing dog-dig motion, make sure the second, third, and fourth are right behind it. If he pulls back against the dog-dig, use his energy to pull your strikes into his face. If he pushes them away with superior force, skim over them or circle in the opposite direction and use rising spear hands to the throat. By rolling with his energy, not against it, you avoid tightness and wasted motion.

The Drac Entry

While relatively close, jump in sideways with your lead arm's elbow extended out horizontally in front of your face, so that you're peering out from behind it like Count Dracula. Keep your rear checking hand underneath by the center of your chest. Simultaneously with making contact with this front-spearing elbow, knock your attacker's lead hand away to your inside with your rear checking hand in a clearing move (figure 8.7a). Instantly thereafter, unbend your Dracula

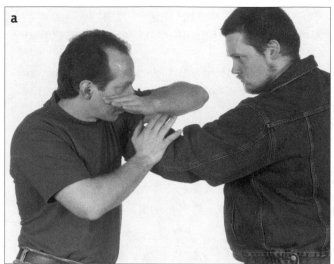 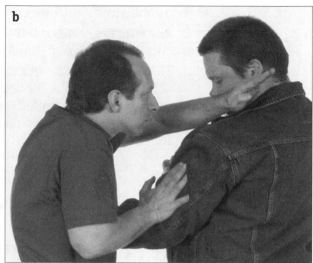

FIGURE 8.7

arm as you turn into him with a dropping, backhanded chop to the side of his head (figure 8.7b), followed immediately in the same turning motion with a palm heel from your checking hand. Your attacker will either eat the elbow when you whip it out or succumb to the chop, because the clearing hand was hidden from view by the Dracula elbow. You can substitute a straight, spearing strike to the eyes with your lead arm for the Dracula elbow if you desire. The spear hand has the advantage of skimming off and deflecting an incoming strike as it simultaneously hits its target. Note the similarity of this move to "Swimming Sidestroke" (page 59), a totally natural motion.

Economy of Movement Drills

Many of the principles in this chapter can really only be practiced during "Contact Flow." They're simply too subtle to be extracted out into separate drills. You can, however, practice shortening the weapon with a drill you already know.

Modified Anywhere Strikes

If you review the "Anywhere Strikes" drills in chapter 2 (pages 34 to 36), you can modify them by imagining that the pole you're hitting is red-hot. Strike from every possible angle, remain close, but don't get burned. You have to hit, instantly relax, and lightly stick. You can also practice isolating your shoulder by shortening the weapon through moving your shoulder joint only. Thus, the rest of your body remains motionless while your shoulder pulls your hand or any other weapon away from the pole by stretching backward dramatically. You can also enhance this movement with rowing the boat.

Row the Boat

Aside from gaining new entry angles for the hand, this motion is also useful for pulsing, raising, and clearing the opponent's arms when you're nose to nose.

1. Touch your hands together in front of you like you're grabbing oars.
2. Leaving the hands relatively stationary, pull both arms back simultaneously by shrugging your shoulders backwards.
3. Roll your shoulders in a circle as far forward, upward, backward, and downward as you can, initiating a rolling movement in your arms. By rolling the shoulders, entry angles are created covertly while the hands are allowed to remain relatively motionless, sticking to the attacker's limbs and safely guarding your centerline.

Preventing Common Mistakes

➤ When zoning, don't step away from your opponent. Instead, step to the side and in.

➤ During "Contact Flow" drills, don't tense up when your partner goes at high speed. Relax, and ride the vortex.

➤ The three-part insurance policy is for explanation only. Don't try to do each part alone. Perform them simultaneously.

➤ Multihitting is not like a combination in boxing. In multihitting, by moving your whole body in loosely for a punch, body parts, like your elbow, simply seem to fall into line during the same motion and strike the opponent as well. This also happens as you pull your arm back. Mulithitting should have a relaxed, bouncing quality, like doing a drum solo.

➤ If you force your movements, they will fail. If a movement doesn't feel natural, as if it could spring out subconsciously, it will fail.

➤ Never force your way in, nor forcibly move a block to get to a vital area. Use as much of the opponent's energy and as little of your own as possible. Slither in like a snake, skim in like a flat stone, or ricochet in like a bullet.

➤ Checking and tool destruction are far more effective with dropping.

➤ Don't overcommit to a check or tool destruction. Splash his weapon, so you can take its space without throwing yourself off balance. Your splashing hand penetrates only a few inches, at maximum, beyond the point of contact.

CHAPTER NINE

GRABS AND LOCKS

Grabs and locks are excellent tools for explaining guided chaos principles for two reasons:

1. They represent opposing forces and condensed combat on a small scale.
2. They are highly revered by many and thus are ripe for a little debunking.

Grabs

Since we never want to be overcommitted and thus involve antagonistic muscles, limiting our ability to flow, an effective grab should be a gentle and elastic maneuver. This is because in guided chaos you almost never grab to restrain someone, and, if you really clamped down when grabbing, you wouldn't be sensitive enough to deal with his response. If your attacker is stronger than you and adrenaline-fired, you'll be crushed. Moreover, don't count on being able to grab at an attacker moving at high speed. It is nearly impossible. Instead, use grabs as a probing tool to instigate a reaction from your opponent that you can flow off of. Grabs need to be subtle to remain undetected and to pass the apples or tool-replace. In gen-

eral, don't take any grab you can't accomplish with two fingers (the thumb and index or middle finger). Striking should always be your priority.

If you need to use more force than you can generate with two fingers, you're too engaged with your opponent. Don't be fooled, however. The fact that you're not clamping down doesn't mean you can't generate a lot of energy. The reason is that the energy comes from your root, and it may feel to the opponent like you're using a lot of muscle strength. What he's feeling, though, is your body weight, sinking into your fingers. This comes from a relaxed elbow that is near your center of gravity in its home position.

You don't necessarily need to use a grab to pull the opponent toward you. Doing so always runs the risk of using antagonistic muscles, leading to a tug-of-war. Instead, use the grab as an energy gauge and distance finder. Now, you walk toward your opponent while simultaneously reeling him in. This type of action is usually so soft and unexpected that you can literally pour yourself over the opponent and crush him. Remember, a grab is not something you hang onto. If you use a grab as a pulse, drop with your whole body weight for a split second, and then release it. Applied this way, it can unbalance him or create an opening. It's often useful to grab an elbow and move it just enough so you can punch right into the spot the elbow just occupied. Your grabbing hand then becomes a target that your punching hand can lock onto. A good example of all this is puppeteering.

Puppeteering involves lightly applying a two-fingered grab (with thumb and middle or index finger) on each of your opponent's wrists and merely following his limbs around without adding any energy of your own. This causes a very curious thing to happen. The opponent panics because he hasn't the slightest idea what you're doing and all he wants is to hit, wrestle—anything to get you off him.

It's doubly annoying to your attacker because you're following him around and can thus easily redirect a strike. You're connected to a control point—as if you were a matador leading a 2,000-pound bull around by a nose hair. Keep your elbows loose, relaxed, and near the home position to keep you structurally strong. As soon as he commits or overextends himself, release, tool-replace, and attack. You can use his first arm strike to block his second by redirecting the first into the path of the second. But the key here is his reaction. Whatever move he makes, flow with him and hit him. Hold on only as long as you need to get a reaction.

If he yanks, you follow him back, release, and hit. If he strikes, you step in, pull his push, extend his arm, pop or check it out of your way with your other arm, then let go with your grabbing hand and strike. If he attempts to pull his hand away behind his back, follow him up and lock his wrist. When you develop the principles, puppeteering can be unnerving to the attacker.

Locks

In any real fight, it's virtually impossible to apply a lock if you're looking for one, when everyone is moving at maximum speed. Under adrenaline, locks, even applied by experts, become less effective (see chapter 1, page 12). The reason you see locks working in ultimate competitions is that, although the combatants are trying to win, they're not necessarily trying to kill each other; as they grapple, they leave limbs vulnerable as they probe for "legal" maneuvers. Also, grappling involves committing and fixating your arms on restraining moves, leaving them static and susceptible to counterlocks; this becomes a vicious cycle. This is not reality. In fact, locks are trained unrealistically in many arts. Often they're worked and reworked cooperatively, flowing from one to the next with the choreography of a dance. When you train in guided chaos, you never cooperate, even in the beginning.

In general, we don't advocate locks because they fixate you. Having said all this, locks can still sometimes be used effectively, but they should be fast, snapping actions that last a millisecond then flow out into a

Never look for a lock. They either happen or they don't.

FIGURE 9.1

strike. You may know of or be shown a lock from some other art, but it's up to you to discover the moment to apply it. This will be dictated by the flow and energy of the movement. If you don't train this way from the start, you'll be lost.

For example, if your opponent punches, you stick and yield, breaking his arm as you pull his push, extend his punching arm, and apply a rising palm to the elbow (figure 9.1a). But suppose he's sensitive and picks up on his overcommitment to the punch and retracts. You might follow him back, tucking his wrist under his armpit (figure 9.1b), thereby breaking it.

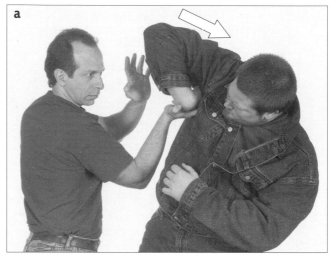

FIGURE 9.1

At any moment, if there's resistance to the movement, fine: he's loading your spring. Don't bear down and hang on. Abandon the lock and release the energy. If you fall into a two-hands-on-one situation, and he fails to do the flipper (chapter 7), his yielding will result in a crushed wrist when you apply inward pressure.

Don't fall in love with locks. They are restraining maneuvers that act as drags to your flow. They make you move as if you were mired in mud. If you bear down on a lock, it employs antagonistic muscles that can start wrestling matches, possibly with opponents twice your size. Bad move.

The Vise

A different type of lock is the vise—a quick, springy action you suspend and release. While fighting, if A's limb gets caught between B's limb and B's trunk, B can quickly drop and clamp down with the elbow (figure 9.2a). This abruptly disrupts A's balance, causing him to resist forcibly with upward pressure. This is great because the vice has acted as a pulse or springboard to further hits. From here B instantly springs up into a chop to the throat. B simultaneously passes the arm he has in a vise to his other hand (figure 9.2b).

If B wasn't loose, but instead only clamped down with the vise and held it with all his might, he would become as fixated and vulnerable as A. This is an obvious display of strength, and its direction gives the opponent a virtual road

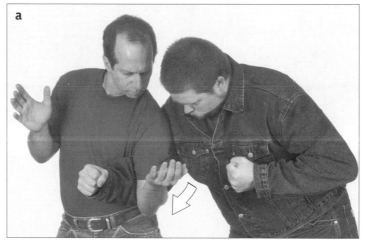

FIGURE 9.2

map of your intentions. This is also the antithesis of stealth energy, guaranteeing an unsuccessful counterattack on your part.

The Cross-Tie

The cross-tie is an opportunistic lock that occurs frequently when you train with someone unskilled in guided chaos. It occurs when one punch is pulsed, passed, deflected, or thrown down and into the path that an anticipated second punch would take (figure 9.3a). In the process of rolling the ball or passing the apples during contact flow, the hand that was doing the deflecting circles under and cross-grabs the second punch while your other hand cross-grabs the first (figure 9.3b). Since his hands are crossed and yours aren't, and since his momentum carried him to this position, you can easily twist his arms up while continuing to roll. Just remember that your body's turning drives the cross-tie, not your arm muscles.

What's interesting is that once he's tied up, you can let go (and strike), because he will actually tense and resist against himself, causing an instant open-

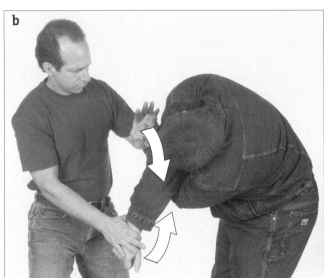
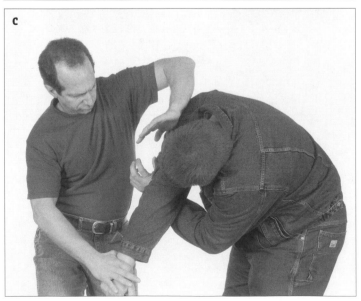
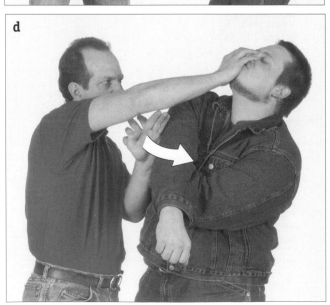

FIGURE 9.3

ing to his torso or head (figure 9.3c). Or you can just twist, drop, and break. If he resists strongly, just roll back with him in the other direction, release one or both grabs, and punch, using his resistance to propel your strike. It's usually easier to let go with the hand that's holding his lower arm (since it's trapped by his own upper arm) and punch. You can also instigate a cross-tie by actually knocking or throwing one arm into the other, then grabbing and twisting. Sometimes it helps to pop-check his elbow with your palm to keep him in the tie a split second longer to ensure your opening (figure 9.3d).

You can avoid being caught in a cross-tie yourself by staying sideways to your opponent, turning 180 degrees, separating the yin from the yang, and not presenting him with two outstretched arms.

Resisting Grabs and Locks

Since you should imagine your enemy as either covered with some foul-smelling slime or as hot as a frying pan, being touched, much less grabbed by him, should put your sensitivity on high alert. This mental image will condition you to avoid entanglement. Resist the temptation to grab back with your other hand. This gives you no advantage; instead, it leaves you with both hands involved and no guard available. At best, you end up in a stalemate. If he's stronger, you lose.

If you're grabbed anyway, his clamping down should be as successful as squeezing an angry alley cat or a handful of mercury: The more pressure is applied, the faster it squirts out through the fingers. Your sensitivity, since it's confined, acts like an incompressible liquid, exploding toward freedom through any convenient opening. Since the move is rapid, you must shift your balance and readapt just as rapidly, with your entire body moving in concert.

Remember, using body unity principles, you'll generate more releasing power by repositioning your whole body to free the grabbed arm than if you strain with all your arm's muscular strength. While driving with your body, your arms can move wildly in any direction to free themselves, as long as it's in the direction of a strike to a vital area. In other words, it makes no sense to release straight up, down, or far out to the side. This leaves you totally open, a sitting duck. The releasing movement by its very nature should be a direct blow to your attacker, satisfying the principles of economy of motion and moving behind a guard.

If you're grabbed anyway, your free hand should go right for his eyes or throat. It's amazing how so many techniques rely on some elaborate maneuver against the grabbing arm when all you need to do is simply poke in the jugular notch or eye socket with your free hand.

Avoid excessive contact from the start and shoot your hand forward through his grasp and into his face. Just say to yourself "Don't touch me," and you'll be in the right frame of mind. Slap his hand out of the way or evade the grab and strike with the same hand or both. Despite all this, you may be successfully grabbed anyway. Read the following material with an eye toward developing the underlying feel of the movements described without necessarily obsessing over their specific components.

Answer the Phone

This is an extremely common, multipurpose movement related to the triangle defense. It can shield against strikes, punches, rakes, chokes, or other harassment to the head. Due to its extremely dynamic use of body unity, it's also a terrific grab-breaker. For example, B is in a left lead, properly standing sideways to A to create a smaller target. A grabs B's left wrist to get control of him (figure 9.4a). B can stab A in the eyes with his right, but if A is ready for it, B can "answer-the-phone" by relaxing and circling his shoulder down, inward, and up, raising his whole left arm from the shoulder. But as B brings the arm up, he keeps it near his side to gain the mechanical advantage of being close to his center of gravity (figure 9.4b). The action is like scraping your ribs with the inside of your palm, forearm, and elbow. As you can see, this involves turning to the right from the waist, stepping in closer with the left foot to take A's space (A's grab was pulling B in anyway), and pocketing the left side of the ribcage in case of an attack to the kidneys and to make room for B's arm to slide past. B's palm moves close by and then past his ear as if raising a receiver to listen (figure 9.4c). Raising the arm this way forms a protective wedge around the side of the head, which can also ward off strikes to the rear. It also tool-replaces the attack or grab from B's wrist or forearm to B's shoulder, freeing his arm.

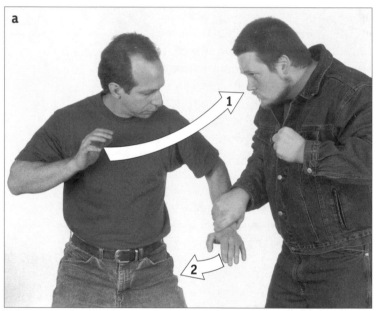

Because A's grab pulled B in, B followed the energy and took A's space, moving behind the guard that the phone motion provided. This, combined with turning away from A as he raises the phone, generates tremendous torque against A's wrist, breaking the grab. After B answers-the-phone, he turns back out to the left, whipping a chop to the left side of A's neck through the huge opening the phone just made (figure 9.4d).

After answering the phone, B delivers the chop as if he were saying "Here, it's for you!" This action is one continuous movement, like swimming. It's also a swinging, yin-yang-type motion, because you twist one way and then immediately whip the other way. This immediately brings in a palm strike with your other hand.

Answering the phone is also a good response any time an opponent's arm contacts your arm between the elbow and shoulder, because he's too high on your arm for you to roll your elbow over (and he's too close for comfort to your face). It's also great for warding off a flurry of strikes to your head by multiple attackers. Under these circumstances, answering the phone looks like you're fighting a swarm of bees.

FIGURE 9.4

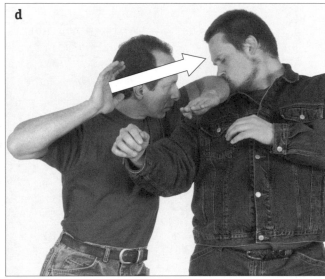

FIGURE 9.4

Swarm of Bees

If you were being dive-bombed by a swarm of angry bees, would you drop into a deep karate stance and throw reverse punches or perhaps use an esoteric tai chi technique such as "grasp the sparrow's tail?" Of course not. While guarding your face, you'd whip your hands around as fast and lightly as possible with great sensitivity to avoid being stung. This is natural. However, if you examine these movements you'll notice they look like multiple answer the phones, combined with short swimming and chopping movements.

Breaking the Double Grab

If both your arms are grabbed despite applying what you've learned so far in this chapter, your looseness just flows into the next available weapon—your elbows. Turn your body and take his space by stepping in deeply and loosen your arm and shoulder muscles, firing one or both elbows sequentially with a rocker motion at one or more of the following targets: the face, upper arm, chest (figure 9.5), or uppermost restraining hand. A nice, multihitting follow-up to this one is to slide straight up and chin-jab with your palm. This works against a single grab also.

When you smash the top restraining arm with your elbow, don't try to pry or wrestle it off. If you simply turn, step, and drop with your whole body, you'll have all the mechanical advantage you need. Multihit, bouncing your elbows from the restraining arm to the face and back again, using both elbows, one right after the other. You can also spear them into the chest.

FIGURE 9.5

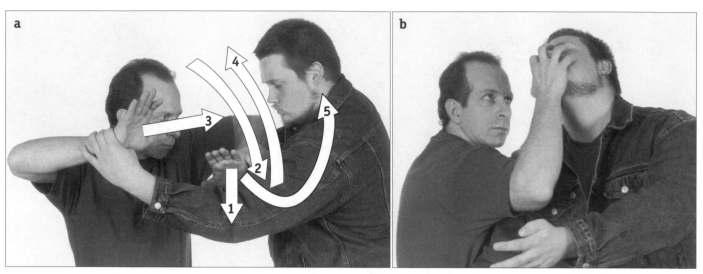

FIGURE 9.6

Tool Destruction

Smashing a rocker into his grabbing hand to liberate your own is tool destruction, as is slamming the knuckles or forearm of an incoming punch with your elbow. Tool destruction is a common martial arts term for attacking the attacker's limbs. What is uncommon is how we use it. Instead of trying to pick an incoming strike out of the air like a baseball or a scud missile, a guided chaos tool destruction often results from either folding or turning your body away from pressure. In the latter case, you should use the principles of taking his space, body unity, the triangle defense, and the box step to turn your whole body and step into a horizontal palm smash at a grabbing arm (figure 9.6a, arrow 1). Within the same movement, your elbow should slash his face—provided the grab was held high enough (arrow 2)—and your now-freed hand should chin-jab (arrow 3). Instantly, using multihitting, your elbow slashes back in the opposite direction (arrow 4), followed immediately by a backhanded chop with the same arm (arrow 5), and another inside palm strike or claw with your freed arm (figure 9.6b). This whole sequence occurs in less than half a second. This works against both regular and cross-grabs. When executed, it looks like an ax tearing through balsa wood. Remember, though, to turn with each movement so you're presenting your side to your opponent.

Grip Exercises

Two parts of your body that can really benefit from a strength-building regimen are your hands. If you think about it, other than our teeth (which are feeble compared with those of most predators), the only raw weapons we have (other than bludgeoning surfaces like knees, feet, and elbows) are our fingers. Lacking claws, we nevertheless have great power in our fingers, relative to the rest of our bodies. This pays off whenever you rip, tear, gouge, and pinch. Training for grip strength is essential when you're totally tied up, and your hands are against your opponent's skin. The amount of pain an iron-like pinch or claw can deliver is sometimes sufficient to create room for further strikes.

The trick is not to hang on. Your hand should have a snapping, biting quality that instantly relaxes to avoid sustained tightness, allowing you to find other targets. That said, here are some exercises for developing your grip.

Finger Creep

The purpose of this exercise is to strengthen the muscles that contract the fingers, which are different from the ones that turn the wrist.

1. Take a full-length broom and hold the stick at the far end with only the fingers of one hand, so the bristles hang barely above the floor.
2. Using only your fingertips, walk your fingers down the handle so you're raising the broom off the floor while your arm stays at the same height.
3. Pull it up till you reach the bottom and start over.

You can weight the broom to make this harder by slipping two-pound barbell plates over the broomstick.

Sand Bucket

You've probably heard that the crushing force of an alligator's jaws are immense, but that an average person can hold the gator's mouth shut. To avoid the gator's dilemma, you need to work the muscles that open the hand, not only the ones that close it. When opening and closing strengths are balanced, they actually augment each other. You need a bucket of sand to do this drill.

1. Form your hand into an "eagle's beak." The tips of your fingers should be pressed together and even with the end of your thumb.
2. Spear your hand into the sand and then twist it 2 or 3 times to drill it in.
3. While continuing to push down, spread your fingers as far as they will go, angling your hand for the most resistance against the sand with all your fingers, including your pinkie and thumb.
4. Repeat steps 2 and 3 at least 10 times per hand, and then try the reverse: spread your palm wide on top of the sand, push down, and try to crush a handful of it into a diamond like Superman. Do this 15 times or until your forearms feel like they're going to explode.

Tendon Strengtheners

The following exercises develop tendon strength, which is far more important for fighting than muscular strength. When moving loosely and powerfully at high speed, large, strong muscles that have been trained purely for strength and size tend to be slow and highly injury-prone. This is why strict bodybuilders can't play in the NFL. Their tendons would simply blow apart. Tendons connect muscle to bone and need to be strengthened carefully along their entire range of movement. Some of the drills are extremely slow and others extremely fast. This trains the tendons (and the muscles they are connected to) to withstand the ballistics of wild and chaotic combat conditions.

Two-Minute Push-Up

High-speed looseness doesn't require big, bulging muscles, but rather tough, elastic tendons that resist tearing.

1. Perform a push-up very slowly, working to increase the time it takes for you to go down and come back up.

2. Continue until you can take (after some significant training) two minutes to go down and two to come up.

Iso-Strike

FIGURE 9.7

These are slow, isometric tension exercises that build strength throughout the entire length of a combative movement, rather than only through the limited range of resistance found in most weight training.

1. Begin with your right arm wrapped tightly around your body in an exaggerated starting position for a backhanded chop.

2. Standing against a wall, exert strong tension against it in a slow, controlled effort to uncoil your strike (figure 9.7).

3. Inch by inch, reposition your feet so you experience resistance against every part of the chop's movement throughout your body until the chop is fully extended.

4. Don't forget to drop in slow motion as well.

5. Try this with every type of strike you can think of, continually repositioning your body to offer the maximum isometric resistance throughout the entire range of movement.

Speed Flow

As well as working your tendons, these exercises promote high-speed muscle strength, which is different from brute strength.

1. Make slow, circular, horizontal chopping motions with your hand and arm. Your forearm should be parallel to the floor. Use a subtle dropping motion with your knees as the chop comes out. Do this for 30 seconds.

2. Increase to three-quarter speed for 30 seconds.

3. Then go to full speed for as long as you can maintain full looseness and relaxation. Whip your arm, making the air move.

4. When you begin to fight against the cramping and stiffening of your own muscles, stop.

5. Repeat with your other arm.

Apply this same procedure of speeding up the flow in increments to the following:

- Dog dig: A repetitive digging motion that is useful for clearing limbs or batting away a knife in a last ditch effort as you backpedal. Similar also to a cat rapidly clawing an enemy in a circular buzz-saw motion. Also try this motion toward your side where it would then look like a swimming sidestroke.

- Stacked spears: Chop straight out in front of you with both hands alternately so your upper hand comes out and then returns underneath in a rapid circular motion (figure 9.8). Once you tire, reverse the motion.

FIGURE 9.8

- Answer the phone and chop combo: Do both motions with one arm and then switch. Performing this as rapidly as possible takes on the appearance of fighting off a swarm of angry bees. Don't overextend on the chop; it should snap out and back like a whip.

- Free flow: Psycho-chimp and small circle-dance at maximum velocity. Be careful not to hit yourself!

Preventing Common Mistakes

➤ In general, don't take any grab you can't do with two fingers.

➤ Don't clamp down while puppeteering. Your hand and arm should be able to loosely rotate around and follow the trapped wrist, allowing the opponent to move as he wishes, without letting go.

➤ Grabs don't necessarily have to pull the opponent toward you. This runs the risks of using antagonistic muscles and getting into a tug-of-war. Instead, grab as an energy gauge and distance finder. Now, you step toward him.

➤ Never look for a lock. They either happen or they don't.

➤ If you treat your attacker's skin as if it is covered with a foul-smelling slime, he'll have a hard time grabbing you in the first place.

➤ You'll generate more releasing power against a grab by repositioning your whole body and dropping to free a grabbed arm, than if you strain with all your arm strength.

➤ It makes no sense to release straight up, down, or far out to the side.

➤ The releasing movement should be in the direction of a straight blow to your attacker's nearest vital area or limb.

➤ Resist the temptation to grab back with your other hand.

➤ Don't just wave your arms around in the "Speed Flow" drill. Move your whole body, drop, and pocket so you don't hit yourself.

CHAPTER TEN

GROUND FIGHTING AND WEAPON DEFENSE

Despite your training, and whether you like it or not, you may find yourself defending your life on the ground. The reason we've saved this subject until now is that ground-fighting principles are actually no different than those you employ when fighting upright, except that you have to translate them to a new dimension where they become even more savage. These principles are very different from the way most other martial arts handle grappling. The ground-fighting principles of guided chaos represent some of the art's most devastating aspects. Developed by John Perkins in his early bouts with his father and uncles, they reflect a great deal of Native American martial arts influence in that they are based on simplicity, sober reality, and actual experience.

Ground Fighting

There are some arts in vogue now that actually prefer to take the fight to the ground and emphasize this in their training. Fans of "ultimate" fighting—no-holds-barred competitions—contend you should practice grappling because more often than not you end up there. Although highly skilled in Native American ground-fighting techniques, John Perkins went to the ground in less than 10 percent of the over 100 serious, violent, armed, and unarmed confrontations he has been involved in.

Intending to go to the ground as a form of self-defense is a potentially fatal way of thinking for at least five reasons:

1. By violating the principle of challenging no one you eliminate the simplest and most effective form of self-defense there is—running away.

2. On the ground, your advantages of upright balance and rooting become negated—bad news if your attacker outweighs you by 100 pounds or more.

3. The real world is not a martial arts school covered with soft mats. In a dogfight, the last thing you want to do is smash your head, tailbone, or neck on car bumpers, concrete sidewalks, fire hydrants, or broken glass to gain a "ground advantage"!

4. Weapons, such as knives, eliminate most grappling techniques. Try wrestling with an opponent wielding a Magic Marker and see how long you can avoid being turned into a piece of graffiti.

5. You might be fighting multiple opponents. With standard grappling, you can only fight one assailant at a time! Meanwhile, his buddies will stomp you into dog food.

Remember, going to the ground to grapple could mean going to your grave. If your opponent falls to the ground, don't follow him. Run away.

People ask "But isn't grappling better than punching? Everybody knows a wrestler can beat a boxer." To answer this, read the following excerpt from a letter the President of the International Combat Martial Arts Federation, professor Bradley J. Steiner, sent to his associates:

During WWII, with the exception of Jack Dempsey, virtually every single unarmed and hand-to-hand combat instructor for the United States, Canadian, French, and British forces had a formidable and core background in wrestling, judo, ju-jutsu—yet every single one of those instructors deliberately minimized, played down, and de-emphasized all grappling in favor of basic, simple blows, when preparing men for war. Why? Well, why do you think? Some of these experts, like Pat (Dermot) O'Neil and William Ewart Fairbairn, were literally the first Caucasian ju-jutsu/judo black belts in the world at that time! They were ranked 5th degree black belt, and 2nd degree black belt, respectively. Fairbairn had personally participated in more than 600 deadly encounters (armed and unarmed) prior to WWII, when he was Commissioner of the Shanghai Municipal Police! Don't you think that man knew what real combat required?

Also consider this from the former Director of Close Combat Training at the Military Intelligence Training Center, Colonel Rex Applegate, who accumulated his experience during wartime and trained over 10,000 military and intelligence personnel for the Office of Strategic Services (OSS) (which eventually became the CIA): "Blows should always be used in preference to throws."

If you've read through the book this far, you already know many of the principles of guided chaos. You already know that if you use only strength, speed, and standard wrestling, boxing, or no-holds-barred fighting skills, the odds of your disabling a larger opponent with the same skills are virtually nil. Unless you're extremely fast or lucky, you'll be crushed, mangled, and torn limb from limb. However, the extremely nasty tactics of guided chaos and close combat can negate an opponent's superior skills and physical strength. Why? Even past ultimate champion Royce Gracie would find it difficult to fight with a finger buried in his eye. This is why they forbid these tactics in ultimate competitions.

You may wonder what might prevent your attacker from using these tactics also. Actually, nothing, except that you will be better at it. Guided chaos levels the playing field. The ability to both deliver and avoid these tactics for survival is based solely on your looseness, body unity, balance, and sensitivity—aspects virtually no one else teaches, especially on the ground.

Ground Avoidance

But how do you avoid going to the ground in the first place? Extend your sensitivity, so you can treat your opponent like a matador treats a bull. Avoid the typical response of squaring yourself and stiffening at the prospect of a collision o-r take-down move. Such tightening would provide a firm handle for him to grapple. Remember, guided chaos is about making yourself unavailable and bnot confronting force head-on. Don't look at him as the enemy. This makes you angry and tense. Rather, regard him as a vile disease, not to be touched. This change in attitude will be reflected in the way your whole body moves. Your looseness and pocketing should accelerate until they turn into a kind of spasming we call "shedding" energy. React to grappling like an angry alley cat. Instead of tensing, squirm and writhe out of your attacker's grasp while you simultaneously rake his flesh.

Let's look at a possible scenario. A threatens B from a distance of about 10 feet. B can back away or run, keeping A in sight as he retreats. If you know you're fast, and the enemy doesn't look it, great. If it's the opposite, a preemptive strike is in order. From this distance, look meek (Jack Benny-style), back away slowly, and wait for him to advance. If he does, explode forward, stomp-step, and kick like you're making a field goal. Immediately spear-hand to the eyes or palm to the face while stepping in with a knee strike. This is basic close combat.

Suppose, however, that he's a grappler, and he dives for your legs. Fine. The forward drop kick becomes a knee to the face. If this doesn't cripple him, you'll be in the same situation as if he were closer in and decided to dive for your legs. You drop strongly, spreading your stance, and jam your fingers underneath and through his eye sockets like clutching a bowling ball. Pocket your vital areas away from his grasp. If you need to, you can use his eye sockets, ears, and hair as handles to wrench and break his neck with. (Remember, you fight to save your life or your loved ones only.)

Because you're striking downward, you can use full dropping energy to power chops, palms, elbows, or hammer-fists against the base of his neck. (Compare with the "Beanbag" drill, page 109.) As your hands come up between blows, take bsomething with you, like his Adam's apple, ears, hair, or his whole head twisted violently (nobody asked him to attack you; he volunteered). If he picks up his head to avoid the initial onslaught, your fingers again seek out and penetrate his eye sockets. This in itself can cause convulsions, unconsciousness, and death. Once again we apologize, but real self-defense isn't pretty. If you die because you didn't finish off your attacker before he regrouped, your grief-stricken family won't be consoled because you showed your assailant compassion.

Falling in Your Favor

If the tactics just discussed fail (for whatever reason), you might still wind up on the ground. Think of a cat, perched on your outstretched arm. If it loses its balance, it digs its claws in and hangs on as it flops over, ripping your skin with its full body weight. The lesson here is, if you're going to fall, fall and take something with you: hair, skin, ears, lips, or the like. Not only may it do some damage, but by borrowing from his balance, you might recover yours (of course, there are no guarantees).

Suppose that as you're losing balance you hook your foot behind his leg and pull (pulse). Sometimes this will allow you to recover your balance and hit him at the same time—kind of like a yo-yo on the rebound. Or sometimes you're in the air, falling, yet your hands are completely free—claw an eye socket or his groin on your way down.

Use your falling momentum to rip at the opponent. Then use your momentum and the moment of weightlessness to shoot your legs out at his or blast your knee up into his groin before your backside hits the ground. This move has great power because your upper body is rolling back while your lower body is swinging out—or up. If you're both going to the ground, get there before him, and prepare to use your butt, back, and sides as your new root points. Just make sure you fall with your head away from the attacker's feet—and keep it away by rolling and twisting. If you fall in a sideways rolling motion like a log, use the momentum to loosely swing out a round kick to his shins as you hit the ground.

Staying Mobile on the Ground

The typical response to a grappling situation is tightness, supreme muscular exertion, and containment. It's when you are both on the ground that you must really understand and feel the principles of suspend and release, loading the spring, shortening the weapon, and spasming (shedding) energy. This is because your mobility, or disengagement energy, is dramatically altered by being off your feet. Not limited—only altered. This mobility is a very important aspect of guided chaos ground fighting. Rather than the posed "sidekick-from-the-ground" kicks you typically see in karate, this is much wilder and looks kind of like a mix of log-rolling, break-dancing, and the moves of Curly from the Three Stooges.

Therefore, your body must now learn to skitter, spasm, and jump around like a freshly caught catfish in a bucket. To shoot your legs out, flip, roll, and change body position by 180 degrees while delivering blows, you've got to be loose, yielding, and sensitive. This is so you can avoid pressure and entanglement, then set up attack positions where you can pulse and react off the opponent's energy, yet remain unavailable. Do not grab or otherwise wrestle your opponent with the intent of containing or pinning him. This is even more important on the ground, because you can be crushed and strangled.

While keeping your head away from the attacker's legs, you can roll sideways like a log at extremely high speeds by pulling in your arms and legs like a figure skater going into a spin. You can violently jackknife your body to reverse your head and legs both to avoid and deliver kicks. Using your hands to help, you can run in a circle on your side on the floor, which powers many of the kicks described in the coming pages.

FIND YOUR ROOT.   One big difference on the ground is that your root is no longer in your feet. The principle of having a root no one can find is never more important than when ground-fighting. Your root can be anywhere your body is in contact with the ground and can change like lightning to any other part as you spasm and skitter. An instantaneous drop and spin onto your backside, back, shoulder, knee, stomach, or elbow can propel you into a completely different alignment and pivot point to facilitate strikes and redirections.

Once you're on the ground, kick and knee-strike, using your buttocks, hips,

When on the ground, your hands work the same as if you were standing. You yield to the slightest pressure, clear the line, shorten the weapon, and tool-replace, going for the eyes, throat, and groin with chops, spears, rips, tears, eye gouges, palm heels, hammer-fists, and elbows. Don't forget to use your teeth.

and hands to balance you like a crazed break-dancer. For a split second, you can root (be in contact with the floor) and kick or hit off your stomach, chest, shoulder, upper back, lower back, hip, or any other body part you land on while spasming and jerking your body, both to remain disengaged from the opponent as well as to find an attack angle for yourself. Don't just hang out like a flipped turtle.

USE BOUNCING AND CONTORTING ENERGY.   To gain power, kick, stomp, or bounce your feet off the floor and kick again. In a flash, contract your whole body into a fetal position (shorten the weapon) and then explode outward. Kick through your opponent's head, bounce the heel off the floor, and kick again. Immediately snap the leg back and hook-kick with the heel to the same target. Bounce parts of his body off the floor like a basketball. Think of it as a form of pulsing, because ricocheting off the floor propels you without requiring you to become entangled—something you must avoid at all costs.

Apply bouncing and contorting energy to all your strikes. Don't linger anywhere; when your attacker is on the ground also bounce a shot off his head, bounce your knee off his spine, or your forehead into his nose. Twist your body around and mule-kick to the chest, knee, throat, back of the neck, and so forth. Lying on your backside, shoot your leg into the air and then drop your heel down onto his neck. Bounce off the neck and drop your heel again onto his thigh or groin.

SUSPEND AND RELEASE.   The suspend-and-release principle is uniquely effective when you are both on the ground, because most people are hell-bent on controlling and overpowering you. Think of the bony protrusions on your opponent as tiny foot- and handholds a rock climber might use. Use your toes, heels, knees, elbows, and hands to "climb" around your opponent's body. Do not, however, take and maintain a wrestling hold, either with leg scissors or your arms. Instead actually stretch him out like a rubber band with your feet and hands (suspend and release) and wait (usually a millisecond) for the response. Let his panic propel your whole body into a snap-back reaction (as if you're doing a jackknife off a diving board) either in the form of a strike or a ripping, throttling action. The possibilities are endless. The simple action of digging the heels of your shoes into his ankles or knees and stretching him out for a split second by straightening your legs causes such a bizarre feeling in your opponent that he may freak out and forcibly pull his body in. You anticipate this energy and use it to propel you like a stretched rubber band into horrifying multihitting strikes that are virtually unlimited. Just remember, deliver your crushing or choking assault as an instantaneous blow that you immediately abandon as you move on to the next attack. This way, he never gets a fix on you until it's too late for him.

If he grabs and twists your leg, don't resist, roll your whole body with it like a log, kicking while rolling. If you find yourself on your back and him on top, your sticking comes back into play because your back is rooted to the ground and your hands are free. If you're on your back and he's sitting on top, you can crush his testicles, even if he weighs 300 pounds and there seems to be no room to insert your hand. Convulse your stomach in and slide a spear hand, palm down, under his crotch. Now make a fist. The amount of power you can generate closing your hand far surpasses the resistance created by his weight. Now twist your fist over and crush. He'll probably get off you first.

While your attacker is still upright, keep your head away from his legs. When you're both on the ground, remember that if he concentrates on throttling or pinning you, you can always snake a finger into his eye or crush his windpipe or testicles.

Defeating Chokes

One way attackers often bring their victims to the ground is through choking. Obviously, the best defense is to prevent them in the first place. If you're aware, sensitive, and yielding, an assailant will find it difficult to choke you. The tendency when you're all yang energy is to tense your neck and shoulder muscles against the attack. This, of course, makes you even more susceptible to choking and other mayhem. When you're yielding, retract your head and neck like a garden snail's antenna. If you get choked from the front, it's better to simply step back than to start wrestling with the offending arm. Or, you can poke him in the eye with the other hand. No fancy moves. If it's too late for this, turning sideways and shrugging one shoulder up into the choking arm can break the choke, while leaving both of your arms free.

Defending a Front Choke

When he's choking you from the front, you can gouge or chop at his eyes, kick his shins, smash the points of your elbows into his arms, and springboard off them into his face, then back to his arms, biting and kicking until you're free. You have lots of options, although the simplest is the poke in the eye.

Defending a Rear Choke to the Ground

Despite all your training, a real predator can pounce on you undetected and choke you from behind. If this is a serious assassination attempt and your awareness has not prompted the fright reaction (page 19) or an answer the phone (pages 165-166) to prevent him from locking down, you'll probably be unconscious before you can try anything else. Nevertheless, if you have a split second before passing out, there are some things you can do, but they each depend on the energy he's giving you. Remember, it's a panic from the start, and there's no time for thought. You have to be explosive and flow with the energy wherever it goes. You simply try to augment it.

The instant response is to drop, turn and chop, gouge, or palm heel his face. If your arms are already obstructed and the choke is locking down, you'll feel this as you turn and flow into a chop to his groin or an elbow to his gut. If he's on you fast like a steel vise, however, you'll probably be throttled before you can react. This is why it's important to train your awareness and sensitivity—you have only a split-second-long window to effectively mount a response. Turn your head and throat away from the bone of his forearm and into the crook of his arm and bite and grab his forearm (or his fingers if you can). Stomp on his toes. Do this all simultaneously. A backward head butt is possible, but a powerful assailant will pull you back and stifle the movement. We're talking about a possible assassination here, not simply restraint. It may already be too late for backward finger pokes in the eye, but try these simultaneously. Adopt the attitude that you're not going to die without taking him with you.

If you're falling backward, actually help him and launch yourself that way by driving back explosively with your legs. There's a good chance you'll make him hit something hard, and you'll roll over him. Then you're both on the ground, and things are more even. Rolling over your assailant at high speed is often a good tactic because there's usually a limb sticking out that can get crushed or dislocated with your full body weight.

If you're falling forward, go with it and turn on your side, keeping your head away from his feet. Snap into a fetal position (loading your own spring) and immediately explode outward, kicking. Like the "Anywhere Strikes" drills, you need to practice all the various ways of delivering strikes with your feet, knees, and legs while lying on the ground.

Avoiding the Sleeper Hold

The sleeper hold, also known as the mugger's yoke or carotid choke, has been outlawed by most police departments because, although intended only to induce unconsciousness, the carotid arteries of some people will not reopen once the hold is released. We advise extreme caution when practicing the hold and its counters.

The hold is performed by placing the arm around a person's throat from behind using the biceps area and the inner forearm of one arm against the carotid arteries on either side of the neck. The hand of the choking arm hooks into the inside elbow of the other arm (figure 10.1), which goes behind the neck, locking it in. Press the hand of the locking arm forward against the back of the victim's head to cinch it tighter. If you are aware of your surroundings and know the principles in this book, however, you are unlikely to encounter this deadly hold.

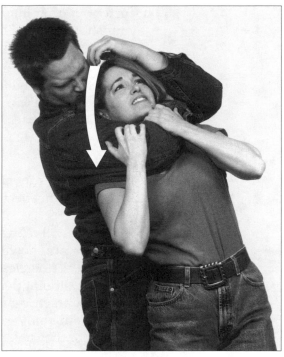

FIGURE 10.1

There are a number of escapes to combat this technique *before* the attacker can fully apply it (not all of them may be available in a particular circumstance):

1. Stick your arm in front of your neck and tuck your chin as someone attempts to apply the lock. Your arm will prevent a solid lockdown (figure 10.2). (This is what the fright reaction is for.) You can now use your free hand to reach back and gouge his eyes out, which usually causes him to release the hold.

2. Slam the assailant's groin with a chop or hammer fist.

If you find yourself fully in the grip of this hold because of various factors, such as being attacked by multiple assailants or being stunned by a blow to the head, you could attempt one or more of the following releases. (When practicing them, have your partner hold with full power without pressing on your arteries.) You must perform the releases in less than five seconds.

FIGURE 10.2

1. Turn your chin into the crook of the choking arm. Simultaneously raise your shoulders and bear down with your chin to relieve some of the choking pressure. Try to bite his forearm.

2. While holding the fingers of his front hand, practice reaching backward and peeling off the fingers of the arm that is behind your head. This will make the choke weaker if you are standing or being pulled off your feet.

3. When an attacker feels that you are releasing his grip, he may try to change tactics. You must seize the opportunity and instantly twist out of the choke as you do this.

Remember, you can easily be killed with this choke. It's you or him. Eye-gouge to maximum effect. If necessary, push your fingers into his eye to hit the brain.

Most people will release their grip once their fingers or thumb are pulled or twisted. There are, however, some rare individuals who possess prodigious strength and will not release. Here is where you need a sharp weapon or a handgun. Even a ballpoint pen will do. If you are someone who carries a knife or gun, you must practice getting these weapons into play in five seconds or less or he'll take it from you. A man can't squeeze you if you cut through the muscles and tendons of the choking arm. He won't hold on long if shot in the head either.

Using Anywhere Kicks on the Ground

There's nothing flashy about the kicks you can use when on the ground; they're simple and more wild, varied, and savage than you might imagine. Here are several kinds of kicks you should try:

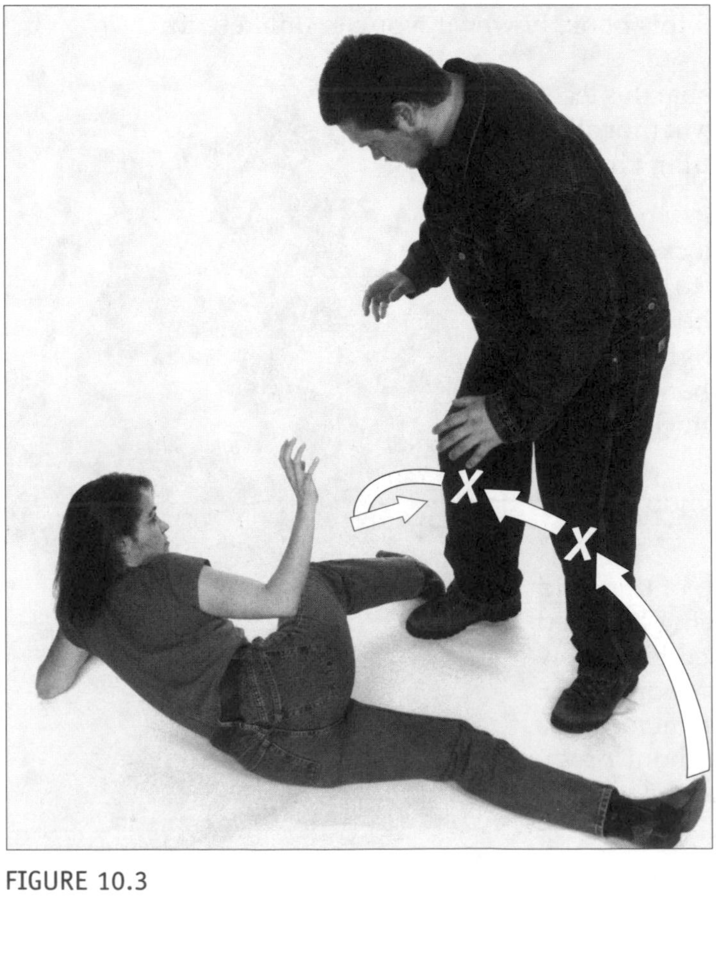

Scissoring. By gripping the ground with your feet as you lie on your hip, you can launch into a cleaving action. This should propel you instantly into something else. By positioning yourself sideways on your hip instead of your butt, you can anchor one foot on the floor to drive the other one through horizontal round and hook kicks. The anchored foot then launches and kicks while the other one returns, making for a devastating scissors effect. A method unique to guided chaos is to anchor the top foot when lying on your side and use it to power a round kick with the bottom leg, which bends just enough to clear the anchored top foot (figure 10.3). You are, in effect, running on the floor while lying on your hip (like

FIGURE 10.3

you've seen Curly from the Three Stooges do).

Hooking and crushing. With your hip on the floor, you pull one leg in, taking some part of your opponent with it, and you smash the other out.

Round-kicking. Lying on your side, drive your foot off the floor in a low horizontal kick that either arcs through or over the target. At the end of its arc, bounce the foot off the floor and heel-kick back into the target.

Vertical ax-kicking combo. With your butt on the floor, raise your leg straight up and then drop the heel like a guillotine onto a floor target; bounce off and kick up into a higher target like the groin or a kneeling attacker's chin (figure 10.4).

Mule-kicking. With your chest facing the ground and your hands in a push-up position, drive the heel of one foot straight back into its target. As with dropping, you should be able to, if necessary, switch your kicking and supporting legs instantaneously.

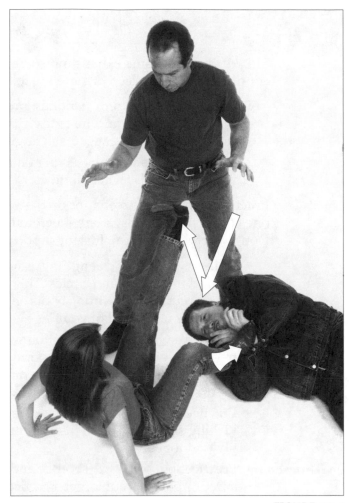

FIGURE 10.4

Shredding. Like scissoring, but you use the feet and legs to scrape and crush against each other and anything in between them. This can be sideways or along their length (figure 10.5).

Remember, you can shorten the weapon on any kick to increase power or gain a different entry angle. Make sure every kick rebounds into another kick.

All this may tempt you into wanting to go to the ground, especially if you get good at the following drills. Don't be foolish. No matter how formidable you may get, escaping multiple attackers on the ground is no picnic. Looking to ground-fight could spell your doom.

FIGURE 10.5

Leg Mania

This drill can become exhausting so be sure you're in relatively good aerobic condition first. Just keep in mind the following two principles of guided chaos:

1. Don't clamp down or maintain pressure on any kick or scissoring move. Splash the target and instantly ricochet off it into something else. Grappling with your legs against a larger opponent is suicide.

2. Whether he's standing or lying on the ground, keep your head away from your assailant's feet at all times.

Practice each of these scenarios on the floor. For simplicity, you can practice any one component against a target before moving onto or combining with others. Don't worry about form. It's not supposed to look pretty.

- Roll on the ground lengthwise while intermittently sending your legs around in big arcs and circles. This looks a little like break dancing, but it's more focused. With strong boots on, you have the equivalent of two sledgehammers at the end of your legs.

- Practice a wide bicycling motion with your legs. Use it to scissors-kick at a tree, pole, or heavy bag. Now bring your legs in contact with the floor so the bicycling action makes you spin in a circle on your hip or butt (it helps if you've seen the Three Stooges in action).

- Practice rolling (lengthwise like a log, not curled up like a ball) and straight-kicking simultaneously. Just contract and shoot your legs straight out singly and together.

- Practice scissoring with both round and hook kicks while on your hip. Use a tree or post as your target. Practice explosively bouncing your heel off the ground and target to add energy. Brace the other foot on the floor while you do this, then launch that foot out into a kick while the other one hook-kicks back in.

- Crescent-kick through the target (narrowly missing it) and rebound back to scissors-kick it. The crescent kick from the ground is when you are on your backside and your foot sweeps up and over in an arc. (An ax kick is straight up and down.)

- Immediately pull your knees to your chest into a fetal position and, with no pause, explode them both out with heel kicks. This action should be so convulsive that for a split second your whole body comes off the ground. Try this on a mat. Be careful. Start slowly. As your legs fly out, twist your body onto your chest (almost a squatting posture), pull them back in, and blast them out again either singly or together, this time as a mule kick, while bracing your palms on the floor.

- Pull in your legs fast as lightning while simultaneously landing on your left hip. Split them into a wide scissors with the bottom leg forward and the bottom foot anchoring you to the ground. Arc the upper leg forward, upward, and then backward in a sweeping circular motion clockwise toward 12 o'clock as you simultaneously switch to your rear end. Smash the heel straight down for an ax kick, bounce off the ground, and kick straight up with your toe into a tree, wall, low heavy bag, or some other sturdy object. Can you visualize the targets? The arcing kick could be to the head of a kneeling foe, the ax to the thigh muscle, neck, or kidney of a recumbent one, and the toe kick to the groin of a standing one.

- Roll like a log or spin on your butt over to a kicking shield that is lying on the ground. While on your side, smash it by clapping your feet together with the shield in between. Commence grinding the heels and soles of your boots together as if to rip the skin off the shield. Do this by moving your legs in and out, pulling your knees alternately to your chest. We call these "shredding kicks." Roll onto your butt, shoot a leg into the air, and ax-kick down onto the shield, stomping it with your heel.

- Instantly, tuck your arms and roll like a log to another tree or heavy bag and use the momentum to spin out a round kick into it as part of the rolling motion, then roll back and scissors-kick the first tree, lying on your hip.

- Snap your legs back into a fetal position, then shoot them straight out into the tree, snap in again, and simultaneously round-kick forward with your rear foot and hook-kick back with the heel of your front foot. Go wild. You get the idea.

Gang Attack III

Ideally, do this drill with at least three partners. You'll need a low, swinging, heavy bag and a bag lying on the ground (recumbent bag).

1. Dive onto your hip and roll horizontally like a log, using your momentum to spin out a kick to the recumbent bag. You can try ax and shredding kicks. You can roll over the bag, smashing your elbows backward and chopping into it with your full, loose body weight.

2. One partner swings the hanging heavy bag at you, which you must kick no matter what positions you get into. Roll or spin off the hanging bag to the recumbent bag, kick it, and roll back into the swinging hanging bag (whose position has already changed). The wildly different angles are very instructive.

3. Another partner simultaneously charges you randomly with a kicking shield.

4. A third partner throws assorted kicking shields at you on the ground while he flicks the room lights on and off. It's vital to keep reorienting yourself so your head stays away both from the swinging dummy and the attacking shield.

This drill is very disorienting as well as exhausting, and you need to be in good physical condition to do it for longer than 10 seconds. You can drill all the ground-fighting principles discussed here, including mobility, scissoring, rolling, jack-knifing, shortening the weapon, disengagement, and so on. It may help to break some of them down; for example, experiment with only scissoring or only mule-kicking against the various targets. In general though, you should just go wild.

Guided Chaos Kicking

Although the close combat kicking described in chapter 2 is very nasty, it is merely a small component of guided chaos kicking methodology. This is because close combat kicking primarily addresses the offensive aspects of kicking and defending against assaults. If, however, you are fighting someone who is also a skilled kicker (street or classically trained), you'll need to flow immediately into a guided chaos approach without thought. This is why we've saved this information for now. One thing you need to know right off the bat is, if you are in love with spinning-wheel kicks and other flashy maneuvers, you'll be in for a rude awakening on the street.

In general, the same guided chaos principles apply to the legs, once contact is made. The difference is that you're not in a position to stick with your legs unless you are very close and kicking or responding to being kicked. Here's where your "Vacuum Walk" drilling applies (page 79). You can probe, stick, pulse, redirect, or tool-destroy with your legs the same as with your arms. The "Ninja Walk" (page 77) develops the one-legged balance required for multiple kicks.

When you're out of range and the opponent kicks, it shows he's either inept or not serious, so simply walk away carefully. If you're out of range and need to enter (because you can't escape), follow his kick back instantly as if you're glued to it and attack to smother any further kicks. You may get hit anyway, but it's better than staying outside in the ideal range for a long-distance kicker, such as a taekwondo expert. If the opponent jumps backward as if he's sparring, you should also jump back (if you can't get in on time) or run away. Force him to charge you (if he means business). When he does, jump toward him and stomp-step and drop-kick to the groin, while unleashing a barrage of full-power palm heels, eye gouges, and chops to the head and neck.

a

FIGURE 10.6

If you're already in range of a kick, take your opponent's space. Never give a good kicker what he wants—a cooperative target. He'll kick your head off if you stay outside. Most people hate to fight nose to nose, where our methodology gets the nastiest. If he's jammed, the tool is eliminated. Jamming kicks with your knee rather than with your foot is more efficient, because the knee is harder to turn aside and closer to your center of gravity than the foot. It's also harder to get your foot into play when close, since it has farther to travel to intercept an attacker's kick.

Deliver the kick with no setting up, rising, or chambering of the knee. Simply shoot the foot out in a relaxed, low trajectory, straight from the floor. You may not kick like a horse, but you will get it there faster. With a sturdy shoe on, that's all that matters. Another approach if you're in kicking range is simply to kick immediately. No matter what kick your attacker uses, kick straight ahead into the groin area. Notice the simplicity of this. He kicks with his leg, and his leg is attached to his pelvis. No matter what part of you he aims at, the base of his kick comes from the same now-unguarded place.

If he round-kicks, you'll hit his groin first and short-circuit his kick (figure 10.6a). Same for an ax, crescent, or sidekick. If he tries a spinning kick, you'll hit him in the butt, knocking him down. If he tries a front kick, you'll intercept it. Now all the principles you've studied come into play: sticking loosely to his leg, using your body's mass and balance rather than muscle, guide his leg to a new root point for yourself, either outside or inside (figure 10.6b).

This is almost always in a bad place for the opponent, since his root, if he ever had one, is committed to his kick. If you deny him a place to land, he is likely to stumble. Worse, since his leg is unprotected and his balance disturbed, you have the opportunity to break his leg with yours by dropping and driving your knee into the back of his leg, sweeping his leg out with a motion similar to the vacuum walk and stepping on his Achilles tendon. If your groin kick intercepts his kick but glances off without sticking, continue through (see "Skimming Energy," page 102) and attack the supporting leg. When intercepting or kicking his shins, use multihitting and ricocheting principles. Your relaxed knee loosely but power-fully swings your foot into his leg. Your foot then bounces off and hits the same or a different spot on the same or different leg multiple times. You can do this with or without bouncing your kicking foot off the floor. By the way, you can also use your hip and backside as sticking and pulsing tools.

By adding dropping energy, you increase the delivery speed of your kicks. If you remember the skiing analogy with down-unweighting's making the fastest type of turn, you can see why. By instantly dropping your weight, as if your knees were trying to beat your feet in a race to the floor, you can shoot out a close-range kick to the shins with no chambering, stepping, hopping, telegraphing, or any other kind of preparation.

This gives you a precious millisecond's advantage. Moreover, you can fire the kick with either leg, weight-bearing or not. This is because your body becomes weightless when you drop. Accordingly, you can rapid-fire one drop kick after another, since no chamber is necessary. When you drop-kick on the supporting leg, you catch yourself by falling into the other or both legs. When you drop-kick on the nonweight-bearing leg, you can catch yourself by falling into either or both legs. Try these variations against a pole or low heavy bag. Once again, the drop kick is an incredibly fast, highly effective close-range kick that you can do in the context of the Mexican hat dance.

b

FIGURE 10.6

Fighting Multiple Opponents

There are various scenarios in which you may encounter multiple opponents. First, of course, if you see a loitering gang ahead, don't try to show you're a graduate of assertiveness training and walk past them with your head held high. Remember, don't merely cross the street. Go down a different street.

If, however, you're suddenly confronted and immediately feel endangered, don't wait. Attack the attacker, shooting your fingers straight for the eyes of the closest person. Keep your body spinning (like you did in the "Whirling Dervish Box Step" drill, page 84) to get behind the first person you hit and keep him between you and the next attacker. Keep up a barrage of chops to the head and neck with palm heels and eye gouges using a swimming sidestroke motion to get behind your attacker. Don't just back up or you'll be tackled. As you attempt to get out of the circle and run away, hit, change direction, hit, change direction, like a running back in football. As you spin, lift your knees and stomp, stomp, stomp. This gives you balance, crushes insteps, and makes it more difficult for someone to grab your legs.

If you grapple for even a second with one of the attackers, you're finished. They'll all pile on. React as if they all have a contagious disease. It's hard to get a grip on you with spinning chops and eye stabs flashing out while your feet are stomping the Mexican hat dance. You can also hope that spinning will get you in range of some environmental weapon you can hit with. Of course, if you've already got a knife or gun, spinning will give you the precious space you need to pull it.

However, simply because you're carrying a weapon doesn't mean you're protected. Many police officers have been shot with their own weapons because they couldn't get to them first. If you're suddenly confronted with an interview situation (as opposed to an immediate ambush), without drawing too much attention, look around for accomplices while you assume the Jack Benny. If a circle is forming, step toward the outside of it. Don't let it close on you. Don't let anyone get behind you. An important point is to keep your eyes, feet, and body moving. Don't settle into a motionless stance. Sway, shuffle, and talk with your hands. These little points keep your attackers from getting a fix on you when they decide to dive in. You deny them the cues of prey frozen in panic.

If you're brought to the ground, you'll need everything you've practiced in the ground-fighting section to keep them away from your head and stay alive. If you ever want to see your family again, have the attitude that this may be your last fight, so you might as well take as many of your attackers with you as you can. This is why going all out in the "Gang Attack" drills (pages 33, 37, and 183) is so vital—and why most classically trained fighters' skills go out the window under these conditions.

Stick-Fighting

The advantages of using a stick or other object are that it can physically extend your arm and that it is strong, relative to its narrowness, which allows it to be thrust through small defensive openings. We've briefly summarized the basics here; however, for more on this subject, see John Perkins's video *series, Attack Proof,* listed in the resources at the end of this book (page 208).

The reality of the stick is far different than that presented in many traditional arts. Flashy patterns and spiraling, circling movements will get you killed. If your opponent has a stick and you don't, your only defense other than running is getting inside on him as fast as possible. If you attempt to time his swings, and dance outside, you'll be pummeled. Think of it this way: if you absorb one glancing blow as you dive inside, you stand a better chance than trying to survive and fight at a distance, which would only prolong the inevitable. Once inside, the opponent's tendency is to fixate his attention on freeing his weapon. This actually hastens his demise as you fight empty-handed. This principle also applies in reverse. If you both have sticks, and you get inside where you want to be, if you can no longer get clean shots, immediately abandon the stick and go straight for his eyes and throat with your hands. It's remarkable how instinctive it is for most people to hang onto their weapon as if it's a life preserver when it's no longer advantageous to possess.

If you have a cane (which is legal to carry), simply raise it into the palm of your other hand, which you should position like a horizontal chop in case he is too close to be speared with the cane (figure 10.7a). If there is still enough room between you and your attacker, grab the cane with the chop hand and jab with a flat thrusting motion, using both dropping energy and a jackhammer-like delivery. Hit him like a crazed sewing machine (figure 10.7b). Because of the penetrating power, directness, and narrowness of the attack angle, this procedure stops a whirling, twirling stick-wielder cold. Once he is stunned, you can swing the cane, but not in the way you might expect. Hold it like a short ax with your hands apart, and take short, rapid, hammering swings that limit your opponent's openings (figure 10.7c). Don't change the direction of your attack. Break whatever you're hammering. With this wide grip, you have more leverage, enabling you to hit with either side of the stick by simply twisting your body.

FIGURE 10.7

Remember, wide swings are slow, wasteful, and dangerous. Once you're inside, you can use short, chopping, hammering, or thrusting strikes with your cane. Remember, though, if it gets in your way, abandon it immediately and go for more damage hand to hand, where you have more options and sensitivity.

Knife Defense

Despite what you've read or seen about elegant, wonderful knife defense techniques, don't kid yourself. Put a knife in the hands of a 12-year-old kid, and he or she becomes an automatic 12th degree black belt. Tell a 50-year-old, nonathletic woman you're kidnapping her grandchildren, and we don't care if you're Grandmaster Moe, if you put a butcher knife in her hand, you'll be sliced up faster than a Thanksgiving turkey. If you need evidence of this, reread "Overqualified?" in the introduction to this book (page xi).

An important point with both knife and gun defenses is, if you can't run away after the initial strikes, your only recourse is to be merciless and keep on striking until you render the assailant unconscious. Keep hammering with palm heels, chopping strikes, and eye gouges over and over. It's you or him.

That said, what can you do to survive a knife attack? First off, if it's a simple mugging, be super polite, give him your whole wallet (don't stand there counting out bills), and do it quickly. You can't spend your money if you're dead. If he wants more than your money, if he wants to take you somewhere, if it's an ambush, or if you're with your family, you all must either run away (if possible) or you must make your stand—right now. Police reports show that if you go with a captor, you'll most likely die or wish you had. So don't think you'll be able to get away later, like on TV. And don't count on being rescued. Instead, train your family to scatter in different directions when in danger.

First, though, a reality check: if someone sneaks up on you successfully and attacks with a knife with the intent to kill, you're dead. That's it. No martial art in the world will save you, nor will a gun. This is an unfortunate fact. Recidivist felons in prison do little else but practice surprise assassinations. Luckily, this is not the intent of most attacks. The goal is to rob, rape, or injure, and then get away. This is why awareness is always the first line of defense.

When you're in a secluded area such as a parking lot at night, always scan the area as you approach your vehicle. One tip is to look into the glass of other parked cars as you pass for the hint of a reflection of an imminent attack. If you see anyone approaching from behind, get a vehicle between you and the stranger as soon as possible. If you see a knife or gun, run. Now, let's address what to do if you are cornered by an assailant who has a knife.

FIGURE 10.8

Knife off Your Body

If your attacker is close and facing you, but the knife isn't against your body, you need space so you won't be sliced. Skip backward as if you were a fencer, lunging in reverse to keep you from crossing up your feet and tripping. In our tests, nearly half fall down if they don't do this. Keep your hands rapidly rolling in a "dog-digging" motion as if searching for a buried bone (figure 10.8). This aids in keeping the knife away from your vital areas. If your hands get cut, remember, it's better than getting sliced across the throat.

Look around for anything you can throw at your attacker to slow him down or hit him with. Gain distance so you can turn and run. If you have a gun, you'll die groping for it if you can't fight hand to hand or get far enough away to pull it and shoot. If you have a knife, you'll get a chance to whip it out, in which case, the attacker may change his mind. If you have neither, and you're trapped, kick like a Rockette, with your foot tapping against the ground only long enough to bounce back up and kick again. Remember to use only your lead leg to kick. Don't change feet unless your opponent backs up. Aim for the shins and keep firing until you do some damage.

If you wind up on the ground against a knife-wielder, you're toast, unless you know how to ground-fight. Even so, you can't stay there; you'd still only be trying to get enough room so you could get up and run.

Knife Against Belly or Chest

This is the robbery method most often given as a scenario in martial arts schools. In real life, it is seldom used. Holding the knife to the neck while holding on to another body part or clothing with the free hand is actually the most common technique. Here, however, we'll show you the defense for the former.

If the robber asks for an item you can give him, hand it over. If you feel he wants to go further or that he's deranged and going to cut you anyway, you must act as B does here. B gets her body off line, or out of danger, by twisting her torso out of the way of the knife. Simultaneously, B strikes at and pushes the knife away toward A's body. While keeping his knife hand in check, B strikes with the opposite hand into A's eyes with a clawing spear hand strike (or any basic strike described in chapter 2, pages 20 through 26). All three actions occur simultaneously, which is why it's shown in only one picture (figure 10.9). If they were depicted sequentially and practiced that way, they would be sure to fail. Don't forget the crucial last step: run away immediately, screaming.

Knife on Back

The escape here is the same idea as for knife on belly or chest: a robbery situation gone bad. If you're not boxed in or being restrained, run.

You can practice kicking against a moving heavy bag that is low to the ground. The faster you kick, the better. Remember to practice dog-digging simultaneously.

FIGURE 10.9

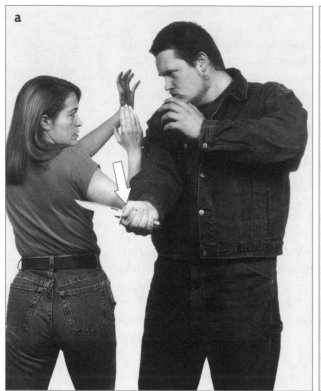

FIGURE 10.10

Otherwise, when you have complied with A's orders, but the attacker wants to go further by taking you somewhere else or begins to give orders that might be a prelude to rape or worse, you must quickly do as B demonstrates here. B twists her torso out of the way of the knife, simultaneously pushing it further off line, left or right (figure 10.10a). Instantly, B palm-heels A's head once or twice, dropping into each strike (figure 10.10b). B runs away immediately. As earlier, getting off line, pushing the knife, and striking are done in one movement. Don't break it down when you practice; you have to keep it simple if you want to live.

Knife on Your Neck From the Front

If the knife is on your neck, it becomes another game. When you're in imminent danger of being abducted, you must act immediately. One tiny advantage you have is that the assailant didn't choose to assassinate you immediately. Thus, he has other intentions. If a knife is pressed against your neck from the front and you're being held by his other hand from the front also, you must train to do two things simultaneously: deflect the knife to the outside and perform the drop-step palm-heel combo from chapter 2 (see also John Perkins's video series, *Attack Proof*).

For example, A holds the knife with his right hand against the left side of B's neck. After B has offered his money and anything else the attacker wants, A decides to move B to another location (where he or she will probably be killed, raped, or tortured). B, not without reason, acts scared and helpless and then, in an instant, simultaneously smacks the knife hand away to the outside from the inside with his left hand and drop-steps forward with a right palm heel or eye gouge. B's right hand should work like a jackhammer, blasting out three or four strikes in one second while his left maintains control of the knife hand. By "con-

Even with a successful escape, you still could be cut, perhaps seriously, but you'll survive. The point is, don't try to be fancy and don't go with your abductor to a second crime scene.

trol" we mean anything that keeps it away from vitals (stick, parry, smack, or grab if necessary). B should then immediately run away, screaming. When you practice this defense against a target, use full howling intensity to be effective. Practice using your adrenaline so it propels you to safety, not paralysis.

Knife on Your Neck From the Rear

The usual manner in which attackers use a knife is to reach around from behind the victim and hold the edge of the knife against the throat. This is an extremely difficult position to get out of. The assailant will also use his other hand, either holding the victim's hair or shoulder or covering the mouth; this is scary, to say the least. This is a method taught to specialized members of various armed forces for "taking out" sentries (and similar to the method used on Nicole Simpson). In this case, we're assuming the victim is not killed outright, but that the knife-wielder is attempting to control and abduct him or her.

The method used to extricate yourself takes a great deal of practice, and you should use it only as a last-ditch effort. The first step to getting free is to get the blade away from your neck by moving several ways simultaneously. Picture the knife being held by a right-handed attacker. His wrist and forearm encircle your neck with the blade pressed against the left side of your throat. At the same time, his left hand is covering your nose and mouth. The attacker is also usually pressed close to your body to control you.

One option, and only you can make this decision, is to wait until the instant he tries to move you to another place, like a car. This tends to loosen the blade and restraining hand for a split second. Just don't wait too long, because the clock is ticking. When you do act, it must be with total commitment. Dramatically lift your right shoulder toward your right ear while turning your head to the left and tucking your chin. This will exert pressure against the knife hand, forcing it away from the neck. Simultaneously reach up with your right hand and grab the hand and/or blade and pull it down with dropping energy. The action should feel like you are doing a pull-up with your full body weight on his hand. The combined up-down effect of raising the shoulder and dropping into the hand creates a powerful levering pressure against the knife arm. Simultaneously, with full extension, drive your left elbow repeatedly into his face, throat, or solar plexus like a jackhammer (figure 10.11). Depending on his body position, you might alternately strike with left hammer-fists or chops to his groin, then turn back to your right with a dropping left palm heel to the side of his head. This should get you free of the blade and

FIGURE 10.11

allow you to run for your life, screaming "Fire! Fire!" Your ability to adapt to changing circumstances is imperative here, because there are no precise formulas. For example, if the attacker grabs your left arm instead of your mouth, your ability to strike may be impeded. Without struggling against his grip, it would be easier to simply turn your left hand toward his groin and crush. You would follow this immediately with elbows to the face. But suppose he has angled his hip to cut off access to his groin; this would tend to bring his head to the side of yours, which is perfect for a sideways head butt into his face like you practiced in your "Anywhere Strikes" drills in chapter 2. You never know how an attack will go down. Sometimes an inexperienced assailant with an extra-long knife will actually keep his wrist against your throat instead of a blade. Since the point of his knife would then be mere inches from his face, your best recourse might be to grab his knife hand and drive it back straight into his eyes.

There are a few key points in practicing knife drills. The first is obvious—train against both right- and left-handed attacks. The second key point is variability. By being creative you will develop more subtleties than we can elaborate here. However, the three things you must usually do with rear-choking knife attacks are

1. drop and pull,
2. lift the shoulder, and
3. hammer repeatedly.

Furthermore, recognize that at any time the situation could change into a scenario like the one presented next.

You should know that unless they're in vital areas, you can keep on fighting for a period of time even with multiple stab wounds. Kick, eye-gouge, and bite. Unless you are facing an assassin with a death wish he'll probably lose interest because he never intended to get hurt in the first place. Don't give up. You can survive.

Knife Skip Drill

Use soft rubber knives, eye goggles, throat protection (a foam collar), and shin guards when performing this drill.

1. Stand with your eyes closed while your partner surprises you with a rubber knife in the stomach. Open your eyes.
2. Dog-dig at the knife while skipping backward as fast as possible, using the fencer's step (pushing off with one leg, leaping, without crossing your legs).
3. Once you're at a sufficient distance, turn and run.
4. If you can't get a sufficient distance away for whatever reason, skip backward and unexpectedly stop, drop, and kick into the knife-wielder repeatedly, like a Rockette, with your front leg only.
5. If you can't get away, and there is a wall, run straight at the wall that is trapping you, brace your body for impact with your palms flat on the wall about chest-high, and then mule-kick backward with your heel at him repeatedly. Bounce the foot off the floor and at your attacker repeatedly like a Rockette. This has enormous power.

6. If you trip and fall, use your ground-fighting kicking skills. Keep your head away from his feet and the knife and kick mercilessly. If you practice this against a partner who is holding a rubber knife and a kicking shield, and wearing shin guards, you will find that the ground kicks are very effective.

Using a Knife for Self-Defense

If you're using a knife for self-defense, you'd better know how to use it well and be seriously determined to defend yourself. Many men who have spent time in prison see the knife as a symbol of power. If you display a knife to a hardened criminal, and he perceives you're not resolved on cutting him, he may go for you and try to take your blade.

Forget about fancy techniques. Miyamoto Musashi, the great Japanese swordsman, taught himself how to fight and killed hundreds of samurai, many from the greatest schools in Japan, using only a wooden sword. Keep in mind that the knife needs to become a deadly, free extension of your body, moving with all the principles of guided chaos.

Using one of the newly available heavy bags shaped like the human body (see resources), learn to thrust into the softer targets—the throat, groin, solar plexus, kidneys, eyes—as well as the chest. Slash at extended targets like the arms and legs. Learn to cut the main arteries of the upper inner arm, the carotid arteries of the neck, and the femoral arteries near the groin.

If he also has a knife, run. If you can't, all your yielding training must come into play, except that now, instead of imagining that the attacker is holding a knife to make you pocket his punches, you've got the real thing to deal with. Try to cut his knife arm and keep your body away from him. Remember, you can kick also. Don't try any kamikaze moves.

If you're forced to hide in your home or elsewhere, and you're not physically strong, hold the weapon (whether a strong-lock back-folding knife or a stout chef's knife) in your strong hand in a shake-hands grip with your other hand over it for reinforcement. If you're discovered, stomp-step, scream, and simultaneously drive the knife straight forward into the assailant over and over like a sewing machine needle, so you won't be disarmed. Drop your body and thrust your arms rapidly, pulling them back faster than you send them out.

Basic Knife Fighting Drill

Using very soft rubber knives or a piece of rolled newspaper, eye goggles, and throat protection (a foam collar), have one or two partners rush you from behind or any random direction.

1. Hold the knife firmly in front of you and slash, chop, and stab at your partner(s) from every conceivable angle. Don't patty-cake with this drill. Actually make contact (which is why your "knife" must be very soft). As with the "Anywhere Strikes" drills (pages 34-36), spontaneity is the key; don't try to emulate some fancy attack you've seen in a movie. Move your whole body and strike with the knife in a blinding flurry like a sewing machine.

2. To avoid being cut yourself, yield and gyrate dynamically as you strike simultaneously.

3. Flow at high speed. Your knife hand should be like a snake weaving in and out. If your wrist is grabbed, twist the blade into the attacker's hand and forearm. Stomp-step and stab like a jackhammer.

4. Your other hand is always available to strike as needed. Note that you can spit in their eyes anytime as well as kick.

5. There's no magic to this. By simply practicing freely in the manner outlined, your subconscious will learn more useful information than if you crammed your higher brain with 50 fancy knife techniques.

Gun Defense

The gun is a unidirectional (single-direction) weapon (as opposed to a blade, which can slice sideways also), but it can penetrate you or your loved ones anywhere from contact distance to at least the length of a football field. Defense against the gun is absolutely dependent on the gun's angle and distance from you.

Always remember when dealing with any life-and-death situation that almost all attacks are dynamic, easily flowing from one position to another without warning. If you're ordered by the gunman to do something that would allow him further control of you, if he hasn't already grabbed you or put the gun on your body, and if you're in a public area, such as a parking lot, run away immediately, even if the gun is already drawn. The chances of his firing at you in public are slim. If he does, the probability of your being fatally wounded are even slimmer.

Everything changes if the gun is right on you, if he's holding you, or if there's no place to run. First, remember that most assaults occur without a weapon, at least initially. Second, you need to know there's no way to defend against a gun if it's out of reach. Defense is feasible only if the weapon is in close proximity or in contact with your body. The best you can do is cooperate until it comes within close range. Sometimes you can encourage this by feigning paralyzing fear (although this will probably be closer to your true reaction than you'd like). The gunman may need to come closer to move you if you no longer seem to be in control of your muscles (voluntary and involuntary muscles, if you know what we mean; you could also use this as a ploy).

Make no mistake, if you aggressively resist moving, he probably will fire, and you may be hit. At the very least, you'll be deafened by the noise or suffer burns. He may fire even if you don't resist. But your chances of survival are more reasonable if you fight back than if you go with your abductor.

As opposed to bare-handed combat, gun defenses are specific techniques you must practice thoroughly, because they change with the angle of the weapon and there's no margin for error. Not surprisingly, bullets are much less forgiving than hand strikes, especially when the barrel is already on you. Because of limited space, we can't go into all the variations of gun defenses. Many of them are more appropriate for video or personal instruction and are simply too advanced to convey practically in a book. The principles, however, are similar. We have included the most elementary ones here. (For more information, consult the resources at the end of this book.)

FIGURE 10.12

Gun Extended Toward Face or Front of Body

If the attacker is extending his gun hand away from his body but the barrel is within easy reach, move your body off line while using the same-side hand to hit his arm from the outside-in (figure 10.12a). The reason you don't do this from the inside-out is that the joints of the body are designed to fold inward, so there's a slim chance the gunman's arm may simply bend with the strike and shoot straight at you anyway (figure 10.12b). Simultaneously strike to the face, chin, or throat with your other hand in a dropping motion and run away, screaming.

Gun Against Front of Torso

The gun is against the front of your stomach or chest. You press the gun off line and against the attacker's body with the same-side hand. Immediately palm-strike, eye-gouge, or yoke hand-strike the throat three or more times with the other hand like a jackhammer (figure 10.13). Drop on each strike and run when you can. If you're in a confined area, you'll have to keep hitting until the gunman is disabled.

Gun Against the Back

Here you may want to see which hand is holding the gun. Say, "Hey! What's going on?" as you turn and look. Then, turn in the direction of the gun hand so your same-side arm and hand strikes the gun arm and hand (10.14a). As you twist around, you step into the assailant, pressing the gun arm against his body while pummeling him with chin jabs to the jaw (figure 10.14b).

FIGURE 10.13

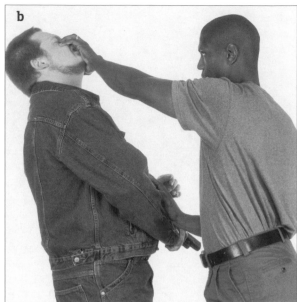

FIGURE 10.14

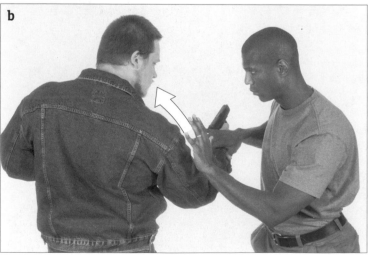

FIGURE 10.15

Gun Against Back of Head

Put your hands up in the air. Throw your head off line by twisting it back and toward the side you're going to turn toward (figure 10.15a). When you whirl, your lead hand (which is already up) pushes the gun further off line, while your rear hand palm-heels two or three times like a jackhammer against his face (figure 10.15b). Run.

Gun-Choke From the Side or Rear

This very dangerous scenario involves an attacker behind you, covering your mouth with his left hand, pointing the gun in his right hand to the rear or right side of your head. With a lot of practice, you can do the following: In one movement, drop your weight while you simultaneously raise your right shoulder and arm (figure 10.16a) and turn in toward the right, so your right elbow clears the gun, driving it into the attacker's face (figure 10.16b). Instantly, drop your right elbow into his face while whirling to the right with your

FIGURE 10.16

left hand chopping to the side of his neck, striking his eyes, palm-heeling into the corner of his jaw, or smashing into his ear. Check his gun hand with your right hand immediately after it strikes the first time and continue hitting with your other hand.

Gun-Choke From the Front Side

Here, the gunman is in the same position (figure 10.17a), but the gun itself is pointing at you from an angle somewhere between the side and front of your head. Simultaneously drive your head backward out of the line of fire (your head might hit his nose as a bonus), bring your right hand up, and pull the gun hand forward and down (figure 10.17b). You need to drop as you do all these things simultaneously. Instantly, switch your grab on the gun arm from your right to your left hand as you whirl to the right with hammering elbows to the face or ribs (figure 10.17c). Remember to move into him while striking. Keep stomping while striking to maintain your balance.

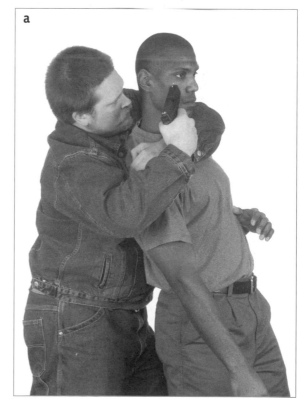

FIGURE 10.17

FIGURE 10.17

There are also techniques for taking guns away from assailants that require grabbing the weapon and twisting it out of their hands. These techniques are more difficult to apply under real adrenaline-rush conditions. If the gun is held with a choke combination behind your back, remember that the gunman still has a free hand and his feet to attack you with. Twisting the gun has some value when the gun is in front of you, but is dangerous when the gun is held behind you. It's far simpler to push the muzzle away from you and into the attacker while simultaneously jumping off line and striking.

Gun Defense I

Practice this drill with a partner and a plastic gun. If you have one that shoots toy darts, you can actually see if you'd get hit or not. Note that you typically have a half-second delay in the response time of your attacker. This amount is increased by obvious paralyzing fear or feigned submissiveness and decreased by assertiveness or apparent "setting up" for a counterattack on your part.

1. While spinning slowly with your eyes closed, have your partner press the plastic gun against any part of your body he can think of. Variation is vital to your practice.

2. Open your eyes and comply with your partner's command to give him money.

3. If he says or indicates he wants you to move someplace else, be totally submissive (in real life you can cry, beg for your life, or whatever), and then like lightning, twist around off line while simultaneously getting in and press-

ing the gun toward and against his body. At the first sign of your physical counterattack, your partner should fire the toy dart. Be aware when you practice that you should not try to push the gun in a direction where, when it goes off (and it probably will), the bullet can strike an innocent bystander. This is a split-second decision, and only you can make it at that moment.

4. Stomp-step and drop while delivering feigned blows to his head.

5. Practice similarly against all the various gun-choke combinations. You will eventually develop subtle nuances in your responses that are more detailed than can be elaborated on in a book. Note: This drill can be modified to practice against knife attacks also.

Gun Defense II

Now practice with both a partner and a heavy bag. You can draw a face on the bag or purchase one of the lifelike dummies commonly available through martial art supply distributors (see resources).

1. Spin with your eyes closed.

2. As you spin, your partner will touch you with a padded stick from behind the bag.

3. Twist off line and drive the stick (gun-arm) against the bag while delivering screaming, full-power dropping strikes.

4. Run away.

Using Handguns for Self-Defense

A well-trained person with a pistol in hand, ready for action, is a rarity. All too often, people buy a gun and some ammunition and go to the nearest range or empty lot and fire off a few rounds, thinking they're now ready for anything. Conversely, a person can train for years firing at static targets, get high scores, and still not be ready to defend him- or herself with a handgun. Over 90 percent of gunfights occur within 21 feet. More than half of these occur within 5 feet. Most people, when put to the test, can't even get their guns out in time to defend against a person rushing them from across a large room. You must also know hand-to-hand combat.

The first step toward carrying a handgun for self-defense is to find a competent trainer through the NRA. After you've learned some basic home defense and how to handle a gun safely, you should practice simple marksmanship for 10 to 20 hours. Once you can hit a man-sized target with sighted fire (i.e., using the gunsights), you can graduate to the more serious aspects of shooting for self-defense. At close range (0 to 21 feet), it's not necessary to bring your handgun up to eye level. Here is where point-shooting, or what's called instinctive shooting, comes into play. This information is not as widely available. Presenting this serious self-defense methodology would take more space than is available here. Consult the resource list at the end of this book.

Attack With Close Combat, Defend With Guided Chaos

When the attacker is unarmed, simple, basic close combat strikes will cut through almost everything, unless he or she is also skilled in guided chaos or similar training. Close combat strikes consist of repeated, jackhammer chin jabs, eye gouges, chops, hammer-fists, head butts, foot stomps, knee strikes to the groin and thighs, and kicks to the shins. They should be delivered in a whirlwind, augmented by the dropping principles you've now trained into every strike.

If you are mugged, keep your defense simple. Don't block; it takes too long. In one movement, hunch your shoulders and shoot palm after palm into his chin, dropping and turning fully with each strike. The hunching and turning automatically takes most of your body off line, and the arc of your arms while palm-striking occupies the only line the attacker could take toward your face. The instant your strikes meet with a block or resistance, your guided chaos training automatically turns on. Remember, a snake can't drill through a rock, but it can twist around it and bite you in the throat.

You're covered and unavailable as you get closer and strike. By attacking the attacker and taking his space, you occupy his line, and thus the deflection of his attack becomes incidental to your delivering your own. This is faster and more efficient, bewildering your opponent.

There are many more principles contained within guided chaos. This book, detailed as it is, represents only about 10 percent of ki chuan do, the art that guided chaos is drawn from. If you train diligently and realistically, absorbing only a small part of this material will yield remarkable improvements in your fighting skills, whatever the style. You may surprise a few people with diligent training in the following ways:

"Attacking the attacker" is guided chaos in a nutshell. Using stealth energy, if you can slide through your opponent's attack while dropping, multihitting, yielding, and moving behind a guard, your defense is actually an attack.

- You'll be more aware and better able to avoid dangerous situations. When you're in one, you'll seem vulnerable to the assailant, which calms him slightly, but you'll actually explode into him preemptively.
- As the attack ensues, you go on autopilot. It seems like you have no idea what you're doing or what you're going to do next. To your assailant, you seem invisible (which is why we call ki chuan do "ghostfist").
- Nevertheless, you're dishing out tremendous mayhem. To your opponent, you feel like a sponge with steel spikes buried in it. A spring-loaded multiple of your entire body weight is behind every blow, no matter what the angle.
- You're without thought, tension, or form. You generate colossal force, because you're not fighting your own muscles or balance. Your higher brain is a mute witness to the melee, a mere bystander. Your primitive brain, the one that houses the million-year-old animal, does what evolution created it to do, except now the instincts have been electrified and tuned.

Train and ingrain these instincts into every fiber of your being. Ultimately, you'll be able to create what you need, when you need it, without thought, until you become pure, unbridled energy.

Common Faults Practicing Two-Person Contact Flow

After reading part III you now have many more ingredients to add to your "Contact Flow" drilling. Since this is your most important training tool, it's important to approach it constructively. Actually "common faults" is too judgmental a term, because "Contact Flow" drilling should be above all a method of experimentation. We're not looking for "perfect" execution or, for example, the exact position of the left pinkie toe. We're not looking to "score points." You're training to become an expert at relaxed, random, and powerful movement, with the accent on random.

Don't actually think about any of the following while practicing. In fact, don't think of anything at all. Just feel. Later, during a quiet moment, relax your mind and visualize the sensations each of the following ways of moving would trigger:

➤ Don't linger. Don't fixate. Keep moving; don't stop the flow.

➤ When sticking, don't follow an opponent's limbs out farther than the perimeter of his or your body.

➤ If he blocks wide, simply slide straight in. Once you become aware of this, you won't believe how many openings it creates. Of course, the same thing applies in reverse. If you swing your arms wildly and wide in order to attack or block, you make as many holes in your defense as Swiss cheese.

➤ Don't reach across your body if your body is not turning with it. If you do, you're violating yin-yang principles by adopting a double-yang position. For example, you're in a left lead, and you reach all the way across your centerline to the left with your right hand to block a strike. You'll wind up folded like a pretzel. This unbalances you, because both sides are sending energy out and neither is receiving. This leaves you open to being tied up, locked, and uprooted, as well as hit. This also violates body unity and moving behind a guard.

➤ Don't hang out with an arm in a horizontal position. It's OK if it occurs temporarily within the movement of sticking or striking, but it leaves your midsection unprotected by your elbows. Also, your wrist and forearm become susceptible to crushing, jujitsu-style breaks. Finally, it violates guard and home principles.

➤ Except within a strike or a "Drac," don't raise your elbow above shoulder level. This leaves everything too open and it unbalances you. There are times when it may become the only block available, but in general, the hello block is much more efficient.

➤ Don't back up when fighting a kicker. A really excellent kicker loves it if you do this, and will take your head off. Always take his or her space.

➤ Don't have a guided chaos upper body and a karate lower body. Train your legs to be as sensitive and versatile as your arms.

➤ Don't merely reach across your centerline to take a grab. Turn with it.

➡ Drop on everything.

➡ Develop more lateral movement with zoning and box-stepping. Generally maintain a sideways L-stance.

➡ Step and hit simultaneously.

➡ If you need to step, then step fully. Avoid the floating sensation of being on your toes, heels, or halfway between roots.

➡ Don't move unnecessarily unless impelled to by your opponent.

➡ Don't clamp down when grabbing. Let the strength of your grip remain constant and loose; as it slides down the limb, let it snag itself on bony protrusions. If he pulls back, snap in. If he pushes back and attacks, pass the apples.

➡ Don't fall into patterns. Be creative, inventing your own strikes. For example, try backhanded eye pokes. They're very sneaky (figure 10.18).

➡ To break a tie-up, drop, turn, and step in, using your whole body. Don't muscle it. Smash and spear with your elbows.

➡ Try to keep your fingers on top of his arms as you stick.

➡ Stick with your elbows to free your hands.

➡ If your partner merely backs up, follow him and keep hitting. Never give him an inch to breathe. (If your attacker falls or becomes disabled, however, run away.)

➡ Drop and pocket at the same time you absorb the strike.

➡ Don't forget your knee can pulse also. When close, drive it into his side or between his legs.

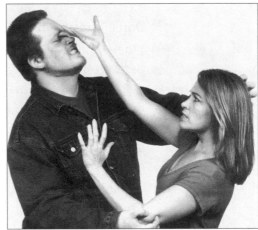

FIGURE 10.18

Preventing Common Mistakes

➡ Don't grapple with a grappler. Let your body react like an enraged alley cat or like your attacker's body is covered with some foul-smelling slime.

➡ When on the ground, keep your head away from your attacker's feet.

➡ If you're falling, take him with you.

➡ If you're the victim of a mugging, be the most cooperative victim your attacker has had all day. If he tries to move you to another location, feign paralyzing fear and then attack mercilessly and run.

➡ Practice the gun and knife drills with an eye toward randomness, versatility, and creativity. Don't just go through the motions or fall into routines.

➡ Skip the gang attack drills at your own peril.

➡ It's better to drop your stick at close range and go hand to hand than to wrestle over a weapon.

➡ Whether you understand guided chaos or not, don't neglect the close combat drills in chapter 2.

CREATING A TRAINING REGIMEN

To help you create a training regimen, we'll make two assumptions:

1. Your primary interest in this book is in improving your self-defense skills, not impressing your friends with flashy moves.

2. You're not a monk living in the mountains, and your free time is probably limited. To reduce your training time we advocate training smarter, not harder. If the drill doesn't increase your power, balance, looseness, or sensitivity (i.e., your combat effectiveness), it's superfluous.

It's better to train frequently for short periods than infrequently for long periods. Studies show that reducing down time, even between short workouts, aids retention. Remember, you're reprogramming your nervous system, so consistency and repetition are cru-

cial. It's also more convenient for most of us to squeeze in a few minutes every day than to schedule a large block of time for training.

Most of the drills don't require a Herculean amount of strength; however, some drills (such as the "Gang Attack" drills on pages 33, 37, and 183 and "Leg Mania" on page 182) can be very exhausting, so it's important to know your condition and limits. Any time you start a new training program, you should first consult your doctor.

All the drills are valuable and build on one another. Some are more specific to training a single attribute, like the dropping drills, while others train many or all the guided chaos principles simultaneously. The absolutely essential exercise is "Contact Flow" (page 118) and its variations (page 121), something you should start to do early in your program and often. While the best thing you can do for yourself is

203

to get a training partner, you will find that even if you get to do "Contact Flow" only once a week, if you regularly do the solo exercises, you will derive the maximum benefit from these sessions, retaining and augmenting the attributes you've already developed.

Variety is important in your drill-training to keep your enthusiasm high as well as to focus and build on all the different nuances of self-defense preparation. This book provides a wide range of drills to work with. Keep in mind, however, that you should continue to review the close combat drills in part I even as you become more advanced.

Moreover, if you're highly trained in a martial art, don't abandon what you already know. We have many students with high-ranking belts from other styles who, because they're in law enforcement or the military, find guided chaos to be the "grease" that makes their other skills work better.

If you have only a limited amount of time to train, "Polishing the Sphere" (I, II, or III, pages 111-112) and "RHEM" (page 116) are drills you should do every day—ideally, for 10 minutes each. You can do these drills by yourself, and they concentrate the most principles in a practical way. Include "Contact Flow" as often as you can. If you have a variety of partners and can do this drill every day, your development will be phenomenal.

We believe the best way to arrange your guided chaos program is to perform five or six drills each day: "Polishing the Sphere" (I, II, or III) and "RHEM" as well as three or four different drills—one from part I, two from part II, and an occasional drill from part III. This allows you to hit every neural pathway and keep things interesting.

Work your way down the drill finder on page xiv, and after a few weeks, start from the beginning again. Don't get too crazy with this; after a while you may decide to skip some drills and double up on others. That's OK. Once you understand the principles and what you're working toward, you may even devise your own drills.

PRINCIPLES GLOSSARY

anywhere principle—In a real fight, a strike can come from or be delivered anywhere.

anywhere strike—Any kind of strike from any angle and any body position.

attack the attacker—A philosophy of striking preemptively without blocking; refusing to be a victim and fighting offensively instead of defensively.

awareness—Being in the moment when out in public as opposed to lost in thought; achieved through calm visualization and learning to extend your tactile sensitivity outward beyond your skin so your nervous system actually begins to recognize and flow with the movement and people around you; learning to trust your gut feeling about dangerous situations and people.

balance—The ability to maintain your center of gravity over your root point no matter what your body position or root point— your foot, back, backside, shoulder, or even your hip when lying on the ground; also refers to the balance of each bone and its relaxed relationship to every other bone.

blind attack—An assault with no interview or warning of any kind, with the intent to mug, rape, or kidnap; this is defensible, as opposed to an assassination attempt, which is virtually impossible to defend against no matter your training and size.

body unity—Having your entire body weight behind every movement you make, no matter how small or subtle, by perfectly aligning all the skeletal joints while still keeping them relaxed.

box step—An effective way of moving that keeps you close to your attacker while enabling you to avoid being attacked.

chambering—A method of striking that wastes time by requiring you to pull back your weapon (object or body part) before moving it forward to strike with it.

close combat—A simplified system of striking culled from methods used to train United States soldiers in World War II to deal with Japanese troops proficient in judo and karate.

counterturning—Turning to strike with the opposite side to that being attacked. For example, driving out a left palm strike when you're punched in your right shoulder.

disengagement principle—Applied by remaining in close physical contact with your attacker while exerting the least pressure.

dropping—A method of delivering energy by a spasmodic lowering of your entire body weight into a current or new root. When you drop you create a shock wave of energy that travels down your body and rebounds explosively off the ground and back up your legs to be channeled any way you desire.

external energy—A source of energy that relies solely on muscular power and is usually characterized by whole-body tension.

fright reaction—Your body's natural adrenaline-fired response to sudden shock or fear in which your whole body instinctively drops its center of gravity, your back curves out protectively, your head sinks low between your upraised shoulders, and your arms come up around your face and neck.

guided chaos—A way of training that accepts that all fights are hell-storms of unpatterned, unchoreographed chaos. By augmenting natural animal and human movement with an awareness of physics you make chaos work for you instead of against you. Guided chaos is culled from an art created by John Perkins called ki chuan do (KCD), which translates to "way of the spirit fist" or simply "ghostfist."

instant balance—An extremely brief period of balance created by dropping into a new root, which is then instantly abandoned for a new, better root as the balance point necessarily shifts.

internal energy—A source of power that is a byproduct of muscular and mental relaxation, perfectly and economically aligned bones, and an attuned nervous system that conducts fear impulses without tension. Contrast with external energy, which relies on pure muscle power.

interview—The verbal banter a scam artist, rapist, kidnapper, mugger, or harasser will use to distract your attention, gain your trust, draw you closer, and further gauge your ability to defend yourself.

inward pulse—A method of pulling against your attacker to provide a reaction.

Jack Benny stance—A position that protects your face and neck without tipping off a potential assailant that you might be about to strike preemptively; looks different when done by men and women.

looseness—The ability to change direction with any part of the body with the smallest possible impetus, with no conscious thought or physical restriction.

moving behind a guard—Keeping some part of your body between an impending strike and its target. The guard should be as fluid as the body position.

multihitting—Striking as many times as possible within the flow of any one movement.

neutral balance—A 50/50 weight distribution over the feet. An intermediate position that is returned to again and again as in the balancing of a scale.

personal comfort zone—An area surrounding your body that you determine you do not allow suspicious strangers or hostile relations to enter. The area is usually as far as you can reach with your arms, however in tighter spaces such as subways, your personal comfort zone may necessarily contract. An intrusion of your zone prompts you to attack the attacker.

pocketing—Stretching only the target area away from a strike while keeping your body close to your attacker.

pulsing—Pushing against your attacker to instigate a reaction.

puppeteering—Lightly applying a two-fingered grab (with thumb and middle or index finger) on each of your opponent's wrists and following his limbs around without adding any energy of your own.

ricocheting—Bouncing a strike off a target to create additional strikes.

root—Your loose, balanced, and sensitive connection to the ground. Usually you use your foot, but you can use anything (e.g., your backside when ground fighting).

sensitivity—The ability to detect and create changes in the type, amount, or direction of energy through your skin without conscious thought.

shortening the weapon—Instantaneously pulling back a blocked strike while continuing to step in and strike at a slightly different angle.

skimming energy—Skipping a strike through an intended block in a flat trajectory, like a stone across the surface of a pond.

sliding energy—Slithering around a block like a snake. Also allowing your attacker's body to slide past your contact point while maintaining your guard position.

slingshotting—Increasing the speed of a circular strike by shortening its arc.

splashing energy—Hitting a target so that your strike penetrates only a few inches and then relaxes immediately, allowing you to stick.

stealth energy—Sensitivity so high that you can stick to the heat emanating from your attacker's skin and react to changes in his intent before he actually moves.

sticking—Remaining in contact with your opponent's body.

sticking energy—Creating suspend-and-release situations with a subtle stretching of the opponent's skin.

stomping drop-step kick—Stomping straight down onto your lead leg to close the gap, adding power to a strike or kick. Prevents you from slipping on ice, blood, beer, oil, sweat, or similar substances.

suspending and releasing energy—Exploding like a mousetrap, in response to a deliberate or accidental pulse.

tactile sensitivity—Using your skin to stick to an opponent.

taking something with you—Using the backward movement of your strike to hit, rip, gouge, or pulse your attacker.

taking your opponent's space—Expressed through attacking the attacker, moving in on your opponent while remaining unavailable to him by your looseness and pocketing.

tool-replacing—Transferring your opponent's energy by passing his strike to another contact point that allows you to take more of his space. For example, folding your arm so that your elbow contacts his arm instead of your palm.

vibrating—High speed dropping and multihitting that results in you striking with the frequency of a machine gun firing.

yielding—Moving your body away from pressure being exerted on you; exerting zero resistance to your attacker.

zoning—Taking his space by moving to the side of your attacker and *in*.

REFERENCES AND RESOURCES

de Becker, Gavin. 1999. *The gift of fear: Survival signals that protect us from violence.* New York: Dell.

Kuo, Lien-Ying. 1994. *The t'ai chi boxing chronicle.* Translated by Guttman. Berkeley, CA: North Atlantic.

Liao, Waysun. 1990. *T'ai chi classics.* Boston: Shambhala.

Strong, Sanford. 1997. *Strong on defense: Survival rules to protect you and your family from crime.* New York: Pocket Books.

Sun Tzu. 1963. *The art of war.* Translated by S.B. Griffith. London: Oxford University.

Yang, Jwing-Ming. 1996. *Tai chi theory & martial power.* Boston: YMAA.

The principles explained in this book are drawn from an art created by John Perkins called ki chuan do (KCD). This is translated as "the way of the spirit fist," or simply "ghostfist." To purchase detailed videos on close combat and ghostfist, for information on classes that teach ghostfist, close combat, or modified Native American ground fighting, or to enroll in a point and instinctive shooting seminar called "Barehands to Handguns," visit our website at **www.attackproof.com**.

The focus gloves, kicking shields, bean bag fill, and much of the other equipment described in this book can be purchased at most martial arts supplies stores.

An essential training tool is the Fighting Man Dummy, a human-shaped heavy bag. It, as well as other resources, can be purchased at I & I Sports (**www.iisports.com**) or by calling 1-800-898-2042.

INDEX

About the Authors

John Perkins has been called America's foremost self-protection expert by the Trends Research Institute. He has been training and teaching martial arts and self-defense for over 42 years. Perkins has taught hand-to-hand tactics to members of Marine Combat units, Marine Scout Sniper units, and military counter drug forces. He also has instructed law enforcement personnel from the New York City Police Department, New York State Police, and the New York City Transit Police.

A bodyguard to the late Malcolm Forbes, Perkins is a forensic crime scene expert and a master handgun instructor and marksman. He has extensive experience in the martial arts of hapkido, taekwondo, kyukushinkai, kempo karate, judo, jujitsu, goju, and tai chi chuan. He has trained in Native American fighting principles since the age of five. Perkins has battled in unlicensed pit fights—a savage forerunner to today's Ultimate Competitions. He is the founder of ki chuan do (KCD), which translates to "the way of the spirit fist" or simply "ghostfist," and from which the guided chaos principle detailed in this book is drawn. KCD is recognized by the International Combat Martial Arts Federation through which he holds a fifth-degree black belt in combat martial arts. Perkins lives in Nyack, New York.

© Timothy J. Carron/TLC Photo, Inc.

Al Ridenhour, a major in the United States Marine Corps Reserves, has been training in the martial arts since 1985. He has studied tai chi, isshinryu karate, and ken jitsu. An all-conference wrestler in high school and later a boxer in the Marine Corps, Ridenhour is now a fourth-degree black belt in ki chuan do. He is a veteran of the Gulf War, where he commanded a 50-man infantry unit and served as an instructor in unarmed combat for his Marine unit and for the battalion's Scout Sniper platoon. He has also worked with various law enforcement agencies—U.S. Customs, U.S. Border Patrol, and the Drug Enforcement Agency—during counter drug missions. Ridenhour has received numerous honors, including the Navy Achievement Medal, a combat action ribbon, the National Defense Medal, and the Kuwait Liberation Medal. A member of the International Combat Martial Arts Federation, Ridenhour lives in White Plains, New York.

Matt Kovsky is an editor for CBS Television. His work has earned him two Emmys—one for outstanding editing and another for producer of an outstanding entertainment series—as well as many other awards. His list of honors includes a gold medal presented at the New York Film & TV Festival, a gold medal presented by the National Mature Market Media Festival, and a bronze medal presented by the National Educational Film Festival. He is the chronicler whose notebooks laid the foundation for *Attack Proof*. He is trained in isshinryu karate and jeet kune do, and he has a third-degree black belt in ki chuan do. Kovsky resides in Ossining, New York.